The Story Behind Alberta Names

How Cities, Towns, Villages and Hamlets Got Their Names

Harry M. Sanders

Red Deer Press

The Publishers
Red Deer Press
813, MacKimmie Library Tower
2500 University Drive N.W.
Calgary Alberta Canada T2N 1N4

Credits
Cover design by Jamie Heneghan
Text design by Red Deer Press
Cover photographs courtesy of the Glenbow Archives
Printed and bound in Canada by AGMV Marquis for Red Deer Press

Acknowledgments
Financial support provided by the Canada Council, the Department of Canadian Heritage, the Alberta Foundation for the Arts, a beneficiary of the Lottery Fund of the Government of Alberta and the University of Calgary.

THE CANADA COUNCIL | LE CONSEIL DES ARTS
FOR THE ARTS | DU CANADA
SINCE 1957 | DEPUIS 1957

National Library of Canada Cataloguing in Publication

Sanders, Harry Max, 1966-
The story behind Alberta names : how cities, towns, villages and hamlets got their names / Harry Sanders.

ISBN 0-88995-256-6

1. Names, Geographical–Alberta–History. 2. Alberta–History, Local. I. Title.
FC3656.S26 2003   971.23   C2003-910256-4
F1075.4.S26 2003

To my young son Jonas, with whom I will someday visit Jonas Creek, Jonas Pass and Jonas Shoulder in Jasper National Park

Preface

A lifetime spent living, working and travelling in the province of Alberta is fair preparation for an historian to write a book about its place names—but not nearly enough. Before this project began I had already crisscrossed the province, both for pleasure and in pursuit of history—whether in archives, libraries and interpretive centres, or in collapsing barns, small-town mainstreet projects or in the memories of old-timers waiting to be recorded. Towns and villages had become familiar to me, but their names teased with few intrigues and offered little more than identification.

In the course of writing this book, with every trip between research institutions in Edmonton and my home in Calgary, I developed a deep appreciation for Alberta's toponymy. Highway signs became interpretive panels and the names and distances they announced became a history lesson about the province itself. Even common surroundings took on new meaning. With each visit to the University of Calgary library, I walked past a stone brought from Calgary Bay, Isle of Mull, and placed in an ornamental garden. At the Legislature Library in Edmonton, I researched only a few steps away from the provincial librarian's office—once occupied by Eric J. Holmgren, who co-authored a previous work on this subject, and who served on the Geographic Board of Alberta, the Canadian Permanent Committee on Geographical Names and the first United Nations conference on the standardization of geographical names. I photocopied material about J.R. Boyle, for whom the village of Boyle was named, under his official portrait as Alberta's opposition leader.

Existing works on the origin of Alberta's place names inspired my interest and my curiosity. Further research in primary and secondary sources convinced me there was more to add to the story. This book is the result. It is by no means the final word, but in the spirit of Victorian optimism, every step forward represents progress.

Author's Note

For any work of local history, consistency and accuracy in formatting is only as consistent as the diverse and sometimes fragmentary sources allow. Every effort has been made to establish proper spelling of names and places and to reconcile variations.

North-West Territories (to 1905), North-West Mounted Police (to 1904), Royal North-West Mounted Police (beginning in 1904) and the North-West Rebellion are spelled with the hyphen in line with common use, even though it might not have appeared in the original establishing legislation or been used consistently in the past. When referring to the period after 1905, when Alberta and Saskatchewan were created as provinces, the long form of NWT is expressed as Northwest Territories, following the spelling used in the amended legislation.

Measurements have been converted to metric, although Imperial measure would have been the standard before the 1970s. Dates have been supplied if they are known and "circa" has been added for approximate years. Life spans are expressed in parentheses with year of birth and year of death; where only one is known, the year is preceded by "born" or "died." If a person's year of death and age at death are known, an approximate year of birth has been supplied, preceded by "circa."

Author's Acknowledgements

In Alberta, as around the world, the timeless appeal of toponymy—the study of place names—has resulted in a rich body of source material and published works on the subject. My first obligation is to thank those who preceded me in researching and writing about the origin of Alberta place names. A century ago James White, chief geographer of the Department of the Interior, and Katherine Hughes, provincial archivist of Alberta, recognized and acted upon the need to document the origin of Alberta's place names. Robert Douglas, secretary of the Geographic Board of Canada, authored the original *Place-Names of Alberta* (1928), and his work has been a source for every subsequent book on the subject. Eric and Patricia Holmgren, Ernest and Austin Mardon, Aphrodite Karamitsanis, Tracey Harrison and Merrily Aubrey have my gratitude and admiration for their works on the subject. I also wish to thank the thousands of Albertans who have contributed to hundreds of community history books, an important source for any work of local history. Since these community histories and previous works on Alberta place names are readily available in libraries across the province, I have not weighted this book heavily with footnote references to them. Likewise, not all works consulted are included in the selected bibliography. However, I relied extensively upon these sources and I acknowledge my debt to them here.

Particular thanks go to Bill Yeo, the former head of toponymic research for the Department of Energy, Mines and Resources, to Merrily Aubrey, head of the Geographical Names Program, Alberta Community Development, and to my mother, Miriam Sanders, a born editor who missed her calling. Each of them read the manuscript and its revisions both critically and constructively. Heather Wylie provided valuable assistance in bibliographic formatting and Shannon Lee Rae, John Olson and Joseph Thywissen contributed original photography. I also wish to thank Dennis Johnson of Red Deer Press for his patience and his confidence.

Many people across Canada and the United States helped on this project, and they are too numerous to name here. However, I wish to single out the following people and institutions: Hugh Dempsey, who offered valuable advice and drew my attention to an important collection at the Glenbow Archives; David Leonard, project historian with Albert Community Development, who provided valuable comments on the naming of northern communities; John Gray, a descendant of the Turners of Turner Valley, who helped me with that section of the book; Hagit Hadaya, who conducted valuable reasearch for me at the National Archives of Canada in Ottawa; Judy Larmour, for her research at the Provincial Archives of Alberta; the staff of the Glenbow Library and Archives in Calgary (particularly Lindsay Moir and Jennifer Hamblin); the Humanities Department of the Calgary Public Library (particularly local history librarian Jennifer Cook Bobrovitz, who was enormously helpful); Jonathan H. Davidson and Connie Yaroshuk of the Provincial Archives of Alberta; Bruce Ibsen and Kim Christie-Milley of the City of Edmonton Archives; Michael Dawe and Garth Clarke of the Red Deer Archives; Marilyn Mol of the Athabasca Archives; Greg Ellis of the Sir Alexander Galt Museum and Archives in Lethbridge; Brock Silversides of the Medicine Hat Museum and Art Gallery; Farley Wuth of Kootenai Brown Pioneer Village; Alex Wackett, Andrew Waller and Ji Zhao of the University of Calgary Library; and Diane Lamoureux of the Missionary Oblates, Grandin Archives in Edmonton.

The images used in this book come from archival, library and private sources, and a serious effort has been made to ensure copyright clearance. I am grateful to those who offered photographs from their private albums, and to those who made it possible for me to use images from institutional collections. Particular thanks go to John and Rebecca Breckenridge, Vera Brown, the Calgary Public Library (for the use of its historic postcard collection), the CIBC Archives, Shirley Corenblum, Hugh Crossthwait (whose generosity allowed the use of Sir Donald Mann's photograph), Thomas Eckford, the Jewish Historical Society of Southern Alberta (which sponsored the use of Henry Frank's photograph), Toni Kennedy, Jesse Knight, Vi Larsen, Frances Moravec, Ted Parker, Gordon Prest, Don Rimbey, John Roberts, Morris Sanders and V.W.M. Smith.

Most important of all, I wish to thank my loving and supportive wife, Kirsten Olson, who during the course of this project gave birth to our son. All I did was write a book.

Introduction

For Albertans—and for that matter, all Canadians—the name of this western province is inseparable from the maverick attitude it connotes. Alberta conjures images of honest, backbreaking work and freedom from the restraints of propriety and status in older settled lands. Alberta invokes the notion that reward comes from ability and hard work, not from title or position. That the name of the province originated with a pampered princess, wife of a governor general seated in distant Ottawa, might seem incongruous. But Alberta's majestic natural beauty and its people's loyalty to old traditions soften the contradiction. The verse of the Marquess of Lorne—the governor general who named the old provisional district of Alberta for his wife, Princess Louise Caroline Alberta (1848–1939)—could justify the regal name to the most republican of westerners.

Princess Louise Caroline Alberta, 1871. The fourth daughter of Queen Victoria and Prince Albert was married to the Marquess of Lorne. GLENBOW ARCHIVES NA-47-37

In token of the love which thou has shown
For this wide land of freedom, I have named
A province vast and for its beauty famed,
By thy dear name to be hereafter known.
Alberta shall it be. Her fountains thrown
From Alps unto three oceans, to all men
Shall vaunt her loveliness e'en now; and when
Each little hamlet to a city grown,
And numberless as blades of prairie grass
Or the thick leaves in distant forest bower
Great peoples hear the giant currents pass,
Still shall the waters, bringing wealth and power
Speak the loved name—the land of silver springs
Worthy the daughter of our English kings.[1]

The Marquess of Lorne, governor-general of Canada from 1878–1883, named the provisional district of Alberta, North-West Territories, for his wife. Notman & Sandham National Archives of Canada C-003622

The district of Alberta, North West Territories (NWT), constituted much of what is now the southern half of the province. The rest of modern Alberta lay within the districts of Assinniboia, Athabaska and Saskatchewan. Before the separate provinces of Alberta and Saskatchewan were created in 1905, NWT Premier Frederick W.G. Haultain proposed a single, massive province to be known as Buffalo.[2] But the Conservative Haultain was outmaneuvred by his federal Liberal counterparts, and the province of Buffalo was stillborn. When Princess

Louise, a daughter of Queen Victoria, died in London at the age of 91, provincial librarian John Blue remarked that "he could not recall ever having heard of the late princess having visited Alberta."[3]

Sarcee (Tsuu T'ina) camp in southern Alberta, 1880s. Aboriginal names for physical features and places long predated contact with non-native culture. Glenbow Archives NA-395-10

As with the province, the names of its cities and towns, villages and hamlets, and boulevards and back roads, reveal attitudes, values and history. They illustrate broad themes as well as successive overlays of historical periods: pre-contact (including such aboriginal names as Ponoka and Okotoks—albeit adapted or Anglicized—or translated names like Cold Lake and Red Deer); the fur trade era (Edmonton, Fort McMurray and Rocky Mountain House); Christian missionary activity (Lacombe, St. Albert, Vegreville); French-Canadian settlement (Brosseau, Duvernay, Girouxville); American whiskey traders (Robber's Roost, Stand Off, Slide Out); the arrival of the North-West Mounted Police (Calgary, Fort Macleod, Fort Saskatchewan); railway construction (Gleichen, McLennan, Wainwright); ranching (Cochrane, De Winton, Stavely); agricultural settlement (Granum, Nobleford, St. Isidore); and resource development (Beaver Mines, Cadomin, Devon).

Roost, Stand Off, Slide Out); the arrival of the North-West Mounted Police (Calgary, Fort Macleod, Fort Saskatchewan); railway construction (Gleichen, McLennan, Wainwright); ranching (Cochrane, De Winton, Stavely); agricultural settlement (Granum, Nobleford, St. Isidore); and resource development (Beaver Mines, Cadomin, Devon).

Captain John Palliser (left) and Sir James Hector (right), n.d. On the Palliser expedition in the late 1850s, these men recorded the names of many features and created new names for others. GLENBOW ARCHIVES NA-588-1

Members of Calgary and Edmonton Railway (C&E) survey party playing poker, 1890. Through its land subsidiary, the C&E determined the location and naming of townsites along its right-of-way.
GLENBOW ARCHIVES NA-1905-13

This book examines the names of inhabited places in Alberta, from its largest cities to its tiniest hamlets, as they exist at the dawn of Alberta's second century.[4] To achieve a manageable scope, certain categories of inhabited places have been excluded, such as counties and rural municipalities, improvement districts, special areas, summer villages and native reserves. Unfortunately, some of the more interesting names and many with interesting stories behind them, fall outside of these parameters. More names have disappeared from highway maps than those that remain (although many still exist officially), and localities that are now smaller than hamlets have been left out of the present volume. (Hamlet, for one, a locality approximately 55 kilometres east of Calgary and named for railway employee William Hamlet, is too small to be a hamlet.) Regrettably, the richness of aboriginal names for places that have become Alberta communities—a broad subject in itself—is only touched upon in this volume. In many cases, native peoples developed their own names for these new centres, such as Olds (*kisaynew-otsinus* in Cree, *ishagwin-oyadíh* in Stoney, both translated as "old man town") and Raymond (*eetiyah-ponowukop* in Blackfoot, meaning "where we make sugar," referring to the sugar refinery). One important work on this subject is Hugh A. Dempsey's *Indian Names for Alberta Communities*.

Grand Trunk Pacific Railway station at Hubalta, east of Calgary, 1912. William Lowry promoted this subdivision as the "hub" of Alberta. It became part of the village of Forest Lawn in the 1930s, and is now within Calgary's city limits. GLENBOW ARCHIVES NA-2025-1

It has long been cliché to ask, in Shakespeare's words, "What's in a name?" A more appropriate question might be, "What is a name?" Is a name simply the term that people use for a place, or does it require an establishing authority? Does the name belong to the local railway facility, to the post office, or to the incorporated municipality? In many cases the three were not always in agreement. Such inconsistencies were inimical to good government, postal service and railway operation and the desire for standardization led to the establishment in 1897 of the Geographic Board of Canada, later renamed the Geographical Names Board of Canada. Responsibility for geographical naming shifted to the provinces and territories in 1961, while the federal body remains a coordinating entity. Alberta's Geographical Names Program maintains and continues to develop a database of information on existing and proposed geographical names, and the Friends of Geographical Names of Alberta Society, established in 1987, promotes awareness of Alberta's place name heritage.

Place names of Alberta have been the subject of study and the object of publication since the province was created. In Alberta's first decade, both James White, chief geographer with the Department of the

Interior and Katherine Hughes, the first provincial archivist, solicited postmasters for the origin of place names in their jurisdictions. Based in part on White's research, Robert Douglas, secretary of the Geographic Board of Canada, authored *Place-Names of Alberta* (1928), published by the Department of the Interior. Provincial librarian Eric J. Holmgren and his wife, Patricia, built upon this volume with their *2,000 Place Names of Alberta* (1972), updated in 1973 as *Over 2,000 Place Names of Alberta* and in 1976 and 1981 as *Over 2000 Place Names of Alberta*. Other works include Ernest G. Mardon's *Community Names of Alberta* (1973) and its second edition, co-authored with Austin Mardon (1998) and the four-volume *Place Names of Alberta* (1991–96), edited by Aphrodite Karamitsanis, Tracey Harrison and Merrily K. Aubrey. Many Alberta place names are also included in William B. Hamilton's *The Macmillan Book of Canadian Place Names* (Macmillan of Canada, 1978) and Alan Rayburn's *Dictionary of Canadian Place Names* (Oxford University Press, 1997).

What often appears in the pages that follow is, in part, how and why a place name was selected, but also how local people or other Albertans have decided to remember it. The story that a numbered siding was named on the spot by visiting railway dignitaries, or that townspeople gathered in the general store to draw a suggestion out of a hat, creates an exciting mental image and a powerful local myth. A railway executive or post office bureaucrat sitting at a rolltop desk and choosing names from a list does not. Still, there is some middle ground. Townspeople did gather to choose names to suggest to the postal department and they sometimes petitioned railways or governments to adopt a certain name or to change another.

In many cases it is possible to read too much into the significance of place names. Railway officials and their townsite agents had wide latitude to impose their personal or corporate identity on the landscape, naming hamlets and towns after now-forgotten secretaries, nieces, or faraway hometowns. Often the names they selected represented their whimsy, unrecorded inspirations, or simple convenience. Sir William Cornelius Van Horne, president of the Canadian Pacific Railway from 1888–99, indicated as much in 1897, when he wrote that possible names had been rejected if they were easily blurred in Morse code, if they were hard to pronounce, or if they closely resembled another station name. "I am not particularly proud of our station names as a whole," Van Horne lamented, "for there is not much originality in them. When we were building at the rate of 100 or more miles per month the stations frequently ran ahead of the names."[5]

Van Horne's pessimism notwithstanding, the origins of Alberta's place names represent a story worth telling—and telling again whenever additional research casts a new light on the subject.

Names By Category

The origins of Alberta's place names are as varied and rich as the imagination and life experience of those who provided the names. Nonetheless, the tapestry of community names—whatever their source—can be broadly categorized by type: names of aboriginal origin; descriptive names; euphemistic or promotional names; names commemorating a concept, event or incident; literary, mythological or religious names; manufactured or hybrid names; names brought from other places in Canada and around the world; shift names—those applied originally to a natural feature, business or institution and subsequently applied to a nearby community; and places named for people. Some are of forgotten origin or else defy categorization. In the list below, an asterisk indicates a possible, but uncertain, explanation.

These categories, applied after the fact, are necessarily artificial, and many names can fall under more than one heading. Ohaton, for example, is named for three people—the partners in the firm of Osler, Hammond and Nanton—but it is also a manufactured name. Some names will fall under an unexpected category. Cold Lake, for example, is descriptive when applied to the lake, but is a shift name when it comes to the city named for that feature. Likewise, Seven Persons Creek is named for an event, but the hamlet of Seven Persons has a shift name derived from the name of the creek.

Names of Aboriginal Origin

Amisk
Athabasca
Carcajou
Etzikom
Fort Assiniboine
Fort Chipewyan
Kananaskis
Keoma
Kinuso

Meanook
Metiskow
Michichi
Namaka
Namao
Nampa*
Nestow
Nisku*
Notikewin

Okotoks
Onoway*
Ponoka
Seebe
Tawatinaw
Wabamun
Wabasca–Desmarais
Waskatenau
Watino
Wetaskiwin

Descriptive Names

Alder Flats
Amisk
Athabasca
Bayview Beach

Beaumont
Beauvallon
Beaver Crossing
Beaverdam

Bellevue
Bellis
Benalto
Benchlands

Big Valley
Bircham*
Blue Ridge
Bluesky
Bluffton
Brant
Brule*
Buffalo Head Prairie*
Cairns*
Carbon
Carbondale
Carseland
Castor
Cherry Grove
Chin
Chinook
Coalhurst
College Heights
Del Bonita
Dewberry
East Coulee
Etzikom
Fairview (hamlet)
Flatbush
Fort Vermilion
Goose Lake
Grande Prairie
Grassland
Grassy Lake
Grovedale
Hairy Hill

Half Moon Lake
High Prairie
Hill Spring
Indian Cabins
Iron Springs
Kinuso
La Crête
Lodgepole
Longview
Looma
Lowland Heights
Manyberries
Marlboro
Meanook
Metiskow
Mountain View
Mulhurst Bay
Namao
Newbrook*
Nisku*
North Cooking Lake
Paddle Prairie
Pine Sands
Pinedale*
Pipestone
Poplar Ridge
Priddis Greens
Red Willow
Redcliff
Redland
Rich Valley

Richdale
Ridgevalley
Rivercourse*
Riverview
Rocky Rapids
Rockyford
Rolling Hills
Rolly View
Rosebud
Round Hill
South Cooking Lake
Springbrook
Spruce Grove
Spruceview
Stony Plain*
Sturgeon Valley
Sunnybrook
Sunnynook
Sunnyslope
Three Hills
Thorhild
Tulliby Lake
Twin Butte
Two Hills
Valleyview
Violet Grove
Waskatenau
Water Valley
Widewater
Wildwood

Euphemistic or Promotional Names

Acme
Cereal*
Compeer
Enchant
Foremost

Gem
Goodfare
Granum*
Indus
Myrnam

Paradise Valley
Rich Valley
Richdale
Star

Names Commemorating a Concept, Event or Incident

Anzac
Bon Accord
Bruderheim
Condor
Consort
Coronation
Dead Man's Flats

Ensign
Fleet
Grande Cache
Harmattan
High Level
Hussar
Hylo

Loyalist
Medicine Hat
Mirror
Monarch
Monitor
Mundare*
Niton Junction*

Orion
Penhold*
Pibroch
Pipestone
Provost

Sherwood Park*
Skiff
Stand Off
Standard
Tangent

Turin
Veteran
Viking
Vimy
Warspite
Wostok

Literary, Mythological or Religious Names

Aldersyde
Balzac
Bruderheim
Carvel
Cowley
Darwell*
Galahad

Marie Reine
Onoway
Rosalind
St. Albert
St. Edouard
St. Isidore
St. Lina

St. Michael
St. Paul
Thorhild
Thorsby
Valhalla Centre
Vulcan
Westward Ho

Manufactured or Hybrid Names

Abee
Altario
Benalto
Cadomin
Carmangay
Carway
Cherhill
Claresholm
Conrich

Dalemead
Drayton Valley
Ellscott
Elnora
Enilda
Glenwood
Hemaruka
Irricana
Lousana

Lundbreck
Lyalta
Marwayne
Minburn
Mossleigh
Ohaton
Rosalind
Sangudo
Westlock

Names from Other Places

Acadia Valley
Aetna
Airdrie
Alberta Beach
Alhambra
Alliance
Altario
Ardenode
Ardley
Ardmore
Ardrossan
Ashmont
Atmore
Banff
Barrhead
Berwyn
Bircham*

Blackfalds
Bodo
Bowden*
Buford
Byemoor
Calgary
Calmar
Campsie
Camrose*
Canmore
Cardiff
Carolside
Carstairs
Cessford
Chestermere*
Claresholm
Cluny

Coaldale
Colinton
Craigmyle
Cremona
Dalroy*
Deadwood*
Derwent
Didsbury
Eaglesham
Edmonton
Egremont
Elk Point
Endiang
Fabyan
Falun
Ferintosh
Forestburg

Fort Kent
Gainford
Glenevis
Green Court
Halkirk
Hughenden
Hythe
Innisfail
Innisfree
Islay
Jarrow
Josephburg
Keephills
Kirkcaldy
Kirriemuir
Kitscoty
Lanfine
Lisburn
Lomond
Lousana

Mallaig
Manola*
Mearns*
Morningside
Musidora
Nampa*
Neerlandia
New Brigden
New Dayton
New Norway
New Sarepta
Penhold*
Peoria
Pincher Station
Queenstown
Rainier
Reno*
Rivercourse*
Rosyth
Scandia

Sedalia
Sheerness*
Stanmore
Streamstown
Strome
Sundre
Taber
Tomahawk
Torrington
Vauxhall
Vilna
Vimy
Wanham
Warburg
Wardlow*
Wembley
Westerose
Wimborne
Woking
Worsley*
Wrentham

Shift Names (Drawn from Nearby Natural Features, Businesses or Institutions)

Antler Lake
Arrowwood
Beaver Mines
Beaver Lake
Beaverlodge
Bittern Lake
Black Diamond
Blackfoot
Bow City
Bow Island
Brule*
Buck Creek
Buck Lake
Cadomin
Cadotte Lake
Calling Lake
Canyon Creek
Clairmont
Cleardale
Cold Lake
College Heights
Crowsnest Pass
Cynthia
Devon
Diamond City
Dickson

Eagle Hill
Elkwater
Fairview (town)
Fort Saskatchewan
Fox Creek
Hastings Lake
Hay Lakes
High River
Hines Creek
Imperial Mills
Kananaskis
Keg River
Kipp
Lac des Arcs
Lac La Biche
Lake Louise
Little Buffalo
Little Smoky
Long Lake
Loon Lake
Lottie Lake
Marten Beach
Meander River
Meeting Creek
Michichi
Milk River

Namaka
Nevis
Notikewin
Okotoks
Peace River
Peerless Lake
Pelican Point
Picture Butte
Pigeon Lake, Village at
Pincher Creek
Pine Lake
Priddis Greens
Purple Springs
Rainbow Lake
Red Deer
Red Earth Creek
Redwater
Ribstone
Rivière Qui Barre
Rocky Mountain House
Saddle Lake
St. Vincent
Sandy Lake
Seven Persons
Slave Lake
Smoky Lake

Spirit River
Spring Coulee
Spring Lake
Steen River
Swan Hills
Sylvan Lake

Tawatinaw
Teepee Creek
Thunder Lake
Trout Lake*
Vermilion
Wabamun

Wabasca-Desmarais
Wandering River
Welling Station
Wetaskiwin
Zama City

People

Abee
Alcomdale
Alix
Andrew
Balzac
Barnwell
Barons
Bashaw
Bassano
Bawlf
Beazer
Beiseker
Bentley
Bezanson
Bindloss
Blackie
Blairmore
Bonnyville
Botha
Bottrel
Bowden*
Boyle
Bragg Creek
Breton
Breynat
Brooks
Brosseau
Brownfield
Brownvale
Bruce
Burdett
Busby
Cadogan
Calahoo
Cardston
Carmangay
Caroline
Cayley
Champion
Chancellor

Chauvin
Cheadle
Cherhill
Chestermere*
Chipman
Chisholm
Clandonald
Claresholm
Clive
Clover Bar
Clyde
Coalhurst*
Cochrane
Coleman
Conklin
Conrich
Coutts
Crossfield
Czar
Dalemead
Dalroy*
Dapp
Darwell*
Daysland
De Winton
DeBolt
Delacour
Delburne
Delia
Dixonville
Donalda
Donatville
Donnelly
Dorothy
Drayton Valley
Drumheller
Duchess
Duffield
Duhamel
Dunmore

Duvernay
Eckville
Edberg
Edgerton
Edson
Edwand
Ellscott
Elnora
Empress
Enilda
Entwistle
Erskine
Evansburg
Exshaw
Falher
Fallis
Faust
Fawcett
Fitzgerald
Fort MacKay
Fort Macleod
Fort McMurray
Frank
Gadsby
Gibbons
Girouxville
Gleichen
Glendon
Glenwood
Greenshields
Grimshaw
Grouard
Gunn
Guy
Gwynne
Hanna
Hardisty
Hartell
Harvie Heights
Haynes

Hays
Hayter
Heinsburg
Heisler
Hemaruka
Herronton
Hinton
Hilda
Hillcrest Mines
Hilliard
Hoadley
Hobbema
Holden
Huxley
Iddesleigh
Irma
Irvine
Janet*
Janvier
Jarvie
Jasper
Jean Coté
Jenner
Joffre
Johnson's Addition*
Joussard
Kathyrn
Kavanagh
Kelsey
Killam
Kimball
Kingman
Kinsella
La Glace
Lacombe
Lafond
Lamont
Lamoureux
Landry Heights
Langdon
Lavoy
Leavitt
Leduc
Leedale
Legal
Leslieville
Lethbridge
Lindbergh
Linden*
Linn Valley

Lloydminster
Longview
Lougheed
Lundbreck
MacKay
Madden
Magrath
Manning
Mannville
Manola*
Markerville
Marwayne
Mayerthorpe
McLaughlin
McLennan
Millarville
Millet
Millicent
Milo
Minburn
Morinville
Morrin
Mossleigh
Mulhurst Bay
Mundare*
Munson
Nanton
Newbrook*
Nightingale
Niton Junction*
Nobleford
Nordegg
Ohaton
Olds
Opal
Orton
Oyen
Parkland
Patricia
Peers
Perryvale
Pickardville
Plamondon
Pollockville
Priddis
Radway
Ralston
Ranfurly
Raymond
Rimbey

Robb
Rochester
Rochfort Bridge
Rosemary
Rowley
Rumsey
Rycroft
Ryley
St. Albert
St. Edouard
St. Isidore
Schuler
Scotfield
Sedgewick
Sexsmith
Shaughnessy
Shepard
Shouldice
Sibbald
Smith
Spedden*
Stavely
Stettler
Stirling
Strathmore
Suffield
Swalwell
Tees
Telfordville
Thérien
Tilley
Tofield
Trochu
Turner Valley
Vegreville
Veinerville
Villeneuve
Wabasca–Desmarais
Wagner
Wainwright
Walsh
Wardlow*
Warner
Waterton
Watts
Welling
Westlock
Whitecourt
Whitelaw
Whitford

Willingdon   Withrow   Woolford
Winfield   Woodhouse   Worsley*
                                                    Youngstown

Unknown and Miscellaneous

Armena   Johnson's Addition   Tillicum Beach
Caslan   La Corey   Travers
Collingwood Cove   Moon River Estates   Wayne
Heritage Pointe   North Star   Wedgewood
Janet   Pinedale

* This category represents a possible, but uncertain, explanation for this name.

Abee

Hamlet on Highway 63, approximately 86 kilometres north northeast of Edmonton

From 1912–1927, Manitoba railway contractor John Duncan McArthur (1854–1927) built three railways into Alberta's north, establishing himself as the province's answer to the Canadian Pacific Railway's legendary Sir William Cornelius Van Horne and the Canadian Northern's Mackenzie and Mann. J.D. McArthur opened the Peace River country with the Edmonton, Dunvegan and British Columbia Railway (ED&BC, dubbed by its detractors as "Exceedingly Dangerous and Badly Constructed"); he built an offshoot of the ED&BC, the Central Canada Railway, which rolled into Peace River town in 1916; and he built the Alberta and Great Waterways Railway (A&GW), which linked Edmonton with remote Fort McMurray.

McArthur reportedly named this hamlet on the A&GW for his friend Abraham Brower ("A.B.") Donley (1874–1961), manager of the Northwest Lumber Company in Edmonton, a supplier to McArthur's railways. (Some old-timers refused to believe this explanation, asserting the hamlet was named for Abe, a pre-railway Jewish trader.[6]) Donley lived in Edmonton between 1916–40 approximately and died in White Rock, British Columbia, where he is buried. Financial difficulties beset McArthur's carriers, and they were amalgamated in 1929 as Northern Alberta Railways.

Abee made headlines in June 1952, when a meteorite flared across the sky and struck a nearby farmer's field. Abee, as the meteorite itself is known, continues to excite international scientific interest.

Acadia Valley

Hamlet on Highway 41, approximately 125 kilometres north northeast of Medicine Hat

In 1524 Italian explorer Giovanni de Verrazzano explored part of North America's Atlantic coast for the King of France. Verrazzano named the region Arcadie, which later became Arcadia and finally Acadia. This became the name of the French colony in what is now Nova Scotia,

New Brunswick and Prince Edward Island. The British conquered Acadia in 1713 and expelled many of its inhabitants, but the Acadians retained their identity in exile. Acadia Valley's name is traditionally explained as the choice of its settlers, who came from Nova Scotia. The post office at Acadia Valley was so named in 1911.

Acme

Village on secondary highways 575 and 806, approximately 63 kilometres north northeast of Calgary

Around 1903 Ontario widow Elizabeth Smith and her sons Frederick and William, homesteaded northeast of Crossfield. Here Elizabeth opened a post office that she called Tapscot, a family name and one of Frederick's middle names. Tapscot disappeared in 1909 when the Canadian Pacific Railway built its branch line north from Langdon to a new station established near Tapscot. The station was named Acme— a Greek word meaning "highest point"—and remained this branch line's northern limit. Acme became a village in 1910. Fans of Warner Brothers cartoons might imagine Acme's business district as Wile E. Coyote's shopping mecca.

Aetna

Hamlet east of Secondary Highway 501, approximately 68 kilometres southwest of Lethbridge

In 1893 Charles Ora Card (for whom the town of Cardston was named) and other members of the Church of Jesus Christ of Latter-day Saints met to organize a new ward for the church a short distance from its centre at Cardston. John W. Taylor—who served on the church's Quorum of Twelve Apostles, a governing body—suggested the name Aetna, as one of the nearby hills (now called Buffalo Hill) reportedly reminded him of the Sicilian volcano, Mount Etna. A post office opened at Aetna in 1900.

Airdrie

City on Highway 2, approximately 25 kilometres north of Calgary

Before the construction of the Calgary and Edmonton Railway (C&E)

in 1890–91, travellers were familiar with Dixon's Stopping House, which lay "one day's journey" north of Calgary.7 The C&E gave the location a future, and contractor William Mackenzie (1849–1923) reportedly named it Airdrie for the Lanarkshire town east of Glasgow, Scotland, and in keeping with his parents' Scottish origins. (The late John Smith, who preceded Prime Minister Tony Blair as leader of Britain's Labour Party, came from Airdrie.) A staunch Presbyterian, Mackenzie was known for bringing a piano into his construction camps to play hymns for his crews. The Ontario-born entrepreneur came west in 1884 to work on the Canadian Pacific Railway and later went into business with his contracting partner, Donald Mann, in developing the transcontinental Canadian Northern Railway (CNoR). (The village of Mannville was named for Mann, and the village of Donalda was named for his niece.) Mackenzie and Mann were both knighted in 1911 for their accomplishments, but within a few years the CNoR failed; it was nationalized in 1918 and later subsumed into the newly formed, government-owned Canadian National Railways. Airdrie acquired a post office in 1900, and was incorporated as a village in 1909, as a town in 1974 and as a city in 1985.

Alberta Beach

Village on Secondary Highway 633, approximately 60 kilometres west northwest of Edmonton

The Canadian Northern Railway (CNoR) established this station at the shore of Lac Ste. Anne in 1917 and named it for the province. Alberta Beach became a summer resort and watering place for the CNoR's engines. It was organized as a summer village in 1920 and finally became a village in 1999.

Alcomdale

Hamlet on Secondary Highway 794, approximately 48 kilometres north northwest of Edmonton

Around 1965 Toronto lawyer Warner Alcombrack brought his wife and family to visit Alcomdale, a tiny Alberta hamlet where they knew not a soul. But half a century earlier, Warner's father—Dr. Arthur Wellesley Alcombrack (1882–1962), an Edmonton dentist—had founded Alcomdale and named it for himself. (The last syllable was changed to "dale," the English suffix meaning "valley.") Born in Napanee, Ontario, Arthur Alcombrack studied dentistry at Loyola University in Chicago before moving to Edmonton. He acquired property north of the city, which in 1919 he had surveyed and subdivided. He persuaded the Edmonton, Dunvegan and British Columbia Railway to build a line into the new settlement and attracted businessmen to buy lots and set up shop in Alcomdale. Arthur built a family home, farmed in his spare time and drove through Alcomdale's streets in his Willys–Knight automobile. But Alcomdale failed to develop as a major centre, and in the early 1920s the family moved to Toronto, where Arthur practiced dentistry for the rest of his long life. There he made a shrewder investment: he owned property at the corner of Bloor and Yonge streets, where the Hudson's Bay Company store was later built. Dr. Alcombrack is buried in Toronto's Mount Pleasant Cemetery. The framed survey plans of Alcomdale hang in his grandson's Toronto home.[8]

Alder Flats

Hamlet on Highway 13, approximately 32 kilometres south of Drayton Valley

Native alder trees inspired the name of this hamlet between Washout and Wolf creeks. A post office was opened in 1930.

Aldersyde

Hamlet on Highway 2A, approximately 44 kilometres south southeast of Calgary

In 1883 Scottish novelist Annie Shepherd Swan (1859–1943) wrote *Aldersyde: A Border Story of Seventy Years Ago*, set in the fictional place named in the title. According to lore a Scottish settler suggested the name for this hamlet. It was established along the Canadian Pacific Railway's Kipp–Aldersyde line, which was built between 1909–1913. By contrast, the *Calgary Daily Herald* noted in 1937 that J.D. O'Neal, on whose land the townsite was established, had named it for the alder bushes that grew along a nearby coulee.[9]

Both Alhambra and Benalto owe their names to John T. Moore, member of the legislative assembly for Red Deer and president of the Alberta Central Railway. Moore is seen here in 1905. RED DEER ARCHIVES GF-7-8-MAY-80-1

Alhambra

Hamlet north on Highway 11, approximately 18 kilometres east of Rocky Mountain House

Although his proposed town of Deerford (see Red Deer) never got off the ground, Ontario-born businessman and politician John T. Moore (1844–1917) played a significant role in the development of Alberta. The former Toronto alderman and reeve of Yorkville invested in Red Deer, served on its Board of Trade and represented the area as a Liberal in the first Alberta legislature (1905–09). Moore headed the Alberta Central Railway, built west from Red Deer in 1910 and later taken over by the Canadian Pacific Railway. One of the new townsites on that line was Alhambra, which Moore whimsically named for the Alhambra—a Moorish palace in Granada, Spain.[10] The local post office was called Horseguards from 1913–1916, presumably for nearby Horseguard Creek.

Alix

Village on Highway 12, approximately 45 kilometres east northeast of Red Deer

This settlement was originally known as Toddsville, named for pioneer settlers Joseph Todd and his wife, who came from Michigan in 1901. When the Canadian Pacific Railway arrived in 1905, the new post office took the name Alix—the diminutive form of Alexia, wife of pioneer rancher Charles Westhead. According to legend, no less a personage than Sir William Cornelius Van Horne, former president of the Canadian Pacific Railway, provided the name. The story went that Alix met Van Horne on a return voyage from England, that they struck up a friendship (possibly even more than a friendship) and that he asked Alix for permission to name a town after her.[11] The Westheads had settled in the area around 1890, reportedly making Alix the first female settler. They eventually separated and Alix returned to England, where she is said to have worked for banker Lionel de Rothschild in the management of his Exbury Gardens before her death in 1941. Alix was incorporated as a village in 1907.

Alliance

Village on Highway 36, approximately 45 kilometres northwest of Coronation

Settler Tom Edwards (or Bob Edwards, according to another source) hailed from Alliance, Ohio, a city formed in 1854 from the union of three communities—Freedom, Liberty and Williamsport. When the Canadian Northern Railway line from Camrose reached this area in 1916, Edwards suggested his hometown's name. Just as Alliance, Alberta's name has modern political resonance (its voters supported the short-lived Canadian Alliance party from 2000–2003), the original Alliance figures in American political history. President William McKinley, whose assassination in 1901 opened the White House for Vice President Theodore Roosevelt, made his maiden political speech in Alliance, Ohio. Alliance, Alberta, became a village in 1918.

Altario

Hamlet on Secondary Highway 899, approximately 48 kilometres south of Provost

When the Canadian Pacific Railway built its Lacombe–Kerrobert line in 1911, it established a station here and likely supplied its name— Bideford. In 1916, Ontario-born Porter M. Robinson (1857–1951), the postmaster at nearby Wilhelmina, moved his store and postal station to Bideford. (Wilhelmina was named after Robinson's daughter, Paulina Wilhelmina Robinson.) There was already a Bideford in Prince Edward Island, so Robinson had to choose a new name for the post office. Before the railway arrived he had operated the mail stage between Wilhelmina and Alsask, Saskatchewan, a border town that combines the names of the two provinces it straddles. Alsask might have inspired Bideford's new name: Altario, reflecting the former home of settlers from Ontario and the new province they came to build. (Mercifully, another suggested name—Alkatchewan—was rejected.) Altario and Alsask are hardly alone in their hybrid names; others include the nearby Saskalta school district, the former post office of Iowalta (Iowa/Alberta) southwest of Ponoka, tiny Ukalta (Ukraine/Alberta) southeast of Smoky Lake and the Saskatchewan communities of Altawan (Alberta/Saskatchewan), Mankota (Manitoba/North Dakota) and Mantario (Manitoba/Ontario).

Amisk

Village on Highway 13, approximately 21 kilometres southeast of Hardisty

The once-abundant rodent in the Battle River area inspired the Canadian Pacific Railway's name for this village, derived from the Cree word for "beaver." The townsite was surveyed in 1906, and pioneer resident Charlie Phipps reportedly chose the settlement's street names, which included Badger, Gopher, Lynx and Squirrel. Amisk became a village in 1956.

Andrew

Village on Secondary Highway 855, approximately 29 kilometres south southeast of Smoky Lake

This village is located on the onetime homestead of Andrew Whitford (1825–1902), who had served as a guide during the North-West Rebellion in 1885. The father of nine children, Whitford died of smallpox and is buried in a nearby cemetery. The cornerstone in the village office is dedicated to his memory and states he is "Gone but not forgotten."[12] Like nearby Whitford Lake and the former hamlet of Whitford on its eastern shore, the local provincial constituency was also named Whitford and was represented by another Andrew: Andrew Shandro (1886–1942), the first Ukrainian–Canadian elected to the Alberta legislature and the person for whom the nearby former locality of Shandro was named. The Andrew post office opened in 1902, and a Canadian Pacific Railway branch line arrived in 1928. Andrew was incorporated as a village in 1930. Andrew's giant duck, built in 1992 for over $20,000, is reputed to be the world's largest.

Antler Lake

Hamlet northeast of Secondary Highway 630, approximately 35 kilometres east of Edmonton

This village, on the eastern shore of Antler Lake, takes its name from that feature.

Anzac

Hamlet east of Secondary Highway 891, approximately 36 kilometres southeast of Fort McMurray

When the Alberta and Great Waterways Railway (A&GW) reached Willow Creek, as this area was known in 1917, World War I still raged and the 1915 assault at Gallipoli by the Australia and New Zealand Army Corps (ANZACs) was a fresh memory. For some time the track could only be used when the ground was frozen, and it took until 1939 before the Northern Alberta Railways, successor to the A&GW, built a station shelter here.[13]

Ardenode

Hamlet south of Secondary Highway 564, approximately 42 kilometres east of Calgary

The Canadian Northern Railway established this siding north of Strathmore on its Calgary–Drumheller line around 1911. The proposed Scottish name of Hawick would have duplicated another place name in the province, and Major George Davis, the first postmaster, suggested Ardenode, the name of an Irish village, presumably in County Kildare.

Ardley

Hamlet north and west of Highway 21, approximately 40 kilometres east of Red Deer

Originally known as Coalbanks, this hamlet was the creation of the Grand Trunk Pacific Railway (GTP), which built a line through here in 1912. Ardley was named for an Oxfordshire parish about an hour's drive from London.

The GTP, a subsidiary of the Grand Trunk Railway, was one of two new railways built across western Canada in the decade preceding World War I. Construction of both the GTP and its contemporary, the Canadian Northern Railway (CNoR), resulted in the creation of new townsites—with new names—wherever their main lines and branch lines were built. Both new lines met with financial difficulty during World War I and were later taken over by the federal government and amalgamated, with other government-owned railways, as Canadian National Railways.

Ardmore

Hamlet on Highway 28, approximately 23 kilometres southwest of Cold Lake

Original postmaster J.M. Whitley and his wife Clara hailed from Ardmore, Oklahoma. That American city, incorporated in 1898, was itself named for Ardmore, Ireland, a place meaning "great height." (Another Ardmore, on the Isle of Mull in Scotland, is only a short distance from Calgary Bay.) Postmaster Whitley held the post from 1913 until his death in 1917. Clara succeeded him and retired in 1919.

Ardrossan

Hamlet on Secondary Highway 824, approximately 22 kilometres east of Edmonton

On its main line into Alberta, constructed in 1908, the Grand Trunk Pacific Railway chose some of its station names to create a partial alphabetical sequence. As it entered the province from the east, one sequence began with Artland, Saskatchewan, continued with Butze, Alberta and concluded with Uncas, east of Edmonton. Ardrossan, the next station to the west, might have been considered as the starting point for another alphabetical sequence. The townsite was surveyed in 1908, and a post office opened the following year. Jessie Edmiston, a settler from Glasgow, suggested the name Ardrossan after a beloved seaside resort in western Scotland.[14] Jessie had "mothered" her younger siblings after their own mother died, but she never married. When she sold her farm in 1920 and moved back to Scotland, Jessie left behind a row of spruce trees that a man named John Williams—possibly a suitor—had planted for her two decades earlier. A century after they were planted, a couple of those trees still remained.[15]

Armena

Hamlet on Highway 21, approximately 13 kilometres northwest of Camrose

The Canadian Northern Railway arrived in the Thodenskjold district, northwest of Camrose, in 1911. It offered residents a name of now-forgotten origin—Armena—in place of the existing one.

Arrowwood

Village on Secondary Highway 547, approximately 68 kilometres east southeast of Calgary

The brushes that grow along the creek that flows through this village— and the historic use of those brushes by native peoples—provided the name for East Arrowwood Creek and its companion, West Arrowwood Creek. Both flow through the Siksika Reserve, of which this townsite was a part until it was sold in 1911. The name Arrowwood shifted to an irrigation project developed between the creeks around 1905, and when the post office opened in 1909, the name stuck. Arrowwood was incorporated as a village in 1926.

Ashmont

Hamlet on Highway 28A, approximately 55 kilometres west southwest of Bonnyville

This station on the Canadian National Railway's Coronado branch was named for Ashmont, a Boston suburb, home of postmaster Leslie

William Babcock, who homesteaded here around 1906. He eventually
retired to Los Angeles.

Athabasca

Town on Highway 2, approximately 145 kilometres north of Edmonton

In 1848 the Hudson's Bay Company established a trading post on the
Athabasca River as a trans-shipment point between the post and
Edmonton—an overland journey—and points north, which were
accessible by river. The river shares the name with Lake Athabasca,
which straddles the boundary between northern Alberta and northern
Saskatchewan. While the name's origin is uncertain, a common explanation is that it derives from the Cree word, meaning "where there are
reeds," which describes the river's delta at the lake. Athabasca Landing
developed as an important shipping centre and was incorporated as a
village in 1905 and as a town in 1911. In 1913, the town's name was officially shortened to Athabasca.[16]

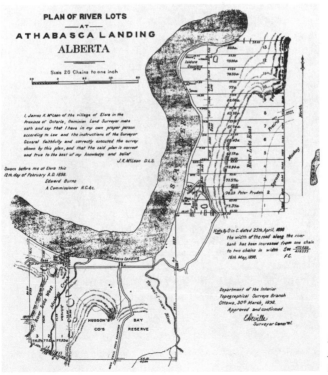

*Plan of river lots at
Athabasca Landing,
1898.* ATHABASCA ARCHIVES

"Gateway to the Great North Country," a Board of Trade booster publication from 1912. ATHABASCA ARCHIVES

Atmore

Hamlet on Highway 55, approximately 38 kilometres west of Lac La Biche

The post office at this hamlet, opened in 1939, was possibly named for Atmore, a town in southern Alabama and the hometown of boxing heavyweight Evander Holyfield. The first settlers arrived in 1914.

Balzac

Hamlet on Highway 2, approximately 18 kilometres north of Calgary

French novelist Honoré de Balzac (1799–1850), author of such works as *La Peau de Chagrin* and *La Comédie Humaine*, was reportedly a favourite of Sir William Cornelius Van Horne, president of the Canadian Pacific Railway from 1888–99. The station at Balzac was named in 1910, long after Van Horne's tenure, but tradition ascribes the choice to him. From 1912–25 the nearest post office was called Beddington, after a London suburb, and the name of a nearby farming settlement now within Calgary's city limits. The post office was renamed Balzac in 1925. Balzac entered the country music lexicon with Leroy Anderson's ditty *Balzac Boogie*.

A bust marks the Paris grave of French novelist Honoré de Balzac, for whom the hamlet of Balzac was named. COURTESY OF JOSEPH THYWISSEN

Banff

Town on the Trans-Canada Highway (Highway 1) in Banff National Park, approximately 92 kilometres west of Calgary

A townsite laid out in 1886 by George A. Stewart, the first superintendent of Canada's first national park, has since become a world-famous resort. Ironically, it had no official name until it was incorporated as the town of Banff in 1990. The name was first applied to the Canadian Pacific Railway (CPR) station in 1883 or 1884, when it was located at Siding 29, about three kilometres east of the government townsite. Until it was moved in 1888 to its present site, Banff station was the nucleus of a small community, which included Stewart's first office, a tent. A log shack was home to Ben and Fred Woodworth, and to the Banff post office. It was established in 1886, and Fred was postmaster. Another post office opened in 1887 at the townsite and was known as National Park. When the station moved to the town, the name Banff moved with it, and National Park post office became Banff post office. Over the years the resort town became popularly known as Banff, and in 1930 the National Parks Act renamed the former Rocky Mountains Park (established 1887) after the town.

Banff Avenue in winter, looking toward Cascade Mountain, 1921. CALGARY PUBLIC LIBRARY PC433

The name Banff comes from Scotland, like many station names along the CPR main line. John MacTavish, the CPR's Land Commissioner, was a Scot and had a role to play in selecting names for stations. It appears that lists of names were approved by the railway company's directors, among who were Sir George Stephen (later Lord Mount Stephen) and his cousin Donald A. Smith (later Lord Strathcona). They were both born in the former Banffshire, in Scotland, so they may well have remarked favourably on the proposed name Banff. This connection, together with the rise of Banff from the obscurity of so many places given Scots names along the railway, forms the basis of the popular legend that Donald Smith chose the name.

Many of Banff's streets and avenues are named for animals found in the park, and to the delight of *Rocky and Bullwinkle* fans, Moose intersects with Squirrel.

The Canadian Pacific Railway built the original Banff Springs Hotel in 1888. Its modern counterpart, pictured here circa 1921, replaced it in stages and was completed in 1928. CALGARY PUBLIC LIBRARY PC366

Barnwell

Village on Highway 3, approximately 40 kilometres east of Lethbridge

The Mormon settlers who founded this community around 1902 named it Woodpecker, after Woodpecker Island in the Oldman River. In 1908 it was optimistically rechristened Bountiful, but the following year the Canadian Pacific Railway renamed it for a family with a long record of service to the company. Richard G. Barnwell, a 50-year employee, served as purchasing agent in Winnipeg. His brother,

William Barnwell (1828–1915) was assistant road master and yard foreman in Maple Creek, Saskatchewan. William's sons Edward and Ernest served as station agents, ending their careers in Fort Macleod and Banff respectively. Barnwell was incorporated as a village in 1980.

Barons

Village on Highway 23, approximately 35 kilometres northwest of Lethbridge

In 1907, John Warnock opened the Blayney post office, named for Ireland's Blayney Castle. When the Canadian Pacific Railway acquired a townsite here two years later, the post office became Barons, understood to have honoured a now-forgotten railway official named Baron. Baron's Bank, as the local Union Bank of Canada branch became known, influenced the spelling, and both the post office and the village—incorporated in 1910—were spelled Barons.

Barrhead

Town on Highway 33, approximately 89 kilometres northwest of Edmonton

At 124 Main Street in modern-day Barrhead, about 13 kilometres southwest of Glasgow, Scotland, stands the James McGuire Building, the old town office named in the 1990s for a popular municipal politician. This is an unremarkable fact, except perhaps to visitors from the world's only other Barrhead: the town in Alberta, named coincidentally by another James McGuire, who in 1906 settled in the Paddle River area north of Edmonton along with his brothers Jack, Tom and Harry. When the post office was established in 1914, both locals and post office officials accepted James' suggestion that it be named for his Scottish hometown. Barrhead saw little development until 1927, when the townsite moved a little over three kilometres southwest to become the new terminus of the Northern Alberta Railways' Pembina Valley branch. Barrhead was incorporated as a village in 1927 and as a town in 1946. The surrounding county shares the name.

Bashaw

Town on Highway 21, approximately 48 kilometres south of Camrose

Eugene Bashaw (circa 1865–1938), an entrepreneur and free spirit with a taste for gambling, has been described variously as a "gallivanter" and a "roaming spirit."[17] At the age of 14, Gene Bashaw left his native Quebec for Seattle, where he later met and married Swedish émigré Annie Lund. The Bashaws lived for a time in Hawaii, where Gene worked as a carpenter for Queen Liliuokalani. In 1904 the Bashaws and their children homesteaded at Lamerton, North-West Territories, in what became the province of Alberta the following year. Gene opened a lumber business at Alix, and helped build the provincial mental hospital at Ponoka and a residence for Irene Parlby, who later became the first woman to serve in the provincial cabinet and was a participant in the 1929 Persons Case that advanced womens' rights in Canada.

Around 1909 Gene bought a quarter section from his friend Andy Allan, who had won it in a poker game from Joe Louis, a Métis homesteader. When he learned the Grand Trunk Pacific Railway would be built through the property, Gene subdivided and established the new railway village of Forster. The name was a duplicate—there was already a Forster in Canada—and the Board of Trade chose the name Bashaw to honour the community's founder.

Gene Bashaw served as president of the town band and, along with his son Vivian, built a grain elevator, the Union Bank and Lyric Hall. The Bashaws moved to Edmonton in 1917 and finally settled down in Empire, Oregon. Though he had left town more than 20 years earlier, the *Bashaw Star* reported Gene Bashaw's death in Spokane, Washington, in 1938.[18] Bashaw was incorporated as a village in 1911 and as a town in 1964.

Bassano

Town on the Trans-Canada Highway (Highway 1), approximately 125 kilometres east southeast of Calgary

While its transcontinental line was still under construction, the Canadian Pacific Railway named this station (a subdivision point) for one of its major shareholders: Napoléon Maret, the Marquess de Bassano. The Italian nobleman had a Quebec-born wife, the former Marie-Anne-Claire Symes. In Alberta, the name Bassano is as much associated with the Bassano Dam—the world's second largest of its type—as with the town itself. In Italy, thirty kilometres northwest of Venice, the city of Bassano del Grappa (the presumed source of the Marquess' name) boasts its famous bridge, *Il ponte degle Alpini.*

In Alberta, the name Bassano is associated with a massive Canadian Pacific Railway (CPR) dam, not an Italian nobleman. The CPR completed the Bassano Dam in 1914 as part of a massive irrigation scheme in southern Alberta. CALGARY PUBLIC LIBRARY PC1206

Bassano's welcome sign boasts the town's slogan: Best in the West by a Damsite. COURTESY OF JOHN OLSON

Bawlf

Village on Highway 13, approximately 27 kilometres southeast of Camrose

"However romantic it might be," wrote the editor of the *Bawlf Sun* in the newspaper's premiere 1907 issue, "the village of Bawlf was not named, as has been suggested after the Indian chief...Big Arm With Long Face."[19] This station on the Canadian Pacific Railway's Winnipeg–Edmonton line was named in 1906 for Winnipeg grain merchant Nicholas Bawlf (1849–1914), a onetime business partner of Manitoba premier Rodmond P. Roblin. The post office was originally Molstad, after postmaster Olaf Molstad (1864–1931). Bawlf was a co-founder and president of the Winnipeg Grain Exchange and pioneered the shipment of Canadian grain to Japan through west coast ports.[20] He established the N. Bawlf Grain Company and later headed the Alberta Pacific Grain Company of Calgary. Bawlf elevators were once a familiar sight on the prairies. Bawlf was incorporated as a village in 1906.

Bawlf elevators were once a familiar sight on the prairies. National Archives of Canada PA-078979

Bayview Beach

Hamlet east of Secondary Highway 858, approximately 23 kilometres northwest of St. Paul

This hamlet's descriptive name reflects the view on the southwest shore of Lac la Biche. Bayview Beach became a hamlet in 1989.

Beaumont

Town on Secondary Highway 814, approximately 20 kilometres south of Edmonton

Among the many colonists Abbé Jean-Baptiste Morin (for whom Morinville was named) brought to Alberta from Quebec were Jean Royer (1856–1935) and his wife Elise, who settled at Sandy Lake in 1894. Soon after his arrival, Jean suggested the name Beaumont—French for "beautiful mountain"—for the nearby hillside settlement overlooking the North Saskatchewan River valley. A post office by that name opened in 1895. Beaumont was incorporated as a village in 1973 and as a town in 1980.

Beauvallon

Hamlet on Highway 45, approximately 26 kilometres east southeast of Two Hills

The French translation of this name, "beautiful vale," describes the hamlet's vista of the North Saskatchewan River valley. Nearby Beauvallon Lake shares this name. The post office opened in 1909.

Beaver Crossing

Hamlet on Highway 28, approximately six kilometres south of Cold Lake

The post office was established in 1910 under the name Cold Lake, which was changed to Beaver Crossing in 1913. It is named for the animal.

Beaverdam

Hamlet east of Secondary Highway 897, approximately 23 kilometres south southwest of Cold Lake

This hamlet on the shore of Angling Lake is evidently named for the structure beavers build. Its post office opened in 1925.

Beaver Lake

Hamlet on Secondary Highway 663, approximately 10 kilometres southeast of Lac La Biche

This hamlet is on the shore of Beaver Lake, the headwaters of the Beaver River. The Beaver Lake post office opened in 1892.

Beaver Mines

Hamlet on Secondary Highway 774, approximately 19 kilometres west southwest of Pincher Creek

Beaver Creek gave this hamlet part of its name and the coal mining industry the rest. The Western Coal and Coke Company opened two mines in 1909, and in 1912 the Kootenay and Alberta Railway, a spur line from Pincher Station, arrived. But a strike during World War I, followed by the condemnation and dismantling of a massive trestle bridge, proved a major setback. A further blow came with the railways' conversion to diesel locomotives in the 1950s. The last mine closed in 1971.[21]

Beaverlodge

Town on Highway 43, approximately 42 km west of Grande Prairie.

The first attempt at group settlement of the Peace River country occurred in 1909, when a party of breakaway Methodists from Ontario took up land along the Beaverlodge River. Although the settlement was known as Beaverlodge, its post office was first named Redlow, after the nearby Red Willow River. This was because the government had already chosen the name of Beaverlodge for a post office it had just established at nearby Lake Saskatoon, even though the community there had always been known as Lake Saskatoon. In 1912 the Beaverlodge post office was renamed Lake Saskatoon, and Redlow was officially named Beaverlodge. When the Edmonton, Dunvegan and British Columbia Railway arrived in 1928, the community moved to a new railway townsite two kilometres downhill. Beaverlodge became a village in 1929 and a town in 1956.

Beazer

Hamlet on Secondary Highway 501, approximately 80 kilometres southwest of Lethbridge

In 1889, Mark E. Beazer (1854–1937), a shepherd from Utah, travelled by covered wagon with his wife, Ellen, and their children to southern Alberta. Beazer homesteaded west of Cardston in 1893 and later opened a post office that became the centre of a new hamlet. Both Mark and Ellen were active in the Church of Jesus Christ of Latter-day Saints, and Mark served as the local Bishop. The Beazers retired to Cardston in 1925.

Beiseker

Village on Highway 72, approximately 50 kilometres northeast of Calgary

Thomas Lincoln Beiseker (1866–1941) was once believed to have been the wealthiest man in North Dakota. He was born in Indiana but grew up in Minnesota, where the one-time reporter became involved in land development for the Northern Pacific Railway. Beiseker later took up similar work in western Canada with the Canadian Pacific Railway (CPR). As part of its incentive to build the transcontinental railway in the 1880s, the CPR received 10 million hectares of land from the federal government. Much of this land was sold to settlers or to colonization companies that would bring in settlers and sell them land. From his seat in Fessenden, North Dakota—where he built a chain of banks, established land companies and owned a weekly newspaper—Beiseker acted in Alberta through the Calgary Colonization Company and its successor, Beiseker and Davidson. He acquired 101,171 hectares for $2.47 per hectare and established a series of colonization farms to assist settlers who had been recruited in North Dakota.[22] The CPR built its Langdon–Acme branch in 1909-1910, along which Beiseker subdivided the townsite named for him and began selling lots.

Welcome sign, 2002. Courtesy of John Olson

A partisan Republican, Beiseker was once suggested as a candidate for the party's gubernatorial ticket in North Dakota. His financial empire crumbled during the Great Depression, but Beiseker retained his flagship Wells County Bank in Fessenden. His death in Fargo, North Dakota, in 1941 evidently went unnoticed in Beiseker, and the Calgary Colonization Company's demonstration farmhouse—possibly the last vestige of Beiseker's investment in the village—was demolished in 1956. However, Beiseker's Victorian mansion in Fessenden is now a bed and breakfast, and was listed on the National Register of Historic Places in 1977. Beiseker is buried in the marble family vault in Austin, Minnesota. Beiseker, Alberta, was incorporated as a village in 1921.

Banker Thomas L. Beiseker (centre, back row) of Fessenden, North Dakota, founded the Calgary Colonization Company and donated the townsite of Beiseker. Courtesy of John Roberts

Bellis

Hamlet north of highways 28 and 36, approximately 23 kilometres east northeast of Smoky Lake

This hamlet's population is overwhelmingly of Ukrainian origin, and the name—applied to the local post office in 1914—reportedly comes from the Ukrainian term for white poplar.

Benalto

Hamlet south of Highway 11, approximately 32 kilometres west of Red Deer

John T. Moore (1844–1917), the politician and railway promoter behind the Alberta Central Railway—built west from Red Deer in 1910—named the townsites of Alhambra and Benalto on that line. This hybrid description means "high hill" from the Gaelic *ben* ("hill") and Latin *alto* ("high").

Benchlands

Hamlet on Secondary Highway 40, northwest of Cochrane

This hamlet along the Ghost River, established in 1978, is situated on a terraced landscape, with housing on three different terraces (or benches).

Bentley

Town on Highway 12, approximately 28 kilometres northwest of Red Deer

Journalist Ken Liddell, who for a quarter century examined rural themes in his *Calgary Herald* column, once observed that "90 percent of the Bentley settlers died in the community."[23] The most obvious exception was George Bentley (1862–1945), a sawyer from Michigan who settled along the Blindman River in the 1890s. When Major William B. McPherson, a U.S. Civil War veteran, opened a post office in April 1900, Bentley's name was the controversial choice. Settlers preferred McPherson's name, but they were outnumbered by the sawmill employees, who wanted Bentley.[24] George Bentley left Bentley around 1905 and is almost certainly the George Calvin Bentley who settled in Stettler that same year. There he operated the Staples Lumber Company and served as the first village reeve and as a school board trustee.[25] In

1922 he left Alberta permanently and, as a real estate promoter, became the "founding father" of Virginia City (now North Long Beach), California.[26] Bentley, Alberta was incorporated as a village in 1915 and as a town in 2001.

George Bentley and family, n.d. Bentley settled in the area in the 1890s but left around 1905.
<small>REPRINTED FROM *Bentley and District Early History* (BENTLEY, ALTA.: BENTLEY & DISTRICT HISTORICAL SOCIETY, 1982).</small>

Berwyn

Village north of Highway 2, approximately 10 kilometres southwest of Grimshaw

From the time the Central Canada Railway arrived in 1922 until its extension to Fairview by 1928, Berwyn served as this northern line's head of steel. The name comes from Wales, where it applies to a village and a range of hills in Wales.

Bezanson

Hamlet on Highway 43, approximately 30 kilometres east northeast of Grande Prairie

In 1907, after pioneering in the Peace River country, Halifax-born A.

Maynard Bezanson (1878–1958) wrote and published *Peace River Trail*, a booklet intended to drum up northern settlement. "[T]he time is now at hand when the landseeker must leave the railroads behind and push out into the more remote regions," wrote Bezanson:

> Imagine a West with no hostile Indians, no sunscorched desert of burning sands, no alkaline plains devoid of vegetation, no lurking dangers of any kind to entrap the unwary traveller: but a West of broad praries [sic] and timbered hills, where both water and feed for horses can always be found in abundance, and where the traveller can make his bed upon the ground, wherever fancy may dictate, with no fear of his rest being disturbed by intruder in any form.[27]

If they paused to think of it, pioneers who endured the hardships of the Edson Trail to the Peace River country might have resented Bezanson's encouraging words. Bezanson promoted an eponymous town-site where he believed a future railway would cross the Smoky River. But when it arrived, the Edmonton, Dunvegan and British Columbia Railway crossed at Watino, and Bezanson abandoned his townsite. Modern Bezanson is located about ten kilometres to the northeast.

Big Valley

Village north of Secondary Highway 590, approximately 33 kilometres south of Stettler

This descriptive name applied first to the post office opened in 1907. Incorporated as a village in 1914, Big Valley became a town in 1920 but reverted to its former status in 1942.

Bindloss

Hamlet north of Secondary Highway 555, approximately 95 kilometres north of Medicine Hat

British novelist Harold Bindloss (1866–1945), who spent part of his youth in western Canada, wrote a series of popular western novels. His books include *A Hinterland Romance*, *The Ghost Of Hemlock Canyon*, *Sunshine and Snow* and *Winston of the Prairie*. Named streets and avenues on the hamlet's early fire insurance plan, such as Lorimer,

Jacinta, Alton and Thurston, appear to be unique in Alberta and might relate to Bindloss's novels.

Bircham

Hamlet north of Highway 9, approximately 60 kilometres northeast of Calgary

The Grand Trunk Pacific Railway established a flag station and siding here just before World War I. The name might derive from Bircham, King's Lynn, England—or possibly from a nearby birch grove.

Bittern Lake

Village on Highway 13, approximately 15 kilometres west of Camrose

The Cree called the nearby lake *mokakasiu*, their word for its plentiful bitterns, a type of bird. Incorporated as a village in 1904, Bittern Lake was known until 1911 as Rosenroll, after Anthony Sigwart de Rosenroll (1857–1945), a Swiss–Italian civil engineer and rancher who represented Wetaskiwin in both the North-West Territories and Alberta legislatures.

Black Diamond

Town on Highway 7, approximately three kilometres east southeast of Turner Valley

According to lore, when this post office opened in 1907, Virginia-born Addison McPherson (1846–1929)—trader, freighter, miner, sheep raiser, gold prospector and possibly early whiskey trader—suggested the name Black Diamond, after his Black Diamond Coal Mine on the Sheep River. The Arnold brothers, who owned a general store, preferred Arnoldville. According to the story, had the draw from a hat gone differently, Arnoldville—and not Black Diamond—would today be associated with the oil and gas fields of the Black Diamond–Turner Valley area. But in a 1908 letter to the provincial archivist, H. Arnold reports simply, "The name of 'Black Diamond' originated from the owner of a coal-mine in this district and was so christened on account of the abundance of coal which is everywhere found."[28] Black Diamond was incorporated as a village in 1929 and as a town in 1956.

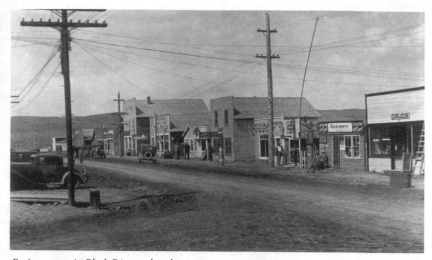

Business street in Black Diamond, n.d. CALGARY PUBLIC LIBRARY PC1229

Blackfalds

Town on Highway 2A, approximately 12 kilometres north of Red Deer

This location's original identity, provided with the 1891 arrival of the Calgary and Edmonton Railway, was "11th Siding." The post office was called Waghorn from 1891–1902, when it was renamed Blackfalds for the Scottish hamlet of Blackfaulds. When queried by the chief geographer of the Department of the Interior about the history of the name, postmaster Walter Waghorn (1849–1930) observed dryly

> I do not know if the name of Waghorn was given in honour of Lieutenant Waghorn the discoverer of the overland route to India
> or
> your obedt. servant,
> Walter Waghorn,
> Postmaster.[29]

A Canadian Pacific Railway engineer from Scotland reportedly suggested the name change. Blackfalds became a village in 1904 and a town in 1980.

Blackfoot

Hamlet north of Highway 16, approximately 12 kilometres west of Lloydminster

The hamlet of Blackfoot, and the nearby Blackfoot Hills for which it is named, lie far north of the present-day reserves of the Blackfoot-speaking people. However, long before they signed Treaty No. 7 in 1877 and subsequently settled on reserves, this area was part of their traditional territory. The hamlet was originally named Blackfoot Hills and dates back to the arrival of the Canadian Northern Railway's main line around 1905. The Blackfoot Hills were historically a battleground between Blackfoot and Cree.

Blackfoot camp on the prairies, 1874. This hamlet is far north of the plains usually associated with the Blackfoot-speaking peoples, but the nearby Blackfoot Hills once lay within their territory.
GLENBOW ARCHIVES NA-249-78

Blackie

Hamlet on Secondary Highway 799, approximately 50 kilometres south southeast of Calgary

How appropriate that this Scottish novelist, professor and publisher is honoured by a place name of his own, adopted by the post office in 1911. "Among the branches of human speculation that, in recent times, have walked out of the misty realm of conjecture into the firm land of science," wrote John Stuart Blackie in his introduction to *A Dictionary of Place Names* (1887), there are few more interesting than Etymology.... Geography, to the young mind, has too often been taught in such a way as neither to delight the imagination with vivid pictures, nor to stimulate inquiry by a frequent reference to the history of names.[30]

Blairmore

See Crowsnest Pass, Municipality of

Blue Ridge

Hamlet on Secondary Highway 658, approximately 20 kilometres east of Whitecourt

This descriptive name evokes the blue haze that can be seen from a distance on the nearby ridge. The post office opened in 1923.

Bluesky

Hamlet on Highway 2, approximately eight kilometres due east of Fairview

Adam Dodge (circa 1852–1928) settled in the area in 1909 and opened the descriptively named Bluesky post office in 1913. The hamlet was relocated five kilometres west of the original site when the Edmonton, Dunvegan and British Columbia Railway arrived.

Bluffton

Hamlet off Highway 20, approximately 13 kilometres north northwest of Rimbey

Bluffs of trees inspired this hamlet's original name, Bluff Centre, and the present name has been in use since 1920.

Bodo

Hamlet on Secondary Highway 889, approximately 25 kilometres south southeast of Provost

In 1928, John Stouse opened a post office known as Scheck; four years later, it was renamed Bodo, after Bodø, a town in northern Norway.

Bon Accord

Town on Highway 643, approximately 30 kilometres north of Edmonton

When settlers in this area north of Edmonton met to organize a school district in 1896, Scottish-born Alexander "Sandy" Florence suggested the name Bon Accord, derived from the motto for his native Aberdeen. (Aberdeen's city council maintains an online newspaper, the *Bon Accord.*) When used as a toast, *Bon Accord* means "Happy to meet, sorry to part, happy to meet again." Bon Accord became a village in 1964 and a town in 1979.

Bonnyville

Town on Highway 28, approximately 122 kilometres north northwest of Lloydminster

In 1908 Father François E. Bonny—a Roman catholic priest and former archaeologist, soldier and topographer—established a church near Moose Lake. A post office opened that year under the name St. Louis de Moose Lake, but it had to be renamed to avoid duplication. Though Father Bonny left the community in 1910, a new post office name adopted that year etched his memory onto the Alberta map. Bonnyville was incorporated as a village in 1929 and as a town in 1958. Bonnyville Beach, a summer village on the shore of nearby Moose Lake, was incorporated in 1983 and named for this town.

Botha

Village on Highway 12, approximately 12 kilometres east southeast of Stettler

Canada's involvement in the South African War (also called the Boer War, 1899–1902) contributed both to national pride and to strained relations between English-Canadians, who supported the imperial war effort, and French Canadians, who opposed it. Albertans contributed through the formation and dispatch of a distinguished cavalry regiment, Lord Strathcona's Horse. After the British Empire defeated its Afrikaner opponents, General Louis Botha—a former enemy—led efforts to reconcile with Britain and helped form a new nation, the Union of South Africa. Botha became South Africa's first prime minister in 1910, a year after the Canadian Pacific Railway (CPR) named its railway station here in his honour. Botha died in office in 1919. Ambassador Matthys Izak Botha, a descendant, visited Botha in 1972 and noted two other South African place names on the same CPR line: Kruger (for Boer president Paul Kruger) and Veldt (Afrikaans for "plain" or "countryside"). He opined that a former South African, or else a Canadian veteran of the South African War, was likely responsible for the names.[31] Botha was incorporated as a village in 1911.

South African Prime Minister Louis Botha, far left, seated, in London to attend the Imperial Conference in May 1911. The other men seated are, from left to right Canadian Prime Minister Sir Wilfrid Laurier, British Prime Minister Herbert Henry Asquith and New Zealand Prime Minister Sir Joseph Ward. National Archives of Canada C-090305

Bottrel

Hamlet west of Highway 22, approximately 50 kilometres northwest of Calgary

When John Thomas Boucher opened a post office here in 1909, it was named to honour pioneer settler Albert Edward Botterel, who had arrived in the district in 1888. Apparently no one noticed the spelling error, which has never been corrected.

Bow City

Hamlet on Secondary Highway 539, approximately 92 kilometres northeast of Lethbridge

Bow City's ambitious name, which replaced the original name of Eyremore in 1958, belies its modest hamlet status. W.T.P. Eyres opened the first post office in 1909 and suggested a name that reflected his own, as well as his wife's maiden name—Moore. The present name evokes the adjacent Bow River.

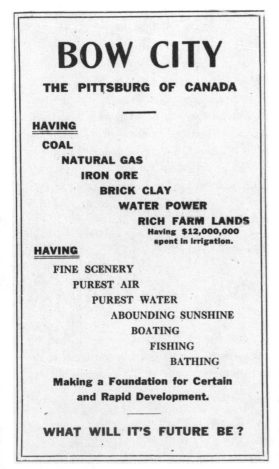

Cover of a pamphlet published by the Prairie Coal Company of Regina. Like so many prairie settlements, the ambitiously-named Bow City aspired to greatness. It remains a hamlet. GLENBOW ARCHIVES NA-789-57

Bow Island

Town on Highway 3, approximately 54 kilometres southwest of Medicine Hat

According to legend, the names of Bow Island and Grassy Lake were accidentally confused and should have been transposed. The island feature whose name this town shares is near Grassy Lake, almost 30 kilometres distant. Bow Island became a village in 1910 and a town in 1912.

Bowden

Town on Highway 2, approximately 42 kilometres south southwest of Red Deer

In a pre-World War I letter to Provincial Archivist Katherine Hughes, Mrs. James Marshall tantalizingly wrote, "I shall endeavor to give you an authentic story of how Bowden (near Olds) got its name, it being a matter of doubt among those now residing in that village."[32] Disappointingly, no explanation follows. Mrs. Marshall might have known whether Bowden was named for Bowdon in Chesterfield, England, or Bowden in Scotland. Bowden's secretary–treasurer in 1970, Marie W. Camney, had another theory: "A surveyor named Williamson who was working on the Calgary and Edmonton Railway was asked when they reached the siding what to name it and he jokingly replied, 'Call it by my wife's maiden name, Bowden.'"[33] A post office opened in 1892. Bowden became a village in 1904 and a town in 1981.

Boyle

Village on Highway 63, approximately 35 kilometres east southeast of Athabasca

Born in Sarnia, Ontario, John Robert Boyle (1871–1936) earned his place in Alberta's history several times over, not least of which as the Member of the Legislative Assembly who helped bring down his own government, the province's first, in 1910.

Boyle moved west as a young man, working as a teacher and journalist while articling for the law. He settled in Edmonton in 1899 and served as an alderman before his election as a Liberal to Alberta's first legislature in 1905. Boyle split with Premier Alexander Rutherford over a 1910 scandal concerning the Alberta and Great Waterways Railway (A&GW) and led a revolt in the legislature that ended Rutherford's tenure and installed another Liberal premier, Arthur Sifton. As education minister Boyle regularly inspected schools, and as Attorney General he was responsible for enforcing prohibition, effective in Alberta from 1916–24. Though a teetotaler himself, Boyle personally opposed the measure, which ultimately proved unworkable. After the Liberal defeat in 1921, Boyle served as opposition leader until his appointment to the Supreme Court of Alberta in 1924. In a 1933 trial, Mr. Justice Boyle admonished a distracted jury, "May I remind the jury that the case may not be altogether interesting, but it is your duty to listen to the evidence. You can go to sleep some other time."[34] Boyle is buried in the Edmonton Cemetery. The A&GW arrived in Boyle in 1914, and the post office opened two years later. Boyle was incorporated as a village in 1953.

Bragg Creek

Hamlet on Highway 22, approximately 30 kilometres west of Calgary

This area was known as Turnbull's Crossing before the arrival of Albert Warren Bragg (1867–1948), a Truro, Nova Scotia native who settled on a creekside ranch west of Calgary from around 1894–96. Despite his brief sojourn, both the creek and the hamlet bear Warren Bragg's name. Bragg later ranched near Rosebud, southwest of Drumheller, and managed farm property there for a Calgary law firm. He is buried in Calgary's Burnsland Cemetery. The name Fullerton, for a longtime family in the area, was often suggested to replace Bragg Creek, but was never adopted.[35] Bragg Creek Provincial Park shares the name.

Brant

Hamlet on Secondary Highway 804, approximately 63 kilometres southeast of Calgary

The Brant goose inspired the name for both this hamlet (established and named in 1905 by E.E. Thompson of High River) and its post office (which Charles H. Kelly opened the same year). Harold and Julia Parker had the new community's first baby in 1905, and they named him Brant Parker. The hamlet relocated when the Canadian Pacific Railway built its Kipp–Alderside line a few years later.

Brant Parker (far left), the first baby born in Brant, stands with his siblings, circa 1913. COURTESY OF TONI KENNEDY

Brant's welcome sign is a rarity: it explains the origin of the name. COURTESY OF TED PARKER

Breton

Village on Highway 20, approximately 36 kilometres east southeast of Drayton Valley

In 1927 the Keystone post office changed its name to honour the area's Member of the Legislative Assembly (MLA), Douglas Corney Breton (1883–1953), a member of the governing United Farmers of Alberta (UFA) party. Born in South Africa, Breton moved to Canada in 1904 with his brother Lawrence, and they opened a store at Telfordville, Alberta. After serving in India and Afghanistan during World War I, Breton returned to Alberta and became active with the UFA. As the MLA for Leduc constituency from 1926–30, Breton pushed successfully for the extension of the Lacombe and North Western Railway. This new railway point on the extended line was named for him in 1927. Breton moved to England in 1953. In the 1980s, Breton's daughter presented a portrait of him for the village council chamber.

Breynat

Hamlet west of Highway 63, approximately 50 kilometres northwest of Lac La Biche

Known as the "Flying Bishop," French-born Gabriel Breynat (1867–1953) flew to remote points in Canada's northern territories during his long tenure as the Bishop of Mackenzie. Breynat was a member of the Oblates of Mary Immaculate, a Roman Catholic order that played a large role in Alberta's missionary activity. The post office was named for him when it opened in 1936. Bishop Breynat is buried in Aix, France.

Brooks

Town on the Trans-Canada Highway (Highway 1), approximately 100 kilometres northwest of Medicine Hat

The Canadian Pacific Railway (CPR) established this station in 1904 and named it for divisional engineer Noel E. Brooks (1865–1926). Born in Quebec, Brooks joined the CPR in 1887 and from 1903–13 he was stationed at Calgary, where he became a member of the exclusive Ranchmen's Club. After serving as engineer of maintenance-of-way in Winnipeg from 1913–17 he returned east. Brooks retired to his native

Sherbrooke, where he is buried. His passing was unmarked by the *Brooks Bulletin*, though the *Calgary Daily Herald* ran a story on his death. Brooks was incorporated as a village in 1910 and as a town in 1911.

Brosseau

Hamlet on Highway 36, approximately 10 kilometres north northeast of Two Hills

Merchant Edmond Brosseau (1842–1917), a Quebec-born veteran of the American Civil War, opened the post office here in 1904 and operated it for the rest of his life. Brosseau fought for the Union cause.

Brownfield

Hamlet on Secondary Highway 872, approximately 26 kilometres north of Coronation

Missouri-born rancher Charles Dee Brownfield (1880–1943), who as a young man drove Texas longhorns from Wyoming to Alberta's Neutral Hills, opened the post office here in 1907 but operated it for only a few months—until it burned to the ground when a lamp overturned. Brownfield was a strong advocate for brand inspection and served as a brand inspector from 1922 until his death.

Brownvale

Hamlet on Highway 2, approximately 161 kilometres west southwest of Grimshaw

In 1924 the Central Canada Railway reached this area of the Peace River country and established a new railway point on property acquired from John Brown, who had settled here in 1913, and for whom the hamlet is named. The slope of the property invited use of the suffix "vale," a poetic form for valley.

Bruce

Hamlet on Highway 14, approximately 20 kilometres northwest of Viking

"Boost for Bruce," an early slogan used to promote this farming community, became possible only after the abandonment of its original name: Hurry. Founded in 1906 by settlers from Michigan, Hurry moved a short distance to its present site when the Grand Trunk Pacific Railway (GTP) established its Bruce station in 1908. The new name honoured A. Bruce Smith (circa 1849–1921), a Montrealer who headed the GTP's telegraph system. The *Toronto Globe* judged Smith "a man of untiring energy and of first class mental power."[36] Smith's son-in-law, financier Edmund Taylor (1871–1929), was a president of the Calgary Stock Exchange and a business partner of Sir James A. Lougheed (for whom the village of Lougheed was named).

Bruderheim

Town on Highway 45, approximately 37 kilometres northeast of Edmonton

In 1895, a group of ethnic German settlers from eastern Europe established Brüderheim, meaning "Brethren's home," a reference to their Moravian faith, and the Moravian Church's identification as the "Brethren's Church." The *umlaut*, confusing to Canadian authorities, was later left out.

Brule

Hamlet on Brule Road west of Highway 40, approximately 19 kilometres south southwest of Hinton

Established in 1912 as a mining town for the Canadian Northern Railway, this hamlet shares the name of nearby Brule Lake. *Brule* was a common term used by surveyors to refer to wooded country that had been burned over.

Buck Creek

Hamlet on Secondary Highway 616, approximately 13 kilometres south southeast of Drayton Valley

This hamlet is likely named for nearby Bucklake Creek. The Buck Creek post office opened in 1925.

Buck Lake

Hamlet north of Highway 13, approximately 30 kilometres south southeast of Drayton Valley

When the post office opened on the shore of Buck Lake in 1910, post-master J.L. Tipping (1860–1936) suggested the names Buck Lake, Minnehik and Tipperary. Tipping's preference was Buck Lake; the postal authorities chose Minnehik, a Cree word for "spruce." But many people had a hard time remembering Minnehik and simply called the settlement Buck Lake. The name changed officially in 1954.[37]

Buffalo Head Prairie

Hamlet on Secondary Highway 697, approximately 69 kilometres south-east of High Level

Approved as a post office name in 1976, it is of unknown origin.

Buford

Hamlet south of Highway 39, approximately 25 kilometres west of Leduc

Tiny as it is, the hamlet of Buford is still larger than its namesake in North Dakota, now a ghost town. Buford, Alberta—so named because many of its settlers hailed from the Peace Garden State—was established in 1903 when its post office opened. "It is a new place and never had no other name," wrote the Buford postmaster to the chief geographer of the Department of the Interior around 1906.[38] The original Buford was once home to civilian personnel of Fort Buford, the American army post where Sitting Bull—whose Sioux warriors defeated Custer in 1876—finally surrendered in 1881 after a four-year Canadian sojourn. Fort Buford was named for John Buford, a Kentucky-born Union general during the U.S. Civil War.

Burdett

Village on Highway 3, approximately 63 kilometres west southwest of Medicine Hat

"After my mother," said King Edward VII of Baroness Angela Burdett-Coutts (1814–1906), "she is the most remarkable woman in the kingdom."[39] Made a baroness by Queen Victoria in 1871, Angela Burdett-Coutts was fabulously wealthy and generously philanthropical, and is the subject of at least three biographies. Charles Dickens dedicated a novel, *Martin Chuzzlewit*, to her. The baroness married William Lehman Ashmead Bartlett (1851–1921), an American-born British politician 37 years younger than her. (By royal licence he took her name, becoming Sir William Lehman Ashmead Bartlett Burdett-Coutts.) The baroness invested in the North Western Coal and Navigation Company, which developed coal resources in southern Alberta, and in the Alberta Railway and Irrigation Company. She is buried in Westminster Abbey. The village of Coutts was also named for her. Burdett was incorporated as a village in 1913.

Baroness Angela Burdett-Coutts, a philanthropist, invested in coal and railway interests in southern Alberta. She donated £50 to each of four Lethbridge churches, and several streets in that city—Ashmead, Bartlett, Burdett and Coutts streets, as well as Baroness Road—were named for her and her husband, Sir William Lehman Ashmead Bartlett Burdett-Coutts. Lethbridge's Westminster Park was named for the area within London, England, that Sir William represented in parliament.
National Archives of Canada C-000639

Busby

Hamlet on Secondary Highway 651, approximately 50 kilometres north northwest of Edmonton

This site was settled by Americans and was boldly named Independence when its post office opened in 1903. By 1915 the Edmonton, Dunvegan and British Columbia Railway arrived and Independence lost to Busby—possibly for a railway contractor or for Edward S. Busby, an

Ottawa civil servant who had been a customs inspector at Skagway, Alaska during the Klondike Gold Rush.

Byemoor

Hamlet on Secondary Highway 853, approximately 44 kilometres north northwest of Hanna

Homesteader Leonard Browne (1884–1952) hailed originally from Stockton-on-Tees, a British port that was "by-the-moors." Browne settled in Alberta in 1904 and became a railway labourer, homesteader and mail carrier. The name he suggested for the local school district—Byemoor, evoking his original home—was drawn from a hat by his son, Buster Browne. The arrival of Canadian National Railways (CNR) in 1925 must have been a familiar sight for Leonard, whose hometown in England was reportedly the birthplace of the modern passenger railway. The CNR purchased a townsite from farmer Jack Wilson, but before long the provisionally named Wilson's Siding became the hamlet of Byemoor. Browne became a real estate, insurance and implement agent and Justice of the Peace in the community that he named. After serving in the army during World War II, Browne moved to Fort Saskatchewan, where he served as town secretary–treasurer from 1945 until his death. He is buried in Fort Saskatchewan.

Cadogan

Hamlet on Secondary Highway 600, approximately 12 kilometres west southwest of Provost

This onetime village was probably named for the 5th Earl Cadogan, George Henry (1840–1915), possibly because of his role as Britain's colonial secretary from 1886–92. He later served as Lord-Lieutenant of Ireland (1895–1902). Avenues in this hamlet originally had such British names as Caversham, Oakley and Reading. The post office opened here in 1909.

Cadomin

Hamlet on Mountain Park Road south of Highway 40, approximately 85 kilometres southwest of Edson

In 1912 Frederick L. Hammond (died 1941) discovered a coal seam in this vicinity and developed it through his Cadomin Mine Company. "Cadomin" was his contraction of the name Canadian Dominion Mine, and the name applies also to Cadomin Creek and Cadomin Mountain. Like the other company towns of the Coal Branch—a Grand Trunk Pacific Railway line that freighted coal from this region for decades—Cadomin flourished until the early 1950s, when the advent of diesel killed the mining industry. More recently, limestone has brought about a revival. Hammond is buried in the famous Forest Lawn Cemetery in Los Angeles.

Cadotte Lake

Hamlet on Secondary Highway 986, approximately 57 kilometres east northeast of Peace River

This hamlet was named for nearby Cadotte Lake, itself named for fur trader Jean Baptiste Cadot (or Cadotte, 1723–1803), who travelled west from Sault Ste. Marie with the likes of Alexander Henry, Thomas Frobisher and Peter Pond. The post office opened in 1969. The Cadotte River also shares the name.

Cairns

Hamlet north of Secondary Highway 600, approximately 19 kilometres west southwest of Provost

This name, meaning "piles of stones," might have been descriptive. The Canadian Pacific Railway established a station here in 1909.

Calahoo

Hamlet on Secondary Highway 633, approximately 35 kilometres northwest of Edmonton

Early in the 19th century, Iroquois brothers Louis and Bernard Callihoo (the spelling varies) came west with the Hudson's Bay Company as voyageurs in the fur trade. The family of Louis' son Michel later received a reserve under Treaty No. 6, but its members later accepted "enfranchisement." This meant equality with nonnative Canadians, including voting rights, but the loss of treaty rights and of the Michel Callihoo Reserve. The Canadian Northern Railway built its Calahoo station in 1915.

Calgary

City on the Trans-Canada Highway (Highway 1) and highways 1A and 2, approximately 297 kilometres south of Edmonton

"As we have now a Post or Fort at Bow River it would be as well if it was known by some name," wrote North-West Mounted Police (NWMP) Assistant Commissioner Acheson Gosford Irvine (for whom the hamlet of Irvine was named) to his superiors in Ottawa on February 29, 1876.[40] Established in 1875 as a communications link between Fort Macleod and Fort Edmonton, the Bow River Fort was commanded by Inspector Ephrem Brisebois (1850–90), a 23-year-old native of South Durham, Quebec. In the pattern set by Fort Walsh and Fort Macleod, named for NWMP Commissioner James Walsh and Assistant Commissioner James F. Macleod respectively, Brisebois called his post Fort Brisebois. But the young officer was unpopular with his men and superiors alike, and within months both he and his name were replaced. In his 1876 letter, Irvine—who had recently succeeded Macleod as Assistant Commissioner—forwarded his predecessor's recommendation: "Colonel Macleod has suggested the name of Calgary which I believe in Scotch means clear running water, a very appropriate name I think."[41] Irvine was mistaken—the original Gaelic form of *Calgary* means "bay farm" or "preserved pasture at the harbour."

Colonel Macleod had once visited Calgary House, the home of John Munro Mackenzie (Macleod's sister's brother-in-law), on Calgary Bay, Isle of Mull, and was struck by the area's beauty. Macleod died in Calgary, Alberta, in 1894 and is buried in the city that he named.

The Canadian Pacific Railway's Imperial Limited arrives at the Calgary station, circa 1907. By 1908 an enlarged structure occupied the site, and the earlier station's two buildings were separated and moved to Claresholm and High River. CALGARY PUBLIC LIBRARY PC604

As for Calgary House, Mackenzie's family lost the property after his death in 1937, and its new owner—the Scottish Board of Agriculture and Fisheries—subdivided the roughly 1,600-hectare estate into smaller farms.[42] Calgary House still stands, however, and tourists can also visit the scenic Calgary Stones and dine at the Calgary Farmhouse Hotel.

Irvine's letter remained in the files of the Department of the Interior until 1921, when Alberta Senator Sir James A. Lougheed (for whom the village of Lougheed was named) removed the document, had it mounted in a leather enclosure with gilt lettering, and presented it to Calgary's mayor, Samuel H. Adams. The letter is now housed in the City of Calgary Archives.

In 1884 the Canadian Pacific Railway (CPR) laid out a new townsite west of the fort and named the principal streets after shareholders and executives of the railway company and its real estate subsidiary. City council changed these names to numbers in 1904, but a few have crept back into use—none more prominent than Stephen Avenue, the downtown pedestrian shopping mall named for CPR President George Stephen (later raised to the peerage as Baron Mount Stephen). A suburban thoroughfare, Brisebois Drive, revived the nearly forgotten name of Fort Calgary's first commander.

The Calgary Brewing and Malting Company, established in 1892, made Calgary's name synonymous with Calgary Beer. Calgary Public Library PC1376

Calgary's Stephen Avenue, seen here in 1912, was named for Canadian Pacific Railway president George Stephen, who was later raised to the peerage as Baron Mount Stephen. CALGARY PUBLIC LIBRARY PC117

In its growth, the city of Calgary has absorbed the villages of Rouleauville (named for Charles and Edouard Rouleau, prominent figures in a Roman Catholic settlement annexed in 1907) and Crescent Heights (descriptive of the heights north of the Bow River, annexed in 1910) and the towns of Forest Lawn (named for the famous Los Angeles cemetery, annexed in 1961), Montgomery (evidently named for Field Marshall Montgomery of Alamein, annexed in 1963) and Bowness (possibly named for a town in England's Lake District, annexed in 1964). Other areas annexed into Calgary include the district of Springbank (descriptive of springs in the area, annexed in stages) and the hamlet of Midnapore (named after an Indian city approximately 100 kilometres west of Calcutta, annexed in 1961).

Calgary was incorporated as a town in 1884 and as a city in 1894.

Calling Lake

Hamlet on Secondary Highway 813, approximately 95 kilometres northwest of Lac La Biche

Calling Lake was named for the adjacent lake, which sounds loudly when its ice freezes up. The post office opened here in 1920. The name applies also to Calling Lake Provincial Park.

Welcome to Calgary: City Hall during the first Stampede Week, 1912. CALGARY PUBLIC LIBRARY PC273

Calmar

Town on Highway 39, approximately 42 kilometres southwest of Edmonton

Though he came to Alberta from Foreman, North Dakota, pioneer farmer Carl John Blomquist (1866–1944) hailed originally from the Baltic port city of Kalmar, Sweden. Blomquist journeyed to Wetaskiwin in 1894 to scout land for a group of Scandinavian settlers in drought-stricken North Dakota. He brought his wife, Maria, and their children the following year, and as the first settlers in the area, their sod-roofed farmhouse—where there was always a fresh pot of rabbit stew—housed many of the other Dakota settlers until they could establish themselves. When Carl became postmaster in 1900, he named the post office for his hometown. Calmar was incorporated as a village in 1949 and as a town in 1954. Both Carl and Maria Blomquist are buried in Calmar's Willow Creek Cemetery.

Campsie

Hamlet on Highway 18, approximately 16 kilometres west of Barrhead

With the name William Wallace—the same as the 13th century rebel, portrayed in film by Mel Gibson—Campsie's original 1909 postmaster could be nothing if not Scottish. When he died in 1942 at 80, the *Barrhead Leader* noted that Wallace "gave up a professorship in a Scottish University to settle in this locality for some obscure reason."[43] Wallace named his homestead Campsie Mains, reportedly for the Campsie Hills near Glasgow and for the Gaelic *maines*, or land. The post office became simply Campsie. Wallace is buried in Barrhead.

Camrose

City on Highway 26, approximately 70 kilometres southeast of Edmonton

The Welsh village of Camrose, Pembrokeshire (now Dyfed), would seem an odd namesake for a centre largely populated by Norwegian settlers. It was originally known as Sparling, possibly for Reverend Joseph Walter Sparling (1843–1912), a Winnipeg clergyman. Because it was confused with Sperling, Manitoba, and Stirling, Alberta, the name was changed when the Canadian Pacific Railway (CPR) arrived in 1905 and the post office opened. The traditional explanation is that a British postal guide yielded the name. Another explanation is that Camrose was named for Cameron and Rose, the children of Canadian Northern Railway contractor Big Archie McKenzie, who built the Vegreville–Stettler line that passes through Camrose.[44] However, the CPR arrived first, so unless Big Archie worked on both railways, the Welsh explanation is the more likely one. Another possibility is that the name refers to wild roses that grow along Stoney Creek, which passes through Camrose. In the 1920s Miss Edith Canham, a schoolteacher from Hull, England, spent a year in Camrose as an exchange teacher. On her return home she built a house and named it Camrose.[45] Camrose was incorporated as Alberta's eighth city in 1955.

Business street in Camrose, n.d. CALGARY PUBLIC LIBRARY PC486

Canmore

Town on the Trans-Canada Highway (Highway 1), approximately 17 kilometres southeast of Banff

Tradition ascribes the naming of Canmore, the first divisional point of the Canadian Pacific Railway (CPR) west of Calgary, to Donald A. Smith (Lord Strathcona), a supporter of the railway and the man who drove the last spike on its completion. Like so many men of influence in the CPR, Strathcona was Scottish. Canmore refers to the Scottish

King Malcom III, who was known as Canmore, meaning "big head" or "large-headed" in Gaelic. However, James White, chief geographer of the Department of the Interior, indicated in 1916 that this town was named "after Kenmore village, Argyllshire, Scotland, which from the Gaelic *ceam mor*, 'big head;' orthography changed in error."[46]

Canyon Creek

Hamlet north of Highway 2, approximately 22 kilometres west northwest of Slave Lake

A nearby creek inspired the name for this hamlet on the southern shore of Lesser Slave Lake. The post office opened in 1928.

Carbon

Village south of Secondary Highway 575, approximately 75 kilometres northeast of Calgary

This coal-rich location was first developed by the Kneehill Coal Company in 1905 and was originally known as Kneehill. Farmer John M. Bogart suggested the current name, inspired by the local coal resource. Carbon was incorporated as a village in 1912.

Carbondale

Hamlet north of Highway 37, approximately 22 kilometres north of Edmonton

This hamlet was so named for the coal mines in the area. The post office opened in 1932.

Carcajou

Hamlet on Secondary Highway 695, approximately 80 kilometres south of High Level

Carcajou comes from Algonkian for "wolverine." Carcajou hamlet is located near Wolverine Point, which explorer and fur trader David Thompson identified on his 1814 map. The post office opened in 1923.

Cardiff

Hamlet east of Highway 2, approximately 27 kilometres north of Edmonton

The area's coal mines obviously influenced the selection of this name, after the Welsh city long known for its coal industry.

Cardston

Town on Secondary Highway 501, approximately 65 kilometres south southwest of Lethbridge

In 1886 Charles Ora Card (1839–1906)—the son-in-law of famed Mormon leader Brigham Young—led a large group of Mormon settlers from Utah into southern Alberta, where they sought both agricultural lands and relief from new American laws against polygamy. Cardston became the centre of Mormon settlement, and Card served as its first mayor. Cardston became a village in 1898 and a town in 1901.

Mormon leader Charles Ora Card was the namesake of Cardston and its first mayor. Sir Alexander Galt Museum and Archives

Dedicated in 1923, the Latter-day Saints Temple in Cardston symbolizes the Mormon faith in southern Alberta. Calgary Public Library PC439 (detail)

Carmangay

Village on Secondary Highway 522, approximately 50 kilometres north northwest of Lethbridge

In 1904 Charles Whitney Carman of Chicago, a civil engineer, acquired 600 hectares of land along the Little Bow River and formed the Carmangay Farm Company, which he named after himself and his wife, the former Mill Gay. The river narrowed at this point, and Carman reasoned correctly the Canadian Pacific Railway (CPR) would

Business section of Carmangay, circa 1910. Calgary Public Library PC483

in future traverse this property. He surveyed the townsite of Carmangay and auctioned town lots once the CPR arrived in 1909.[47] Along with their son, Gay, the Carmans eventually moved back to Chicago—much wealthier than when they came. Carmangay was incorporated as a town in 1911, but reverted to village status in 1936.

Caroline

Village on Highway 54, approximately 34 kilometres south southeast of Rocky Mountain House

From 1908–1921 Minnesota-born merchant Harvey A. Langley (1870–1965) and his wife, Cynthia, operated this post office, which they named for their only child, Caroline Rebecca Nelson (circa 1899–1981). Although the village, which formed in 1951, maintains the name Caroline, its namesake always called herself Reba. She lived in the area most of her life.

Postmaster and storekeeper Harvey Langley with his wife, Cynthia, and their daughter, Caroline Rebecca, 1918. The Langley store served as Caroline's post office, and Reba—as she was known—was its namesake. Courtesy of Vi Larsen

Carolside

Hamlet on Secondary Highway 570, approximately 78 kilometres south southeast of Drumheller

In 1920 the Jethson post office moved from its original location to the vicinity of George and Harry Purvis' ranch, which they had acquired a decade earlier and named for their former home in Scotland.

Carseland

Hamlet on Highway 24, approximately 35 kilometres southeast of Calgary

Originally named for pioneer postmaster Emil Griesbach in 1913, the post office here acquired its present name the following year. It is a Scottish term describing the area's rich alluvial soil.

Carstairs

Town on Highway 2, approximately 82 kilometres south of Red Deer

The original Carstairs is a scottish village in South Lanarkshire, southeast of Glasgow. Its first namesake was Carstairs Junction, a village only two kilometres away from Carstairs, laid out for Scottish railway workers in the 1840s. The second was another railway settlement, this one in far-off Canada and reportedly settled by Scottish émigrés. Alberta's Carstairs developed along the Calgary and Edmonton Railway, built in 1890–1891. It became a village in 1903 and a town in 1966. The original Carstairs in Scotland occupies the site of a mediaval castle, Castleterrs.

Carvel

Hamlet on Secondary Highway 770, approximately 14 kilometres west of Stony Plain

The Grand Trunk Pacific Railway established this railway point west of Edmonton in 1911, naming it Carvel Station after the bestselling 1899 novel *Richard Carvel*. (*Station* was dropped from the name in 1950.) The author was American historian and writer, Winston Churchill (1871–1947)—not to be confused with British historian and writer, Winston Churchill (1874–1965), whose own novel, *Savrola*, was also published in 1899. In a letter that year to his American counterpart, the

British Churchill proposed a solution: "Mr. Winston Churchill presents his compliments to Mr. Winston Churchill, and begs to draw his attention to a matter which concerns them both," wrote the future British prime minister. "Mr. Winston Churchill has decided to sign all published articles, stories and other works, 'Winston Spencer Churchill' and not 'Winston Churchill' as formerly."[48] The American novelist responded warmly. "Mr. Winston Churchill is extremely grateful to Mr. Winston Churchill for bringing forward a subject which has given Mr. Winston Churchill much anxiety," wrote the American. "Mr. Winston Churchill makes haste to add that, had he possessed any other names, he would certainly have adopted one of them." Though they were once equally famous, Prime Minister Winston S. Churchill has far eclipsed the American novelist in popular memory.

Carway

Hamlet on Highway 2, approximately 86 kilometres southwest of Lethbridge

The name of this border hamlet, opposite Montana's Port of Piegan, is condensed from "Cardston Highway," referring to the route from Babb, Montana, to Cardston, Alberta. William Roberts, the first officer in charge of this preventative station (possibly relating to the health of imported livestock), coined the name in 1926.

Caslan

Hamlet on Secondary Highway 663, approximately 38 kilometres southwest of Lac La Biche

This name, of forgotten origin, was probably chosen by the Alberta and Great Waterways Railway, which established a station here in 1914.

Castor

Town on Highway 12, approximately 140 kilometres east of Red Deer

Before the Canadian Pacific Railway line from Stettler arrived in 1909, the local post office was named Williston, after the North Dakota hometown of area settlers. "It appears, however," noted Calgary's *Morning Albertan* in 1909, "that the C.P.R. Co. has an antipathy to words ending in 'ton' or 'ville' as names for stations, and decided on the name of Castor, in allusion to the name of the creek—the Beaver Dam—on which the town is situated."[49] (*Castor* is Latin for beaver.) Early fire insurance plans show the main street as Beaver Street. Castor became a village in 1909 and a town the following year.

Cayley

Hamlet west of Highway 2, approximately 55 kilometres south of Calgary

As a young man, Toronto-born lawyer Hugh St. Quentin Cayley (circa 1859–1934) moved to frontier Calgary, where he became court clerk and published the *Calgary Herald* from 1885–87. Warned not to criticize Magistrate Jeremiah Travis, a temperance advocate, or he would be charged with contempt, Cayley published the headline, "Is This Contempt of Court?"[50] A brass band accompanied Cayley on his way to jail, where he remained briefly. The public had the final say: Travis was forced from the bench and Cayley was later elected to the North-West Territories Assembly. He moved to Vancouver in 1897 and became a judge in 1917. This onetime village was named for him.

Lawyer Hugh St. Quentin Cayley was an early publisher of the Calgary Herald. *He later became a judge in British Columbia.* GLENBOW ARCHIVES NA-433-3 (DETAIL)

Cereal

Village on Highway 9, approximately 138 kilometres east of Drumheller

Reverend R.J. McMillan, who was impressed by this region's agricultural potential, suggested the name, adopted when this prairie post office opened in 1911. Cereal was incorporated as a village in 1914.

Cessford

Hamlet on Secondary Highway 876, approximately 94 kilometres southeast of Drumheller

Axel Anderson and his wife came from Cess Fiord, Sweden, and they named their homestead Cess Fiord, according to the farm's later owner, longtime resident Dorothy Williams. Mrs. M.E. Anderson served as postmistress from 1910–1917 and evidently operated the post office out of her farmhouse pantry. The post office shortened the homestead name to Cessford.

Champion

Village east of Highway 23, approximately 65 kilometres north northwest of Lethbridge

In 1906, Martin George Clever and his second wife Jennie quit their native Iowa to homestead in southern Alberta, north of the Little Bow River. Clever's offer of free lots on his property attracted businesses and created the instant hamlet of Cleverville. When the Canadian Pacific Railway (CPR) started planning its Kipp–Aldersyde line, the company tried to buy Clever's remaining property through a third party. Clever was no dummy; he knew who wanted his land and demanded a better price. The CPR responded by buying another farm west of Cleverville and developing it in 1910 as the new railway townsite of Champion. Cleverville vanished as quickly as it appeared. Its buildings and people moved to Champion, and all that remains is a stone cairn on a lonely highway that reads, "Village of Cleverville—1906–1910."

Champion was named for Henry Thomson Champion (1847–1916), a Winnipeg banker and onetime chairman of the Winnipeg Stock Exchange. Born in Toronto, Champion came west during the Manitoba Insurrection of 1870 as a sergeant in the Wolseley Expedition, then remained in Winnipeg for the rest of his life. If he had no other Alberta connection, at least Champion lived on Winnipeg's Edmonton Street.

Chancellor

Hamlet on Secondary Highway 842, approximately 85 kilometres east of Calgary

In 1913, German settlers provided the name for this new hamlet on the Canadian Pacific Railway: Chancellor, for their homeland's political leader, Theobald von Bethman-Hollweg (1856–1921), who held that title (the equivalent of prime minister) from 1909–17. Within a year World War I broke out, pitting Canada—as part of the British Empire—against Germany and its allies. Although he tried to keep the peace in 1914, the Chancellor's "blank cheque" to Austria–Hungary and his dismissal of Britain's guarantee of Belgian neutrality as "a scrap of paper" were key steps toward world war. While other places in Alberta discarded their German names—such as Carlstadt and Dusseldorf (renamed Alderson and Freedom, respectively), and in the next war, Swastika (which became Gayford)—Chancellor was never renamed. (Bismark, a German settlement 24 kilometres northwest of Ponoka named for Germany's "Iron Chancellor," survived the war without a name change, but after its post office closed Bismark eventually disappeared from the map.)

Chauvin

Village south of Secondary Highway 610, approximately 38 kilometres north of Provost

Like many of the directors of the Grand Trunk Railway, parent company of the Grand Trunk Pacific, George Von Chauvin lived in England. Though he might never have set foot in the province, this village—part of an alphabetical line beginning with Artland, Saskatchewan—bears his name. Chauvin was incorporated as a village in 1912.

Cheadle

Hamlet on Highway 24, approximately 40 kilometres east of Calgary

In 1862, British medical student Walter Butler Cheadle (1835–1910) interrupted his studies in London to join William Fitzwilliam, Viscount Milton (1839–77) on an expedition to western Canada. Milton and Cheadle described their explorations of the prairies and Rocky

Mountains in *The North-West Passage By Land* (1865). Cheadle wrote a separate book under the title *Cheadle's Journal of a Trip Across Canada, 1862–1863*, which was published in 1931. The Canadian Pacific Railway named this siding for Dr. Cheadle in 1884; Mount Cheadle in British Columbia is also named for him.[51]

Cherhill

Hamlet on Highway 43, approximately 33 kilometres southeast of Mayerthorpe

Adolph Peter Stecher opened a post office by this name on Stecher's Hill, his homestead farm, in 1911. The manufactured named Cherhill was fashioned from the last syllable of Stecher's name, combined with a descriptive suffix. In 1914, with the approach of the Canadian Northern Railway, the post office moved about five kilometres to the present townsite. Stecher, along with his wife, Mary, and their children, Gaylord and Alta, moved to California and eventually returned to their native Michigan, where Adolph and Mary are buried in Evart.

Left to right: Mary and Adolph Stecher, with son, Gaylord, and a customer, stand in front of the Cherhill post office on the family farm, Stecher's Hill. REPRODUCED (WITH PERMISSION OF VERA BROWN) FROM VERA A. HOLT, ED., *The Lantern Era: A History of Cherhill, Rochfort Bridge, Sangudo and Surrounding School Districts* (SANGUDO, ALTA.: SANGUDO AND DISTRICT HISTORICAL SOCIETY, 1979).

Cherry Grove

Hamlet on Highway 55, approximately 11 kilometres southeast of Cold Lake

This descriptive name refers to the choke cherries that grow in this district. Dudley James Dow opened this post office in 1932.

Chestermere

Town on Highway 1A, approximately 15 kilometres east of Calgary

In the years before World War I, Calgary's rapid growth led to widespread land speculation and the promotion of distant subdivisions to be connected to the city by streetcar or "inter-urban" trains. Speculators promoted a slough east of town—formerly known as Kinniburgh Slough, and identified on irrigation maps as "Reservoir No. 1"—as Chestermere Lake, a grand-sounding name for a community that existed only on paper. "The coming swell residential district of Calgary," boasted Chestermere Lake's promoters, who foresaw a clubhouse, amusement park and summer hotel.[52] The boom turned bust in 1913, and it took decades before the artificial Chestermere Lake was developed and for the community to grow beyond a few cottages. Chestermere Lake became a summer village in 1977 and was incorporated as the town of Chestermere in 1993. Accounts differ as to the origin of the name—whether it was Lord Chester or Lord Chestermere or Chesterville, Ontario.

Chin

Hamlet on Highway 3, approximately 25 kilometres east of Lethbridge

The name is descriptive, referring to a nearby butte that resembles a chin. A post office opened in 1910.

Chinook

Hamlet on Highway 9, approximately 150 kilometres north of Medicine Hat

This former village, incorporated in 1913 and dissolved in 1977, was named for the warm Chinook winds that descend from the Rocky Mountains and relieve winter's grip.

Chipman

Village on Highway 15, approximately 58 kilometres east northeast of Edmonton

In 1891—only two decades after the Hudson's Bay Company (HBC) yielded its control of what is now Alberta to the Canadian government—Clarence Campbell Chipman (1856–1924) became the company's chief executive. Born in Amherst, Nova Scotia, Chipman enjoyed a distinguished career as a civil servant, notably as secretary to future prime minister Sir Charles Tupper during Tupper's tenure as Minister of Railways and Canals. Chipman was involved in Atlantic fisheries negotiations with the United States and authored *A Treatise on the Fisheries of Canada* (1891). He retired from the HBC in 1911 and died in Leamington, England. In 1905, the Canadian Northern Railway named this station on its new Winnipeg–Edmonton line for him. Notwithstanding its Ango-Saxon name, Chipman's population is overwhelmingly of Ukrainian origin. Chipman became a village in 1913.

Chisholm

Hamlet west of Highway 44, approximately 60 kilometres west southwest of Athabasca

Here is an example where the hamlet was known by one name and the post office by another. Both Chisholm and its post office, Chisholm Mills (as well as Chisholm Creek) were named for Thomas Chisholm (1844–1936), a former Klondiker and tie contractor for the Edmonton, Dunvegan and British Columbia Railway. As the owner of Dawson City's Aurora Saloon and dance hall during the Klondike gold rush, Chisholm once sold milk for $5 a mug—"just five times the price of whisky," according to Pierre Berton.[53] He was reputed to wear a watch chain of gold nuggets, but at 110 kilograms and nearly two metres tall, the Nova Scotia native would have been memorable regardless. Though he left the Klondike with $75,000 to his name, Chisholm was generous to a fault and died penniless. According to his obituary in the *Peace River Record Gazette*, Chisholm had fronted $20,000 to Alexander Pantages, a Dawson City bartender and Greek immigrant who later founded a continent-wide chain of Pantages Theatres. As the story goes, Chisholm's friends later appealed to the impresario to help out his former benefactor, but an ungrateful Pantages had evidently forgotten him.[54] Accounts of Pantages' life make no mention of Chisholm, who is buried in McLennan.

Clairmont

Hamlet on Highway 2, approximately 10 kilometres north of Grande Prairie

In 1916 the Edmonton, Dunvegan and British Columbia Railway established a station on the western shore of Clairmont Lake. The lake was named for Eugene Clairmont, the cook on an early survey party led by noted Dominion Land Surveyor J.B. St. Cyr.[55] The railway took its station name from the lake. Clairmont was incorporated as a village in 1917, and an elevator built that year still stands as the oldest one remaining in northern Alberta. Proximity to Grande Prairie stunted Clairmont's growth, and the village was dissolved in 1945. It remains a bedroom community of Grande Prairie.

Clandonald

Hamlet south of Highway 45, approximately 27 kilometres north northeast of Vermilion

When James Hagen opened the post office in 1909 this centre was known as Wellsdale. In the 1920s a Catholic priest, Captain Reverend Donald MacIntyre (circa 1891–1944), headed a colony of some 120 agricultural settlers under the aegis of the Scottish Immigrant Aid Society.[56] With its new Scottish colony, Wellsdale became Clandonald, honouring Scotland's largest clan. The Canadian Pacific Railway's Willingdon line arrived in Clandonald in 1927–28.

Claresholm

Town on Highway 2, approximately 64 kilometres northwest of Lethbridge

"Old J.N.," as Ontario-born John Niblock (1848–1914) was known, was a railway superintendent like no other. He eschewed cigarettes, placed Bibles on cabooses and, in the words of his boss, General Superintendent D.C. Coleman, "loved the Canadian Pacific with all the

John Niblock, 1890. He named his Medicine Hat residence "Clare's Home" for his wife, Clare. As divisional superintendent for the Canadian Pacific Railway, he gave this station a similar name.

fervor of his rich Celtic temperament."[57] Niblock served as Canadian Pacific Railway (CPR) divisional superintendent at Medicine Hat from 1887–99, and held the same post in Calgary from 1899–1909. While at Medicine Hat, Niblock kept a bear on the train station lawn for the amusement of passengers. After his wife, Isabella, died in 1890, Niblock married Clare Attwood, and he named their Medicine Hat residence "Clare's Home." When the CPR established this station on its Macleod–Calgary branch in 1891, Niblock named it after his house. John and Clare retired to Victoria, where he died less than five years later. Mount Niblock near Lake Louise was named for him in 1904. Clare later moved to Burlingame, California, where she passed away in 1942.[58] Claresholm became a village in 1903 and a town in 1905.

Claresholm business district, n.d. CALGARY PUBLIC LIBRARY PC915

Cleardale

Hamlet on Highway 64, approximately 80 kilometres west northwest of Fairview

The Clear River flows a short distance north of this hamlet on its way from the Clear Hills in the north into the Peace River in the south. The name Clear Hills is of unknown origin; the river is probably named for the hills, and the hamlet takes its name from the river.

Clive

Village north of Highway 12, approximately 20 kilometres east of Lacombe

This settlement on the Canadian Pacific Railway's Lacombe–Coronation branch began as Valley City, as its post office was named from 1906–09. But the railway did not initially stop here, and by the time it did in 1910 the community was renamed—evidently out of Imperial sentiment—for Sir Robert Clive (1725–74), a soldier and administrator who solidified British rule in India, which lasted until 1947. Clive was later charged with corruption. "As he thought of the treasures he might have taken and didn't," wrote D.B. Hanna, the Canadian National Railways executive for whom the town of Hanna was named, Clive remarked under cross-examination, "By heaven, Mr. Chairman, at this moment I stand astonished at my own moderation."[59] Though exonerated, Clive committed suicide.

Clover Bar

Hamlet on Highway 14, approximately 15 kilometres east of Edmonton

The prospect of gold brought Missouri-born Thomas H. Clover (born 1829), a California 49er and recent veteran of the 1858 British Columbia gold rush, to the North Saskatchewan River in 1859. The river sandbar where Clover found success gave the district its early name—Clover's Bar—and the area settlement formed in 1881 became Clover Bar. Clover later farmed at Pembina, Manitoba, and then Leroy, North Dakota, where he was still living in 1917. He later claimed to have been at Red River during the first Riel Rebellion in 1869–70 and recalled fancifully that Thomas Scott—the prisoner Riel had condemned to death—passed Clover on the way to his execution and said, "Good-bye, Tom."[60] Clover Bar was once a village, but reverted to hamlet status in 1970.

Cluny

Hamlet on Secondary Highway 842, approximately 75 kilometres east of Calgary

Trader "Cluny" McPherson Stades operated an early trading post at Cluny, a station established and named by the Canadian Pacific Railway (CPR) in 1884. As a McPherson, Stades might have earned his nickname from Cluny Castle, the Scottish home of the Macpherson clan chief, located southeast of Loch Ness. However, this might all be coincidence; tradition ascribes the CPR's choice of name to Cluny Parish in Aberdeenshire.

Clyde

Village on highways 2 and 18, approximately 15 kilometres east of Westlock

When homesteader George D. Clyde opened a post office here in 1905, settlers suggested three possible names for the post office: Clyde, Kelvin and Summerset.[61] Postal authorities chose Clyde, whose home doubled as a stopping place. Clyde became a village in 1914.

Coaldale

Town on Highway 3, approximately 10 kilometres east of Lethbridge

Like Claresholm, Coaldale derives its name from a house: Coal Dale, the Lethbridge residence of Elliott Torrance Galt (1850–1928). Galt was an assistant Indian commissioner for the North-West Territories and the son of Sir Alexander Tilloch Galt (1817–93), one of the Fathers of Confederation and who became Canada's high commissioner to Britain in the 1880s. Between them they developed coal mines, railways and irrigation systems. The Galts' summer home in Glasgow, Scotland, was called Coal Dale. Elliott chose this name for his Lethbridge home, and the Canadian Pacific Railway used this name for its railway siding here. Coaldale (as the name was eventually formalized) became a village in 1919 and a town in 1952.

Elliott Galt's residence, Coal Dale, was built in the riverbottom at Lethbridge. It was abandoned after a 1902 flood and was demolished in 1908 when the Canadian Pacific Railway built its High Level Bridge. Sir Alexander Galt Museum and Archives

Coalhurst

Town on Highway 3, approximately seven kilometres west of Lethbridge

This name refers to the area's plentiful coal reserves and came into use in the mid-1870s. *Hurst* might have referred to a settler by that name, or it may have been chosen simply as a euphonious suffix. Nearby Lethbridge was named Coalhurst briefly in 1885. Coalhurst was incorporated as a village in 1913, dissolved in 1936 and reestablished in 1979.

Cochrane

Town on Highway 1A, approximately 25 kilometres west northwest of Calgary

Senator Matthew Henry Cochrane (1823–1903), a stock breeder from Compton, Quebec, advised Sir John A. Macdonald's government, in its 1881 amendment of the Dominion Lands Act, to allow large-scale ranching leases. That year Cochrane set up the Cochrane Ranche Company on the Bow River west of Calgary, the first of southern Alberta's massive ranches. The Canadian Pacific Railway named its station for the ranch and Cochrane was incorporated as a village in 1903 and as a town in 1971.

Senator Mathew Henry Cochrane, 1879. His massive eponymous ranch was the first of many large ranches in southern Alberta.
NATIONAL ARCHIVES OF CANADA PA-026579

Cold Lake

City on Highway 28, approximately 133 kilometres north of Lloydminster

With its year-round chill, the lake that straddles the Alberta–Saskatchewan border was known in the Cree language as "Cold Lake." It was recorded on a 1790 map as "Coldwater Lake." The shorter form of the name stuck, and also became attached to the Cold Lake Indian Reserve, Cold Lake Provincial Park and the settlement on its southern shore. Cold Lake was incorporated as a village in 1953 and as town in 1955. Nearby Grand Centre, where a post office opened in 1937 and which became a town in 1958, aspired to the importance that its name connotes. However, Grand Centre disappeared in a 1996 amalgamation that formed a new, larger town of Cold Lake. In 2000, Cold Lake became Alberta's newest city and the last to be incorporated in the 20th century.

Women fishing on Cold Lake, 1936. MISSIONARY OBLATES GRANDIN ARCHIVES OB.8247

Coleman

See Crowsnest Pass, Municipality of

Colinton

Hamlet on Secondary Highway 663, approximately 13 kilometres south of Athabasca

Scottish émigré James M. Milne (died 1984) homesteaded in the Peace River country in 1906, six years before the Canadian Northern Railway built its station here. Much of the townsite was reportedly built upon Milne's land, and it was named for his hometown in Scotland. Colinton Creek shares the name. (Until 1913 the post office was known as Kinnoul, possibly named for Kinnoull Hill in Perth, Scotland.) Robert Louis Stevenson (1850–94), author of *Dr. Jeckyll and Mr. Hyde*, spent his boyhood summers in the original Colinton, which became a suburb of Edinburgh in 1920.

College Heights

Hamlet between highways 2 and 2A, approximately four kilometres north of Lacombe

In 1909 the Alberta Industrial Academy, a Seventh Day Adventist college, moved from the Leduc area to a hillside north of Lacombe. When a post office opened in 1925, its name reflected this institution, which was eventually renamed Canadian University College and still operates today.

Collingwood Cove

Hamlet south of Secondary Highway 629, approximately 23 kilometres southeast of Edmonton

Collingwood Cove, a hamlet established in 1980, is on the shore of Cooking Lake. Its name is of unknown origin.

Compeer

Hamlet north of Highway 12, approximately 57 kilometres south southeast of Provost

Sleepy Hollow was the original name of the post office, located in the home of pioneer settlers William and Ella Young. When asked to explain, Ella is said to have replied, "Why not? It's as good as Stony Plains [sic]."[62] Nonetheless, when the railway arrived in 1915, the settlement was renamed Compeer, a word defined by the *Concise Oxford Dictionary* as "an equal, a peer" or "a comrade". On the prairie frontier, all settlers were on equal footing.

Condor

Hamlet on Highway 11, approximately 13 kilometres west southwest of Eckville

The HMS *Condor*, a British Composite Gun-Vessel built in 1876–77, became famous in 1882 for its role in the bombardment of Alexandria, Egypt. Under the command of Lord Charles William de la Poer Beresford (1846–1919), the *Condor* bombarded forts at Alexandria in response to an uprising against British rule. The Canadian Pacific Railway named this station for the *Condor* in 1914.

The connection to Alberta is indirect. Admiral Beresford's younger brother, Delaval James de la Poer Beresford (1862–1906), was a remittance man. In western lore, the remittance man was a hapless figure— the younger son of a titled English family who emigrated either to make good or to avoid embarrassing the family at home. Unsuited for pioneer life, the archetypal remittance man depended on a remittance of money from home. After ranching in Mexico, Delaval moved to southern Alberta in 1903 and established the Mexico Ranch near Brooks. Admiral Beresford visited Alberta after Delaval's death in a North Dakota train wreck.

Conklin

Hamlet on Conklin Road, east of Secondary Highway 881, approximately 110 kilometres northeast of Lac La Biche

The Alberta and Great Waterways Railway established a station at this remote hamlet in 1916 and reportedly named it for J.D. McArthur's timekeeper, John Conklin.

Conrich

Hamlet on McKnight Boulevard, approximately 10 kilometres east of Calgary on McKnight Boulevard

Tradition ascribes this name to two real estate developers, Connacher and Richardson, who presumably intended to make a killing on this property during Calgary's phenomenal pre-World War I real estate boom. The Grand Trunk Pacific Railway arrived in 1913 and established its Conrich flag station just east of Calgary, but that year the boom turned bust and Conrich failed to develop. City directories list only one Connacher at that time—William, manager of the Bank of Nova Scotia.

Consort

Village on Highway 12, approximately 53 kilometres southwest of Provost

The coronation of King George V, on June 22, 1911, displayed all of the pomp and ceremony that the still-mighty British Empire could muster. The Canadian Pacific Railway showed its patriotism through the choice of station names along its new Lacombe–Kerrobert branch in Alberta, including Fleet, Coronation, Throne, Veteran, Loyalist and Consort, and possibly also Federal and Monitor.[63] The hilltop village of Consort began as Sanderville, a post office named in 1910 for its first postmaster, H.A. Sanderson. Consort's avenues originally included Dowager, Prospect, Loyalist and Railway; among its streets were Mary (the new King's consort and namesake of the famous Cunard ocean liner *Queen Mary*), Alexander, Caroline and Katherine, and the main street, Albert (Queen Victoria's consort). However, street signs were never posted while these names were in use, and in the 1980s the names were changed to numbers. Consort, hometown of country singer k.d. lang, became a village in 1912.

Coronation

Town on Highway 12, approximately 160 kilometres east of Red Deer

The Canadian Pacific Railway named Coronation in 1911 to honour the coronation of King George V that year. Other stations along the new Lacombe–Kerrobert branch named to honour the coronation included Consort, Fleet, Loyalist, Throne and Veteran, and possibly also Federal and Monitor.[64] Coronation's avenues included Alexandra (after the dowager Queen), Imperial, Victoria, Westminster and York; its streets included Albert, Arthur, Edward, George, Mary, King, Queen and Royal, the main street. The hotel was named the Royal Crown, and one of the first businesses, coincidentally, was Crown Lumber. The

Canadian Pacific Railway employed auctioneer Tobias Crawford Norris, who later served as premier of Manitoba (1915–22), to conduct the sale of lots.[65] Coronation became a village in 1911 and a town in 1912.

When King George VI was crowned in 1937, town officials cabled the new sovereign, explaining the origin of the town's name and offering the best wishes of its citizens. Thousands of stamp collectors sent pre-stamped envelopes to Coronation's postmaster, Robert Ellis, to be postmarked "Coronation" and returned to the senders. One local schoolgirl sent hers to the new king, who was a philatelist himself.[66]

By 1953, when King George's daughter was crowned Queen Elizabeth II, Ellis' son had succeeded him as postmaster of Coronation. Like his father 15 years earlier, Robert S. Ellis spent Coronation Day stamping thousands of envelopes and mailing them back to collectors from over 50 countries. As part of its Coronation Day programming, broadcast around the Commonwealth, the Canadian Broadcasting Corporation recorded sounds from Coronation, Alberta. "People around the world will hear the sharp crack of the curler's (ladies) rocks, the shuffle and calling of the square dancers, the roar of the oil drilling rig, the whistle, click and steam of our train as it pulls in," reported the *Coronation Review*.[67]

Coutts

Village on Highway 4, approximately 95 kilometres southeast of Lethbridge

Like Burdett, this village on the Canada–U.S. boundary was named for Baroness Angela Burdett-Coutts (1814–1906), a fabulously wealthy and generously philanthropical Victorian. "After my mother," said King Edward VII of the Baroness, "she is the most remarkable woman in the kingdom."[68] Given her title by Queen Victoria in 1871, Angela Burdett-Coutts is the subject of at least three biographies, and Charles Dickens dedicated a novel, *Martin Chuzzlewit*, to her. She married William Lehman Ashmead Bartlett (1851–1921), an American-born British politician 37 years younger than her. (By royal licence he took her name, becoming Sir William Lehman Ashmead Bartlett Burdett-Coutts.) Baroness Burdett-Coutts invested in the North Western Coal and Navigation Company, which developed coal resources in southern Alberta, and in the Alberta Railway and Irrigation Company. The baroness is buried in Westminster Abbey. Coutts became a village in 1960.

Railway station serving the border communities of Coutts, Alberta and Sweetgrass, Montana. Note the American flag to the left and the Canadian Red Ensign to the right. The station remained in use until 1986 and was moved to Stirling in 2001 by the Great Canadian Plains Railway Society. Sir Alexander Galt Museum and Archives P 1976 0237031

Cowley

Village on Highway 3, approximately six kilometres east southeast of Lundbreck

"The lowing herd winds slowly o'er the lea," wrote poet Thomas Gray (1716–71) in his "Elegy Written in a Country Church-Yard." Rancher F.W. Godsal related that once while watching his own cows he was reminded of this line—and that it inspired his suggestion for the village's name. The Cowley post office opened in 1900, and in 1906 Cowley became a village.

Craigmyle

Hamlet north of Highway 9, approximately 23 kilometres west of Hanna

Known originally as Lillico when its post office opened in 1910, Craigmyle was renamed in 1913 by the Canadian Northern Railway. By one account, Craigmyle was named for Craigmyle House, a 17th-century mansion and the ancestral estate of Violet Eaton, the wife of homesteader Captain R.B. Eaton.[69] Craigmyle was once a village.

Cremona

Village on Highway 22, approximately 28 kilometres west of Carstairs

In Cremona's centennial museum, a miniature violin—presented in 1991 by a group of tourists from Cremona, Italy—evokes this village's namesake, the home of Stradivari (the maker of Stradivarius violins). That visit was Cremona's only Italian connection. Ontario-born Lillian Jackson (1880–1965) and her husband, Smith Jackson, had established the post office in 1906. Smith's brother Squire proposed the name Honley, for the Jackson brothers' hometown in Yorkshire. Postal authorities rejected the name as too similar to Hanley, Saskatchewan. Smith and Lillian then suggested Cremona, after the Italian city famous for its violins. Lillian became postmistress and registrar when Smith died in 1909, and as registrar she earned a 25¢ provincial government fee for reporting her own wedding, in 1910, to farmer Percy Bird.[70] Both Lillian Bird and Smith Jackson are buried in Carstairs. Cremona was incorporated as a village in 1955. The 1991 visit by Gianfranco Carutti and his group was reported by newspapers in both southern Alberta and Cremona, Italy.[71] Though Cremona's official slogan is "Village with Promise," its postal code (TOM ORO) might have suggested another: "Village of Tomorrow."

Crossfield

Town on Highway 2, approximately 45 kilometres north of Calgary

In 1890–91, the builders of the Calgary and Edmonton Railway (C&E) more or less followed the old Calgary-Edmonton Trail between Calgary and Airdrie. The next siding to the north, however, lay west of the old trail, and the railway reportedly named it for railway engineer William Crossfield. Hammond Street, Crossfield's main thoroughfare and once a common street name in towns along the C&E, was named for a partner of Osler, Hammond and Nanton investment and brokerage firm. (The town of Nanton was named for partner Augustus M. Nanton, and the hamlet of Ohaton was named for all three men.) Most Hammond streets have changed to numbers. Crossfield became a village in 1907 and a town in 1980.

Welcome sign, 2002. COURTESY OF JOHN OLSON

Crowsnest Pass, Municipality of

Town on Highway 3, in the Crowsnest Pass

In 1979, the Crowsnest Pass Municipal Unification Act amalgamated the village of Bellevue, the towns of Blairmore and Coleman, the villages of Frank and Hillcrest Mines, and several hamlets. Their original names remain in use as the equivalent of communities or subdivisions.

Bellevue

"Quelle une belle view," exclaimed Elise, daughter of J.J. Fleutot, West Canadian Collieries Ltd. Managing Director, when she visited the Crowsnest Pass and gazed to the west.[72] Her father, a native of France, remembered these words in naming this mining company town in 1905. The village of Bellevue was incorporated in 1957.

Blairmore

On November 15, 1898, the Crow's Nest Railway arrived at the "Tenth Siding," thereafter known as Blairmore. The first community in the Crowsnest Pass east of the British Columbia border, Blairmore was named either for two railway contractors (Blair and More) or, at least in part, for former New Brunswick premier and then-federal railways minister Andrew G. Blair (1844–1907). Incorporated as a town in 1911, Blairmore once had such colourful street names as Cement, Madawaska and Otterburn, but none as colourful as Tim Buck Boulevard, proclaimed in 1934 by a radical town council to honour the general secretary of the Communist Party of Canada.

Honourable Andrew George Blair, federal railways minister and former premier of New Brunswick, 1907. He was possibly the namesake of Blairmore. NATIONAL ARCHIVES OF CANADA PA-027976,

Blairmore Hotel and main street, Blairmore, n.d. CALGARY PUBLIC LIBRARY PC 921

Coleman

Alfred Cornelius Flumerfelt, president of the International Coal and Coke Company which developed the area's coalfields, named this town for his youngest daughter, Norma Coleman Flumerfelt (1885–1975). Norma married violinist Albany Herbert Ritchie (1881–1965) in 1906, and they moved to Seattle where Albany played in the Seattle Symphony and later in the Spargur String Quartet. Both Norma and Albany died in Seattle. Coleman, Alberta, was born in 1904 when town lots first went on sale; the town of Coleman was incorporated in 1910.

Main street, Coleman, circa 1918. GLENBOW ARCHIVES ND-54-468

Frank

Lenny Bruce didn't know Henry L. Frank. In his autobiography, *How to Talk Dirty and Influence People*, the American comic made this observation: "To me, if you live in New York or any other big city, you are Jewish. It doesn't even matter if you're Catholic, if you live in New York, you're Jewish. If you live in Butte, Mont., you're going to be goyish even if you're Jewish."[73] H.L. Frank was Jewish, and he was the *mayor* of Butte.

Born in Ohio, Frank moved to Montana Territory to pursue his mining interests and served as Butte's mayor in 1885–86. He was elected to the state legislature and once ran for the U.S. senate. In 1901, Frank and a partner formed the Canadian-American Coal & Coke Company and began operations in the Crowsnest Pass. Frank established an eponymous village in the shadow of Turtle Mountain—one of the sources of his company's wealth—and staged a grand opening for the town in September 1901.

The town's namesake was a frequent visitor and popular figure in Frank. On April 29, 1903, an enormous chunk of the mountain sheared off, burying half the town and killing at least 76 people. The town was rebuilt nearby, and Henry Frank retained ownership in the mine for another five years. But he was deeply affected by the disaster and died at the 1908 Republican National Convention, which nominated William Howard Taft for the presidency. Frank is buried in Cincinnati. The multimillion-dollar Frank Slide Interpretive Centre, set in a landscape of shattered rock, tells the disaster's story. Frank Lake was formed by the Frank Slide.

Henry L. Frank, former mayor of Butte, Montana and founder of Frank, Alberta. He was deeply affected by the Frank Slide disaster in 1903 and died only five years later.
Butte–Silver Bow Public Archives, Mayor's photo collection

Hillcrest Mines

"I beg to say that the Post Office of Hillcrest Mines was named after your humble servant," wrote Charles Plummer Hill, former U.S. customs officer and managing director of the Hillcrest Coal and Coke Company to the chief geographer of the Department of the Interior in 1909. "I am also glad to report that the town of Post Hill, Idaho was dedicated and the Post Office named for me. Such is the result of 24 years hustling in the Northwest."[74] The hamlet of Hillcrest Mines was founded in 1905. On June 19, 1914, the Hillcrest Mine explosion claimed the lives of 189 miners.

A scarred Turtle Mountain towers over Front Street in Frank after the slide in April 1903. In just 100 seconds, 74 million tonnes of rock crashed down on part of the town and covered a mine entrance, trapping the miners underground. Dozens of miners and townspeople were rescued, but 76 people perished. The community was later rebuilt a short distance away. CALGARY PUBLIC LIBRARY PC 432

Cynthia

Hamlet on secondary highways 621 and 753, approximately 30 kilometres west northwest of Drayton Valley

Cynthia was a product of the 1950s oil boom—a brand-new, planned community intended to house oil company field workers and their families. It was one of several communities incorporated between 1956–1967 under the New Town Act. Oil discoveries led to the creation of instant boomtowns, and the New Town Act was intended to smooth the development of local government and infrastructure.[75]

Developed in 1956 by the Mobile Industrial Development Company of Edmonton, Cynthia was planned to house workers in the Pembina oilfield and was expected to have a population of nearly 3,000. It was named for the Cynthia Crown oil reserve south of Chip Lake.[76] (Another story has it that Cynthia was the daughter of the local hotelkeeper.) Cynthia failed to develop as expected, and its town status was rescinded in 1959.

Czar

Village on Highway 41, approximately 40 kilometres west northwest of Provost

Czar was incorporated as a village on November 12, 1917—242 days after Czar Nicholas II of Russia abdicated and 246 days before he and his family were executed by the Bolsheviks. However, the name dated back to 1910, when the Canadian Pacific Railway established the Czar siding and Joseph Laughy opened the Czar post office. The chief geographer of the Department of the Interior explained the name as that of a "Russian settlement," but Czar was actually settled by English and American pioneers.

Various theories explain the name as a reference to a railway boss, to Premier Arthur Sifton (the Liberal "czar" of Alberta) or to the Russian emperor himself. It might just as well have been the whimsy of a railway official. When the townsite was laid out, the Russian theme was expanded through streets named for Russian royalty—Alexandra, Nicholas and Peter—as well as Kerensky Street, named for Alexander Kerensky, a member of the provisional government that briefly held power in Russia in 1917.

Dalemead

Hamlet south of Highway 22X, approximately 22 kilometres southeast of Calgary

Both the hamlet of Dalemead and nearby Dalemead Lake share their name's origin with Lake Mead, the massive Nevada reservoir formed when the Hoover Dam was completed in 1928, restricting the flow of the Colourado River. Indiana-born Dr. Elwood Mead (1858–1936) earned degrees in science, law and civil engineering, and became an expert in irrigation and water management. As Wyoming's territorial engineer in the 1880s, Mead developed influential and widely used principles of water management and legislation. Mead's impressive career in academia, public service and international consulting included work for the Canadian Pacific Railway (CPR). His career culminated in his tenure, from 1924–36, as U.S. commissioner of reclamation, through which he worked on the Hoover and Grand Coulee dams.

When the CPR arrived in 1914, it used the area's existing school name, Strathmead (which incorporated Dr. Mead's surname), for its station. Strathmead was easily confused with nearby Strathmore, and the local branch of the United Farmers of Alberta petitioned successfully for a name change. The prefix "Dale" describes Dalemead's location in a valley.

Dalroy

Hamlet east of Highway 9, approximately 25 kilometres east of Calgary

By one account this hamlet was named for settler G.M. McElroy, with a prefix meaning "dale" or "valley." By another, it was named for Dalroy, Scotland, which lies 13 kilometres east of Inverness on the River Nairn.

Dapp

Hamlet on Highway 661, approximately 21 kilometres north of Westlock

When the Edmonton, Dunvegan and British Columbia Railway arrived in 1913, Andrew Holm opened the post office of Eunice. In 1917 it was renamed for David A. Pennicuick ("D.A.P.") of Edmonton, the railway's chief accountant. Dapp Creek and Dapp Lake share the name.

Darwell

Hamlet on secondary highways 633 and 765, approximately 42 kilometres west northwest of Stony Plain

The Canadian Northern Railway established a station here in 1915. One tradition purports that it was named for a biblical character, another that it was named for 18th century English vicar and hymnist John Darwall.

Daysland

Town on Highway 13, approximately 40 kilometres east southeast of Camrose

Around 1888, Egerton Winnet Day (1863–1919), a young Ontario merchant (and former stagecoach driver), moved to Winnipeg, where he worked for the Massey-Harris Co., won election to the Winnipeg Public School Board and served as president of the Young Men's Conservative Club. He relocated to Toronto in 1896 to manage a loan company, but returned west after the turn of the century and formed the Alberta Central Land Company. Day's firm amassed 15 sections in what is now the Daysland district, before the arrival of the Canadian Pacific Railway (CPR), and subdivided the land for sale to settlers. According to lore, the town's name arose from Day's extensive holdings. When a newcomer inquired about any parcel of property, the response was likely to be "Oh, that is Mr. Day's land."[77]

When the town of Daysland was incorporated in 1907, Day took office as its first mayor. He lost his bid for a House of Commons seat in 1908 and later settled in Edmonton, where he served as a major in the army's commissariat department during World War I.[78] Day is buried in Edmonton Cemetery.

Newcomers who inquired of area property were frequently told, "Oh, that is Mr. Day's land." Real estate developer Egerton W. Day was the first mayor of the town named for him. PROVINCIAL ARCHIVES OF ALBERTA A.3992

Dead Man's Flats

Hamlet on the Trans-Canada Highway (Highway 1), approximately seven kilometres southeast of Canmore

When the Trans-Canada Highway was constructed along the Bow River west of Calgary in the late 1950s, a new roadside sign identified this hamlet as Deadman's Flats. Local business owners objected, and in 1974 it became known as Pigeon Mountain Service Centre. When the nearby Pigeon Mountain ski area closed in 1983, owners again requested a name change—to Dead Man's Flats. Evidently they preferred being named for a dead man than for a dead ski hill. Two competing legends account for the name. In 1904, dairyman François Marrett killed his brother John with an axe, or two or three natives who had been poaching beaver "played dead" to avoid the park warden. It is also possible that the legend of Kananaskis was the origin of Dead Man's Flats (see Kananaskis).

Deadwood

Hamlet on Secondary Highway 690, approximately 60 kilometres north northwest of Peace River

Deadwood is a name of uncertain origin, possibly referring to the South Dakota hometown of original postmaster John Keller Eggenberger. Deadwood native Carolyn Dawn Johnson won the Favourite New Artist Country Music award at the American Music Awards in Los Angeles in 2003.

DeBolt

Hamlet on Highway 34, approximately 50 kilometres east northeast of Grande Prairie

In 1919, Henry Elbert DeBolt (1888–1969) and his brother George (1884–1961) and their families moved from the State of Washington to homestead in the Peace River country. Their settlement was known early on as American Creek, but when Elbert became the first postmaster in 1923 (followed by his wife, Laura May, from 1927–40), the office

Postmaster Elbert DeBolt later moved to Spirit River and was elected to the Alberta legislature. COURTESY OF FRANCES MORAVEC

was named DeBolt. The couple moved in 1941 to Spirit River, where Elbert served as Social Credit Member of the Legislative Assembly from 1940–52. He ultimately quit the party and was defeated in his final bid as an Independent Social Crediter in 1952.

De Winton

Hamlet west of Highway 2, approximately 10 kilometres south of Calgary

This hamlet was named for General Sir Francis De Winton (1835–1931), Crimean War veteran and military secretary to the Marquess of Lorne (governor-general from 1878–83 and the man who named the province). De Winton established an eponymous ranch south of Calgary.

Del Bonita

Hamlet on Highway 62, approximately 70 kilometres south of Lethbridge

The site of this southern hamlet once lay within the northern reaches of Spain's North American possessions. It's name is evidently Spanish in origin, meaning "of the pretty" or "beautiful valley."

Delacour

Hamlet on Secondary Highway 564, approximately 20 kilometres north-east of Calgary

In a common but difficult to prove naming tradition, Delacour is believed to have been named for a Danish railway construction foreman. The Grand Trunk Pacific Railway reached Delacour in 1914.

Delburne

Village east of Highway 21, approximately 40 kilometres east southeast of Red Deer

One theory suggests that the name was inspired by a woman named Della Mewburne. Another suggests it was a variation on Wilburne, a name first suggested by resident Wilfred Clendenning. When the Grand Trunk Pacific Railway arrived in 1911, the Gaetz Valley post office moved to the new railway townsite and was renamed Delburne. Delburne became a village in 1913.

Delia

Village on Secondary Highway 851, approximately 30 kilometres west of Hanna

Delia's Stopping House, operated by shopkeeper A.L. Davis, was an early landmark before this village was born. Though Davis and his wife, Delia, left this community early on, and their whereabouts remain a mystery, her name is inseparable from this place. The post office took her name in 1909, but the village, incorporated in 1914 following the Canadian Northern Railway's arrival, was originally called Highland (because it was the highest point on the Calgary–Saskatoon line). To avoid confusion, the village became Delia the following year.

Derwent

Village on Highway 45, approximately 27 kilometres south of Elk Point

Named for Derwentwater in England's Lakes District, Derwent was established with the construction of the Canadian Pacific Railway's Willingdon line in 1927–28. The Monkman post office—known as Peguis when it opened in 1909—moved to the new railway townsite in 1928 and was renamed Derwent. The village was incorporated in 1930.

Devon

Town on Highway 60, approximately 30 kilometres southwest of Edmonton

Many Alberta communities were named tenuously for their counterparts in Britain, without much regard for local conditions. Devon, Alberta, provides an exception, because it was *not* named for Devon, England, but for the Devonian formation deep below the townsite. Before the 1947 Leduc discovery galvanized Alberta's oil industry, the present site of Devon was a grain field, its nearest community the agricultural settlement of Glidehurst. By 1949 a model, planned community had been developed for oilfield workers and their families. Its street names included Derrick Drive, Exploration Drive, Oil Patch Drive and Wellhead Street. Devon became a village in 1949 and a town in 1950.

Oil rig near Devon. After the Leduc oil discovery in 1947, a grain field was transformed into the model town of Devon. CALGARY PUBLIC LIBRARY PC 1192

Dewberry

Village on Secondary Highway 893, approximately 43 kilometres southeast of Elk Point

According to lore, residents were in disagreement over names suggested for the post office that Eli Sweet opened in 1907. "Why don't you try *dewberry?*" suggested a woman who entered the local store carrying a bucket of them. Dewberry was incorporated as a village in 1957.

Diamond City

Hamlet on Highway 25, approximately six kilometres north of Lethbridge

This grandiose name belies the tiny hamlet that Diamond City has become. It was intended to be named for the Black Diamond Coal Company, but the post office name Black Diamond had already been taken when the post office opened here in 1908.

Dickson

Hamlet south of Highway 54, approximately 24 kilometres west of Innisfail

In 1903 a group of Danish settlers from Omaha, Nebraska, settled near Dickson Creek, which had been named for an early Norwegian settler named Benedickson. Chris Christiansen opened a store and post office in 1906, and reportedly his wife, Laura, suggested that the first Danish settlement in western Canada be named Dickson. After the store closed in the 1980s, the Danish Historical Society of Dickson restored the building as the Dickson Store Museum, officially opened in 1991 by Queen Margrethe of Denmark.

Didsbury

Town on Highway 2, approximately 70 kilometres south southwest of Red Deer

This farming town's heritage has little in common with its namesake: the onetime township of Didsbury, now a suburb of Manchester, England, and a familiar backdrop for viewers of the British television show *Cracker*.

Alberta's Didsbury was established in 1892 as a stop along the new Calgary and Edmonton Railway. Its first settlers were a group of Mennonites who came from Berlin, Ontario, in 1894. Called Pennsylvania Dutch in error, they were of German origin ("Deutch") and fled the Keystone state as United Empire Loyalists after the American Revolution. Didsbury's streets originally reflected their heritage in such street names as Bismark, Berlin, Hespeler and Liesemer. That German heritage became a liability during World War I, and like the settlers' former Ontario hometown—renamed Kitchener—some Didsbury streets were rebranded with English names: Berlin became Churchill, and Hespeler became King Edward.

Railway Street south, Didsbury, n.d. Calgary Public Library PC642

Dixonville

Hamlet on Highway 35, approximately 39 kilometres north of Grimshaw

Roy "Buster" Dixon, former owner of a Regina baseball team and hockey coach in Rouleau, Saskatchewan, settled in northern Alberta in middle age along with his wife, Ethel. The store they operated through the 1920s became the Dixonville post office in 1930. The popular Buster extended credit during the Great Depression and was known for his friendly smile and brilliant mind. Ethel, a religious woman, was known for her "Jiggs and Maggie" dinners, and the Dixon home became a restaurant of sorts as well as the venue for games of bridge, rummey and whist.

Donalda

Village on Highway 53, approximately 28 kilometres east of Bashaw

As the first postmaster and a pioneer settler of Donalda, D.C. Harker was the namesake of Harker, Alberta, as this post office was named in 1907. In 1911 the name changed to Eidswold—possibly to commemorate Eidsvold, Norway, or its namesake Eidswold in Minnesota. The name changed again when the Canadian Northern Railway (CNoR) arrived. The new name honoured the baby niece of CNoR Vice-President Sir Donald Mann (for whom the village of Mannville was named).

Donalda Crosthwait (1908–99) lived most of her life in Ontario, where she worked as a teacher's assistant and as a violin instructor. She was likely named for her illustrious uncle, who was also her father's employer. Donalda's ashes are buried in St. John's Cemetery, Bancroft, Ontario. The village of Donalda was incorporated in 1912.

Donalda Crosthwait was likely named for her uncle, railway magnate Sir Donald Mann.

COURTESY OF HUGH CROSTHWAIT

Donatville

Hamlet on Highway 63, approximately 30 kilometres east northeast of Athabasca

Donat Gingras, a young homesteader from Joliette, Quebec, was the namesake for this hamlet, whose post office opened in 1914.

Donnelly

Village on Highway 49, approximately five kilometres east of Falher

The Irish name of this small village in the Peace River district belies its Franco-Albertan character. It was reportedly named for an official of the Edmonton, Dunvegan and British Columbia Railway, which established its station here in 1915. Apart from T. Donnelly of Edmonton, a boilermaker's helper in 1916, no Donnelly associated with the ED&BC has been identified. Donnelly became a village in 1956.

Dorothy

Hamlet on Secondary Highway 570, approximately 33 kilometres southeast of Drumheller

Ironically, this hamlet named for a woman was once famed for its abundance of bachelors. Dorothy families tended to have more boys than girls, and available young women migrated to larger centres. Even Dorothy herself—Dorothy Wilson (1904–1988), daughter of ranchers Jack and Eliza Wilson—moved to Calgary and married Eugene Fairbanks. (When Fairbanks opened the post office at what was known as Circus Coulee in 1908, merchant Percy McBeath had wanted to name it Percyville, but postal authorities chose the name of the only child in the community.)

Many of Dorothy's bachelors had come of age during the Great Depression, when their financial (and marital) opportunities were limited. In 1952 a *Toronto Star* reporter did a leap year story on Dorothy, profiling 20 men—over half the community's population—as "The Lonely Bachelors of 'Dinosaur Valley.'" American and European newspapers picked up the story, and before long the bachelor cabins of Dorothy piled high with letters and marriage proposals. New York-based *Parade Magazine* asked bachelor Tom Hodgson to choose three of the letter writers, and the magazine would fly one of them to Dorothy for a three-day visit. He picked Rosa Mae Brewer of Chicago, and *Parade* documented her visit in its next issue. Some of the bachelors married, others moved away, but Hodgson remained—unmarried. Although flattered by the attention, he found many of the women had problems or wrote out of desperation. "Some of the women who sent pictures of themselves half-dressed, you felt kind of sorry for them, too," he said.[79]

Dorothy Fairbanks (nee Wilson), circa 1958. As the only child in the community, the post office was named for her. Glenbow Archives NA-1993-12

Drayton Valley

Town on Highway 22, approximately 105 kilometres west southwest of Edmonton

In 1920, homesteaders Bill and Dora (1902–81) Drake opened a post office at Power House, a settlement named for a never-completed hydro project on the North Saskatchewan River. There was already a Powerhouse in British Columbia, so the Drakes chose a new name, Drayton Valley. The usual explanation is that Dora had come from the village of Drayton in Hampshire, England. In her old age, however, Dora revealed their reasons to the *Edmonton Journal:* "The first part of the name was near to our own and the latter part 'ton' similar to our old hometown."[80] Bill Drake was killed in a 1957 highway accident, along with the couple's son Albert. Dora evidently remarried and is buried as Dora Kynoch in Drayton Valley's Riverview Cemetery.

Drayton Valley was incorporated as a new town in 1956. It was one of several communities incorporated between 1956–1967 under the New Town Act. Oil discoveries led to the creation of instant boomtowns, and the New Town Act was intended to smooth the development of local government and infrastructure.[81] Drayton Valley became a town in 1957.

Drumheller

Town on Highway 9, approximately 100 kilometres northeast of Calgary

But for the toss of a coin, the name Greentree—and not Drumheller—might have been indelibly associated with the badlands of the Red Deer River, the coal mining industry and prehistoric fossils. English-born farmer, cowpuncher and brewmaster Thomas P. Greentree (1870–1956)—whose grandfather, Sir Thomas Doveton Greentree, had reportedly been governor of St. Helena during Napoleon's exile there— became the valley's pioneer homesteader in 1902. There he raised cattle, operated a ferry and discovered a local source for heating his farmhouse: coal. It was a bucket of bituminous coal in Greentree's house that piqued Samuel Drumheller's interest and changed the fate of the valley.

Samuel Drumheller (seated at left, behind the wheel) once reportedly drove his cadillac down the frozen Red Deer River to get down into the valley. GLENBOW ARCHIVES NA-2389-20

Born near Walla Walla, Washington Territory, Sam Drumheller (1864–circa 1949) farmed, managed livestock for a county fair and even established a town named Drumheller in Washington's Franklin County before coming to Alberta. On a winter day around 1909, Sam and his cousin Jerome were looking for suitable ranch and farmland when they came upon the isolated Greentree home and let themselves in. When they saw the coal, Jerome and Sam followed footprints in the snow to the coal's source—a rich seam in the valley wall. The Drumheller cousins hightailed it to Calgary to secure mineral leases.

On a return visit to the badlands—possibly the trip Sam reportedly spent $700 on cab fare—Sam offered to buy Greentree's land. According to lore, Greentree accepted the offer, but when he learned the railway was coming through and that Drumheller had known, he was furious and mounted a legal challenge to the sale. Because the deal had been made on a Sunday, a judge ruled that the land should be split 50-50.

As the story goes, when the post office was about to open, the two men flipped a coin to determine whether it would be named Drumheller or Greentree Crossing. Drumheller formed the Drumheller Land Company Ltd. and the Sam Drumheller Oil & Gas Company, and his son Lee later became head of the local power plant. Though his wife and son remained, Drumheller returned to the United States and evidently settled at Coronado, California. Greentree, on the other hand, remained in Drumheller for most of his life and finally retired to the Peace River country. Drumheller's Greentree Mall perpetuates his name.

Welcome sign at Drumheller flanked by Mounties, 1943. CALGARY PUBLIC LIBRARY PC820

Drumheller was incorporated as a village in 1913, as a town in 1916 and as a city in 1930. Coal fueled the valley's booming economy for years, giving Drumheller the nickname "coal city." But the dramatic growth of Alberta's oil industry after World War II contributed to the decline of the coalfields and the towns that depended on them. Over time Drumheller absorbed many of its satellite mining towns, including Midlandvale (named for the Midland Coal Company), Nacmine (originally named Monarch for its Monarch Colliery, then renamed using an acronym for the owner, North American Collieries, followed by "mine"), Newcastle (from the mining city in England), Rosedale (for the Rosedale Coal & Clay Products Co. Ltd.) and Wayne (origin unknown). In 1998, the city of Drumheller amalgamated with the surrounding municipal district to form a newly constituted town of Drumheller.

Though it has been annexed to Drumheller, Rosedale still boasts a welcome sign. The former hamlet was named for the Rosedale Coal & Clay Products Co. Ltd., which opened in 1911. COURTESY OF JOHN OLSON

Film aficionados will recognize Sam's grandson, set decorator Robert Lee Drumheller (1923–98), whose credits include *Annie Hall*, *Manhattan* and *Dog Day Afternoon*. He was nominated for an Oscar in 1979 for his work on *The Wiz*. Sam Drumheller's uncle, Dan Drumheller, wrote a book titled *Uncle Dan Drumheller Tells Thrills of Western Trails in 1854*.

Duchess

Village on Secondary Highway 550, approximately 117 kilometres north-west of Medicine Hat

When the Canadian Pacific Railway built its "royal line" between Empress and Bassano in 1912, the appointment of Canada's tenth governor-general since Confederation was still a recent memory. Queen Victoria's son Prince Arthur, First Duke of Connaught and Strathearn (1850–1942), held the vice-regal post from 1911–1916. His wife, the Duchess, was a Prussian princess and a member of the German royal family, the Hohenzollerns: Luise Margarete Alexandra Viktoria (1860–1917). Among the avenues originally named in Duchess were Louise and Margaret. Duchess became a village in 1921.

Other place names along this line, chosen for their connections to royalty or aristocracy, include Empress, Iddesleigh, Millicent, Patricia, Princess and Rosemary.

Arrival of the Duke and Duchess of Connaught, possibly in Regina, circa 1911–15. National Archives of Canada C-077583

Welcome sign, 2002. COURTESY OF JOHN OLSON

Duffield

Hamlet south of Highway 16, approximately 23 kilometres west of Stony Plain

A Canadian Northern Railway station, established in 1911 and named for George Duffield Hall of Boston, Massachusetts.

Duhamel

Hamlet on Highway 21, approximately 14 kilometres southwest of Camrose

Originally a trading post known to natives as *notikiwin sipi* (Battle River), Battle River Crossing became known as the Laboucan Settlement when the Laboucan brothers settled there in 1880. The post office that opened in 1893 took the name of Most Reverend Joseph-Thomas Duhamel (1841–1909), the Roman Catholic Archbishop of Ottawa. Duhamel, who was also the first chancellor of the University of Ottawa, once presented a bell to his namesake community in Alberta.

Monseigneur Joseph-Thomas Duhamel, archbishop of Ottawa and the first chancellor of the University of Ottawa. NATIONAL ARCHIVES OF CANADA PA-138828

Dunmore

Hamlet on the Trans-Canada Highway (Highway 1), approximately 5 kilometres southeast of Medicine Hat

The Canadian Agricultural, Coal and Colonization Company was one of many late-19th century British corporations operating in what is now Alberta. One of its major shareholders was Charles Adolphus Murray, 7th Earl of Dunmore (1841–1907). The Earl visited western Canada in 1883, and according to one fanciful story, he inspired the name of Moose Jaw, Saskatchewan, by repairing his Red River cart using the jawbone of a moose. The post office of Dunmore Junction opened in 1886, and in 1898 the name was simplified to Dunmore (from 1905–1957 it was called Coleridge). Dunmore, Pennsylvania, was named for the Earl's uncle, Charles Augustus Dunmore.

Duvernay

Hamlet on Highway 36, approximately 10 kilometres north northeast of Two Hills

This hamlet on the North Saskatchewan River was established by French Canadian settlers in 1905 and in 1907, when the post office was opened, was originally known as South Bend. It was renamed the following year for Ludger Duvernay (1799–1852), a journalist, co-founder of the *Société St. Jean-Baptiste* and participant in the 1837 Rebellion in Lower Canada. Duvernay faces the twin hamlet of Brosseau opposite the river.

Eaglesham

Hamlet on Secondary Highway 739, approximately 90 kilometres northeast of Grande Prairie

The Edmonton, Dunvegan and British Columbia Railway named this station in 1916, possibly for the Scottish village that later made headlines during World War II. In 1941, in an apparent mission to negotiate with Britain, Rudolf Hess—Deputy Führer of Germany—unexpectedly parachuted over Scotland, landing near Eaglesham. He was captured and spent the rest of his life in prison.

Eagle Hill

Hamlet west of Secondary Highway 766, approximately 25 kilometres southwest of Olds

The name belonged originally to a nearby tree-covered hill and is possibly of native origin. The Eagle Hill post office opened in 1903.

East Coulee

Hamlet on Secondary Highway 570, approximately 18 kilometres southeast of Drumheller

This former coal mining community is located east of Drumheller and near a coulee. Its post office opened in 1929.

Eckville

Town on Highway 766, approximately 40 kilometres west northwest of Red Deer

In 1901 Dublin native and Boer War veteran Arthur Edward Thomas Eckford (circa 1878–1961) homesteaded in the Medicine River district west of Red Deer. When the river was bridged three years later, the area became settled and Eckford opened a post office, which the postal authorities evidently decided to name Eckford. At Eckford's request, the name was changed to its present form.[82] With the arrival of the railway, Eckville moved from its original location on Eckford's farm to a new railway townsite farther south. Eckford served as a local justice of the peace, notary public, road councillor and school trustee. Eckford, his wife, Eva, and their children left Eckville for the west coast around 1920, and Arthur is buried in Capilano View Cemetery, West Vancouver.

Eckville became a village in 1921 and a town in 1966. Despite their long absence, the town invited 16 members of the Eckford family for Eckville's 75th anniversary in 1996, when a plaque was erected and a numbered street was renamed Eckford Street to honour the town's founder.[83]

Eckville was named for homesteader, postmaster and Boer War veteran Arthur E.T. Eckford. Courtesy of Thomas Eckford

Edberg

Village on Secondary Highway 609, approximately 25 kilometres south of Camrose

Edberg's namesake was founding postmaster Johan Anton Edstrom (1850–1910), a Swedish émigré who settled here with his wife in 1900 after a sojourn in North Dakota. Edstrom chose the suffix "berg," meaning "hill" in his native tongue, for the post office's name. Both Edstrom and his wife are buried in the nearby New Norway Village Cemetery. Edberg was incorporated as a village in 1930.

Edgerton

Village on secondary highways 610 and 894, approximately 29 kilometres east southeast of Wainwright

On its main line from Winnipeg to Edmonton, the Grand Trunk Pacific Railway used the name of engineer H.H. Edgerton to form part of its alphabetical series of stations between Artland, Saskatchewan, and Uncas, Alberta (east of Edmonton). Edgerton was incorporated as a village in 1917.

One of its most famous sons is historian Hugh A. Dempsey, former curator and chief archivist at the Glenbow–Alberta Institute in Calgary and biographer of native chiefs Crowfoot, Red Crow and Big Bear.

Edmonton

City on highways 2, 16 and 16A, approximately 297 kilometres north of Calgary

At Edmonton his loving wife
  From the balcony espied
Her tender husband, wondering much
  To see how he did ride.

William Cowper penned these words in 1782 as part of his humourous poem, "The Diverting History of John Gilpin." Gilpin's intended destination on his wild horseback ride was Edmonton, a Middlesex village that now lies entirely within the boundaries of London. In 1795, thirteen years after the publication of Cowper's poem, William Tomison of the Hudson's Bay Company (HBC) built a new trading post in Rupert's Land, at the confluence of the North Saskatchewan and Sturgeon rivers. Here the rival North West Company had already built its own post, Fort Augustus. It was likely Tomison who named the HBC post Edmonton House, possibly to honour HBC Deputy Governor James Winter Lake, a native of Edmonton, Middlesex.[84] Both Fort Augustus and Edmonton House shifted locations several times and finally amalgamated as

Edmonton House (later renamed Fort Edmonton) when the two rival companies merged in 1821. Both the Siksika (Blackfoot) and Cree who traded at Fort Edmonton called it "the big house." The final version of Fort Edmonton, a riverbank complex built in 1830, was demolished in 1915. The local post office, which opened in 1877, dropped the word "fort" around 1880 and became known simply as Edmonton.

Fort Edmonton from across the North Saskatchewan River, 1871. Glenbow Archives PB-885-10

Alberta's future capital was incorporated as a town in 1892 and as a city in 1904. However, before 1912 only a fraction of modern day Edmonton lay within the city limits. When the Calgary and Edmonton Railway arrived in 1890–91, it stopped short of the North Saskatchewan River and terminated in South Edmonton, which had been incorporated in 1898 as the town of Strathcona and in 1906 as a city. Strathcona—a name chosen over such other proposals as Minto and New Aberdeen—honoured Lord Strathcona, former HBC chief commissioner and an important figure with the Canadian Pacific Railway.

Before these "twin cities" amalgamated in 1912, Edmonton's main street was Jasper Avenue (named as the road to Jasper), and Strathcona's, was Whyte Avenue (named for CPR executive Sir William Whyte). The name Strathcona lives on as Edmonton's Old Strathcona district and in the name of nearby Strathcona County.

The Legislature building in Edmonton, 1919. The seat of provincial government was built, at least in part, from sandstone quarried in Calgary. GLENBOW ARCHIVES ND-3-207

Edmonton has since annexed the village of Calder (named for founder Hugh Calder, an Edmonton alderman and real estate developer, incorporated in 1910 as West Edmonton and annexed in 1917), the towns of Beverly (named for a township in Wentworth County, Ontario, annexed in 1961),[85] Jasper Place (which straddled Jasper Avenue and was annexed in 1964) and the southern locality of Ellerslie (a name of Scottish origin). Calder's landmark water tower was demolished in 1970. Ellerslie's 'Jesus elevator,' with its quotation from Mark 8 towered over Calgary Trail—"what shall it profit a man, if he gain the whole world, and lose his own soul?"—was demolished in 1989.

Following World War I, school children in Edmonton, Middlesex, raised money to cast an embossed brass shield honouring the Canadian soldiers who fought in the conflict. Thousands of children in Edmonton, Alberta, attended the presentation ceremony on September 1, 1920, when British dignitaries presented the shield and a massive Union Jack. The shield was stolen a few months later and remained missing for 66 years. It was recovered in 1986 and placed on display at the Edmonton Public Schools Archives and Museum.[86]

During World War II, Canadian soldiers in London always found a warm welcome at 27 Sheldon Road, Edmonton, where "Pop" Kempston shared his home, rations and humour. News of his death in 1948 made its way to Edmonton, Alberta, where many veterans remembered his

First train to cross bridge over North Saskatchewan at Edmonton, October 20, 1902. The engineer was James Greenwood Entwistle, for whom the hamlet of Entwistle was named. GLENBOW ARCHIVES NA-1244-1

hospitality.[87] Kempston's Edmonton was absorbed into the Borough of Enfield in 1965, but its residents can still worship at the Edmonton Methodist Church, join the Edmonton Cycle Club and swim at the Edmonton Leisure Centre. London's Edmontonians are fiercely proud

Commemorative shield presented by the school children of Edmonton, Middlesex, England, to their Alberta counterparts, 1920. The shield went missing a few weeks after it was presented and did not turn up until 1986. GLENBOW ARCHIVES ND-3-579

of their community's history and identity, and are keenly aware that a major Canadian city perpetuates the name.

Edmonton itself once had a namesake in Edmonton Beach, a summer village established in 1959 and later renamed Spring Lake.

Edson

Town on Highway 16, approximately 192 kilometres west of Edmonton

As long as it served as the railhead on the main line of the Grand Trunk Pacific Railway (GTP) west from Edmonton, the settlement of Wolf Creek boomed. Land speculators bought all the real estate they could in the expectation that Wolf Creek would become the divisional point. But the railway pressed on another dozen kilometres, placing its station on the future Edson townsite. Authorities initially declined to name the station for GTP vice-president and General Manager Edson Joseph Chamberlain (1852–1924) because of possible confusion with Edison (later renamed Westlock). The station was named Heatherwood in 1910, but it became Edson in 1911, and Edson was incorporated as a town the same year. The Edson River shares the name. Edson Chamberlain took over the Grand Trunk Railway, the GTP's parent firm, when company president Charles M. Hays was killed in the *Titanic* disaster in 1912. Chamberlain died in Pasadena, California, and is buried in St. Albans, Vermont.

Edwand

Hamlet north of Highway 28, approximately 12 kilometres east northeast of Smoky Lake

This hamlet's name came from its first postmaster: Edward Anderson, who held the post from 1904–1917. Edwand Creek shares the name.

Egremont

Hamlet north of Highway 18, approximately 10 kilometres north of Redwater

R.C. Armstrong opened this post office in 1908, and it was named for his wife's hometown of Egremont in what is now Cumbria, England. There is also an Egremont in Ontario. Alberta's Egremont became a hamlet in 1979.

Edson J. Chamberlain, vice-president and general manager of the Grand Trunk Pacific Railway (GTP), left. The man on the right is likely Sir Alfred Waldron Smithers, the GTP director for whom Smithers, British Columbia, was named. NATIONAL ARCHIVES OF CANADA PA-172623

Elk Point

Town on Highway 41, approximately 90 kilometres north northwest of Lloydminster

The original Elk Point, a South Dakota town between the Missouri and Sioux rivers, was established in 1862 on what had been an elk runway surrounded by woods and known as the "elk point." Lewis and Clark hunted there in 1804. Elk Point was the hometown of a man named Highby (or Higby), who resettled in Alberta around 1905. According to lore, Highby worked as a bartender in Vegreville, but to overcome his alcoholism he briefly secluded himself in a cave he dug along the bank of the North Saskatchewan River. Here Highby spent a winter hunting and trapping, and he named the area for his hometown. When the post office opened in 1909, the name Elk Point was chosen over Courtland or Vermilion (the name of a town near Elk Point, South Dakota). Elk Point became a village in 1938 and a town in 1962.

Elkwater

Hamlet west of Highway 41, approximately 45 kilometres southeast of Medicine Hat

This hamlet, whose post office opened in 1901, is named for the nearby lake.

Ellscott

Hamlet east of Highway 63, approximately 34 kilometres southeast of Athabasca

English-born Louis Scott of Edmonton was the secretary and purchasing agent for the Alberta and Great Waterways Railway, as well as the namesake ("L. Scott") for this hamlet on the Carbondale–Lac La Biche branch of the Edmonton, Dunvegan and British Columbia Railway, established by 1918. During World War I he served overseas with Princess Patricia's Canadian Light Infantry and was seconded to the Royal Air Force. In 1920, Scott was among a small group of railway functionaries who gathered in an Edmonton drug store, spread out a map and came up with several railway place names, including Newbrook.[88]

Elnora

Village east of Highway 21, approximately 32 kilometres north of Three Hills

Pioneer settler Alexander Hogg (died 1939) and his wife, Jessie Murdie (died 1936), came from the borders in Scotland and settled in this district in 1906. Two years later, Irish-born William Edwards and his American wife, Catherine Nora (born 1858), settled next to them. Residents applied for a post office in 1908 and proposed that it be named Stewartville, for the local Presbyterian student minister, Reverend Stewart. Postal authorities rejected the name—there was already a Stewartville in Ontario—so residents proposed three alternatives: Lilliesleaf, Ypsilanti and Elnora. Elnora, Hogg once explained, was formed from his mother's name (Elnor) and Catherine Edwards' middle name (Nora).[89] William Edwards was the first postmaster (1908–09), Catherine Edwards the second (1909–10) and Alex Hogg, the third (1910–13). Catherine Edwards traversed the area by democrat, birthing babies and tending the sick. She died relatively young. The Grand Trunk Pacific Railway's Mirror–Calgary line arrived around 1912, and Elnora became a village in 1929.

Empress

Village south of Secondary Highway 562, approximately 108 kilometres north northeast of Medicine Hat

Queen Victoria's death in 1901 was still a fresh memory when the Canadian Pacific Railway built its Empress–Bassano branch line a dozen years later. The railway named this point on the Red Deer River, just west of the Saskatchewan boundary, to honour her role as Empress of India. Other place names along this "royal line" that were chosen for their connections to royalty or aristocracy include Duchess, Iddesleigh, Millicent, Patricia, Princess and Rosemary. Townsite lots were auctioned in Medicine Hat in late 1913, and Empress was incorporated as a village in 1914.

Enchant

Hamlet on Secondary Highway 526, approximately 56 kilometres northeast of Lethbridge

The *Concise Oxford Dictionary* uses the words *charm, delight* and *bewitch* to define *enchant*, and perhaps early settlers felt their new home was enchanting when it began as a Canadian Pacific Railway (CPR) townsite in 1914. Certainly it is more positive than the original name, Lost Lake.

The origin of the name Enchant is unknown, but an interesting theory appears in the local history book *Drybelt Pioneers*. The next locality on this CPR branch line is Retlaw—"Walter" spelled backwards—and said to be named for Walter R. Baker, the CPR general manager's assistant. Enchant, according to this theory, forms part of an acrostic that also spells Walter: Winfield (a water tower siding), Armada, Lomond, Travers, Enchant and Retlaw.

Endiang

Hamlet south of Highway 589, approximately 38 kilometres north northeast of Hanna

At the age of 21, sailor William Henry Foreman (born 1849) left his native England for Muskoka, Ontario, where he worked as a builder and eventually built a new business for himself—the Endiang Hotel, which he named for the Chippewa word meaning "my home." Foreman and his family later moved to Alberta, where he opened a store and post office in 1910 and named it for his old hotel. (A subsequent owner rechristened Muskoka's Endiang Hotel "Arcadia House.") Foreman retired to British Columbia and is buried near Colwood on Vancouver Island.

Enilda

Hamlet on Highway 2, approximately 13 kilometres east of High Prairie

Enilda once had a post office with one name and a railway station with another. Adline Tompkins was the wife of J. Tompkins, the first postmaster from 1913–17. Enilda is the reverse spelling of her name. However, the Northern Alberta Railways station was long known as Grouard Station, as opposed to Grouard, where the Grouard post office was located. The station eventually changed its name to Enilda.

Ensign

Hamlet north of Secondary Highway 534, approximately 60 kilometres southeast of Calgary

Before Canada's maple leaf flag was adopted in 1965, a variation on the British Red Ensign—a red flag with the Union Jack in the upper corner next to the staff, and the Canadian coat of arms in the fly—served as Canada's national flag. It was already in use at the time the Canadian Pacific Railway built its Kipp–Aldersyde line from 1909–12 and established the new townsite of Ensign. The Canadian Red Ensign is believed to be the source of the hamlet's name.

Prime Minister Mackenzie King made attempts in 1925 and 1946 to create a distinctly Canadian flag, and a 1946 House of Commons–Senate joint committee presented a revised Red Ensign with a gold maple leaf. But it took another two decades and the efforts of Prime Minister Lester B. Pearson to push through a new flag design.

The Canadian Red Ensign, right, served as Canada's flag until 1965.
CALGARY PUBLIC LIBRARY PC495 (DETAIL)

Entwistle

Hamlet on Highway 16, approximately 42 kilometres south southeast of Mayerthorpe

As they pass through this hamlet for a weekend at Jasper National Park, Edmontonians might pause to remember James Greenwood Entwistle (circa 1860–1940), the engineer who drove the first passenger train into Edmonton in 1902. The Canadian Pacific Railway (CPR) operated the Calgary and Edmonton Railway (C&E), which had been completed 10 years earlier. But the C&E stopped short of the North Saskatchewan River and made its terminus the new railway town of Strathcona, or South Edmonton.

Fuming after a decade without train service, Edmonton proper finally entered the railway age via the five-kilometre-long Edmonton Yukon and Pacific Railway, owned by the CPR's arch rivals, William Mackenzie and Donald Mann. Engineer Entwistle operated the train on this short line for three years, crossing back and forth across the Low Level Bridge.[90] (Mackenzie and Mann's Canadian Northern Railway reached Edmonton in 1905, and in 1912 Edmonton annexed Strathcona.)

Entwistle retired west of Edmonton by the Pembina River, where he became a postmaster in 1908. Postal authorities rejected the name Pembina and selected Entwistle instead.

It became a village in 1955, but reverted to hamlet status in 2001.

Erskine

Hamlet on highways 12 and 835, approximately 12 kilometres west of Stettler

When its post office opened in 1903, Erskine was named Liberal—not for the political party then in power in Ottawa, but for Liberal, Missouri, hometown of Irish-born postmaster James Sweetlove Steenson (died 1917) and his wife, Elizabeth Wallace (died 1927). With the arrival of the Canadian Pacific Railway in 1906, Liberal became Erskine, possibly in honour of Lady Millicent Fanny St. Clair-Erskine (1867–1955), for whom the hamlet of Millicent was also named. Her husband—Cromartie Sutherland-Leveson-Gower, the fourth Duke of Sutherland (1851–1913)—had extensive land holdings in the Brooks area.

Other sources suggest British jurist Thomas Erskine (1750–1823) and British novelist and politician Erskine Childers (1870–1922) as possible sources for this hamlet's name. In 1910, Erskine merchant John Mitchell met a man named Erskine in Guernsey, Saskatchewan, who claimed to be Erskine's namesake. "One day an official of the railroad came past our gang," Erskine told Mitchell, "and said, 'Well, Erskine, I think we'll name this town after you.'"[91] Nearby Erskine Lake takes its name from this hamlet.

The Liberal Church and Liberal Cemetery are reminders of the hamlet's former name, but Erskine has not elected a provincial Liberal since 1917. It gained an unwanted federal Liberal Member of Parliament when Progressive Conservative Jack Horner crossed the floor in 1977; he was defeated in the next election. Don Getty, another Progressive Conservative, represented this constituency from 1989–93 during his tenure as Alberta premier.

Etzikom

Hamlet on Highway 61, approximately 67 kilometres southwest of Medicine Hat

Around 1914, the Canadian Pacific Railway purchased land from settler J. Becker for townsite development along the railway company's new Foremost–Weyburn line. The name is Blackfoot for "valley" and is shared with nearby Etzikom Valley. Unsatisfied with the name, postal authorities changed it to Endon in 1915, but before long the original name was restored. Etzikom Coulee shares the name.

Evansburg

Village on Highway 16, approximately 39 kilometres south of Mayerthorpe

Toronto-born Henry Marshall Erskine Evans (1876–1973) moved west in 1900, spending four years as business manager of the *Winnipeg Tribune* before coming to Alberta. He prospected for coal along the Pembina River west of Edmonton, worked as an insurance and real estate broker in Edmonton, and was elected as that city's mayor in 1918. Evans later chaired the Alberta Coal Commission and in 1931 became a financial adviser for the provincial government. This former village on the Pembina River, incorporated in 1953, was named for him. The post office name was originally spelled Evansburgh in 1914. The spelling was changed in 1950.

Exshaw

Hamlet on the Trans-Canada Highway (Highway 1), approximately 15 kilometres east southeast of Canmore

Motorists along the Trans-Canada Highway east of Canmore cannot help but notice the cement plant operation at Exshaw, which has been chopping away at the limestone cliffs for about as long as Alberta has been a province. The Western Canada Cement and Coal Company was founded by a group of businessmen that included Sir Sandford Fleming (1827–1915), the prominent railway surveyor and engineer who was instrumental in developing standard time, and his son-in-law, Lieutenant William Exshaw (1866–1927), for whom this hamlet is named. The name is shared with Exshaw Creek and Exshaw Mountain.

Fabyan

Hamlet on Highway 14, approximately 10 kilometres northwest of Wainwright

Someone associated with the Grand Trunk Pacific Railway must have been impressed by Fabyan House, a mountain resort in New Hampshire established by hotelier Horace Fabyan in 1837 (it closed in 1951). Built in 1909 and named for the American hotel, this station forms part of the alphabetical sequence between Artland, Saskatchewan, and Uncas, Alberta.

Fairview

Town on Highway 2, approximately 71 kilometres west southwest of Peace River

Fairview was the creation of the Central Canada Railway, which bypassed the existing communities of Friedenstal and Waterhole (so named because of its natural reservoir where settlers watered their stock) and established its newest siding here in 1928. At the suggestion of E.J. Martin, the new siding took the name of the local municipal district—Fairview—itself named in 1914 for the farm of area homesteader H.L. Propst. Fairview became a village in 1929 and a town in 1949.

Fairview

Hamlet south of Secondary Highway 512, immediately east of Lethbridge

Forty-third street in Lethbridge serves as the border between Lethbridge to the west and Fairview, a hamlet created in 1979, to the east. The Lethbridge fairgrounds, just opposite 43rd Street, are visible from Fairview.

Falher

Town on Highway 49, approximately 20 kilometres west of McLennan

In the 19th century, Roman Catholic missionary activity in what is now Alberta was largely the work of the Oblates of Mary Immaculate, an order founded in France in 1816. The order's first foreign mission was Canada, and Oblate missionaries reached what is now western Canada in 1845. One such missionary was Constant Falher (1863–1939), who was born in Josselin, Bretagne, France, ordained as a priest in 1889 and arrived at St. Bernard mission (now Grouard) that same year. Falher learned the Cree language and remained in what is now northern Alberta for the rest of his life. In 1912 he inaugurated St. Jean Baptiste de Falher, a mission located five kilometres southeast of the present-day town. With the arrival of the Edmonton, Dunvegan and British Columbia Railway in 1915, the mission's population divided between two new railway settlements, Donnelly and Falher. Briefly organized as a village from 1923–26, Falher was reestablished as a village in 1929 and was incorporated as a town in 1955. Falher bills itself as the "Honey Capital of Canada" and boasts the world's largest bee, a sculpture 6.92 metres long and 2.31 metres in diameter. Father Falher is buried in Grouard, where he became principal of a native school in 1935.

Fallis

Hamlet south of Highway 16, approximately 43 kilometres west northwest of Stony Plain

W.S. Fallis, a salesman from Perth, Ontario, eventually rose in position to become president and managing director of the Sherwin-Williams paint company. In a national convention held at Calgary's Palliser Hotel in 1927, the Montreal-based businessman was elected president of the Canadian Manufacturers' Association (later renamed the Alliance of Manufacturers & Exporters Canada). The Grand Trunk Pacific Railway named this station, on the north shore of Wabamun Lake, for Fallis in 1910.

Falun

Hamlet on Highway 13, approximately 30 kilometres west of Wetaskiwin

The name was suggested by John Strom, one of many settlers who had come originally from Falun, the capital of the Swedish province of Dalecarlia. Strom settled first in Minnesota, then homesteaded here in 1902 and was widowed the following year. One morning he awoke to see a bear peering in through his cabin window, watching him sleep. It turned out that seven bears had surrounded the dwelling, and John and his brother Richard bolted the door until they were gone. The Stroms kept the bear's paw prints on the window for a long time as a conversation piece. The Falun post office opened in 1904. In 1906 John Strom returned to Minnesota, where both Fahlun and Falun townships are named for Falun, Sweden. Falun Creek also shares the name.

Faust

Hamlet on Highway 2, approximately 56 kilometres west of Slave Lake

Edward T. Faust, an American railway fireman, moved to Canada in 1912 and worked for the Grand Trunk Pacific Railway until 1914. That year he became a locomotive engineer for the Edmonton, Dunvegan and British Columbia Railway (ED&BC), operating a work train during the company's track construction in the Peace River country. The ED&BC named this station, on the south shore of Lesser Slave Lake, for Faust in 1914. An authority on air brakes, Faust acquired the nicknames "Soft Exhaust" and "The Westinghouse Kid."[92] Faust settled at McLennan and served for years on the local school board.

Fawcett

Hamlet on Highway 44, approximately 46 kilometres north northwest of Westlock

Around 1914 the Edmonton, Dunvegan and British Columbia Railway reached French Creek and established Fawcett, a station named for its resident engineer during construction.

Ferintosh

Village on Highway 21, approximately 29 kilometres south southwest of Camrose

Ontario-born Dr. John R. McLeod (1872–1931) and his family homesteaded in this district in 1903. Dr. McLeod established a medical practice covering an extensive area, which he maintained for a quarter of a century, and was elected as a Liberal to the first Alberta legislature in 1905. McLeod's ancestors had come from the village of Ferintosh in what is now Highland, Scotland, and he suggested the name that the post office adopted in 1910.

Fitzgerald

Hamlet on the Fitzgerald Portage Road, approximately 339 kilometres north of Fort McMurray

In December 1910, Royal North-West Mounted Police Inspector Francis Joseph Fitzgerald (1867–1911) and three companions set out from Fort McPherson to Dawson City. They never arrived. Searchers discovered their bodies and a diary that revealed they had become lost and ran short of supplies. The story is told in Dick North's *The Lost Patrol: the Mounties' Yukon Tragedy*. The Smith Landing post office on the Slave River was renamed Fort Fitzgerald in 1915 in Fitzgerald's memory. The hamlet, near the North-West Territories border, is known simply as Fitzgerald.

Royal North-West Mounted Police Inspector Francis Joseph Fitzgerald, second from left, was part of the "Lost Patrol" that set out from Fort McPherson in 1910 but never reached Dawson City. National Archives of Canada PA-203842

Flatbush

Hamlet west of Highway 44, approximately 55 kilometres west of Athabasca

This hamlet, whose post office opened in 1916, is descriptively named.

Fleet

Hamlet on Highway 12, approximately 15 kilometres southeast of Castor

Originally known as The Hub, this settlement was renamed Fleet in 1911, when the Canadian Pacific Railway (CPR) named a series of stations on its Lacombe–Kerrobert branch to honour King George V's coronation, including Consort, Coronation, Throne, Veteran and Loyalist, and possibly also Federal and Monitor.[93] In this context, Fleet is understood to evoke the British fleet, a keystone of empire in 1911.[94] An alternative explanation is that the name refers to the CPR's fleet of ships, which spanned both the Atlantic and Pacific oceans.

Foremost

Village on Highway 61, approximately 80 kilometres southwest of Medicine Hat

One of the definitions of "foremost," according to the *Concise Oxford Dictionary*, is "the most advanced in position, the front," and this was certainly true of Foremost at its inception as the railhead of the Canadian Pacific Railway's Lethbridge–Weyburn line. The track reached Foremost in 1913 and was not extended farther east for another two years. In 1914 the Foremost post office replaced its counterpart at Webber, established in 1911 a short distance to the south.

Forestburg

Village on Highway 53, approximately 27 kilometres south southwest of Killam

Before World War I the nearest post office for this area was Duxbury, located a few kilometres away and evidently named for the local waterfowl. Postmaster B.L. Thornton moved his office to the present site when the Canadian Northern Railway built its Edmonton–Alliance branch in 1915, but postal authorities rejected the proposed new place name—Highmore—as a duplication. Thornton had once lived in Forestburg, South Dakota, and this is the likely origin of the name.[95] However, many settlers had come from Ontario, where there is another Forestburg. Forestburg became a village in 1919.

Fort Assiniboine

Hamlet on Highway 33, approximately 58 kilometres southeast of Swan Hills

Fort Assiniboine originated as a Hudson's Bay Company post, built in 1823, and was likely named for the Assiniboine people, an alternative name for the Stoneys. Fort Assiniboine became a village in 1958, but has since reverted to hamlet status.

Fort Chipewyan

Hamlet on the Fort Smith Winter Road, approximately 213 kilometres north of Fort McMurray

The Hudson's Bay Company's Fort Chipewyan trading post, pre-1920. It had been a North West Company post before the two rival firms merged in 1821. GLENBOW ARCHIVES NA-2750-1

A North West Company trading post by this name was built on the south shore of Lake Athabasca in 1788 and relocated to the north shore in 1804. It became a Hudson's Bay Company post after the two companies merged in 1821. Named for the Chipewyan people, it was called the "Emporium of the North" for its key role in the fur trade. Fort Chipewyan is considered the province's first nonnative settlement.

Fort Kent

Hamlet on Highway 28, approximately 12 kilometres northeast of Bonnyville

The New England city of Fort Kent, Maine, took its name from an early 19th century wooden fort, itself named for Maine Governor Edward Kent. Alberta's Fort Kent was evidently named for its New England counterpart.

Fort MacKay

Hamlet on Highway 63, approximately 57 kilometres north northwest of Fort McMurray

Originally known as Red River House, this northern post was renamed in 1870 to honour Dr. William Morrison MacKay (1836–1917), a Scottish-born surgeon and fur trader who worked for the Hudson's Bay Company (HBC) from 1864–1898. While serving as a doctor for a massive territory, MacKay became an HBC chief trader and factor. He later practiced medicine in Edmonton, where MacKay Avenue and MacKay School are named for him.

Fort Macleod

Town on Highway 3, approximately 40 kilometres west of Lethbridge

Scottish-born James Farquharson Macleod (1836–94), the man responsible for the naming of both Calgary and Fort Macleod, emigrated to Canada in 1854. He was called to the bar in 1860, but chose instead to join the militia. He fought in the Red River Rebellion of 1870. Macleod joined the newly formed North-West Mounted Police (NWMP) in 1873 and soon became its assistant commissioner. Following the Mounties' Great Trek of 1874, Macleod established his command at Fort Macleod, a post built on an island in the Oldman River, and later rebuilt on the present townsite.

Colonel James F. Macleod, commissioner of the North-West Mounted Police and later a judge of the Supreme Court of the North-West Territories. SIR ALEXANDER GALT MUSEUM AND ARCHIVES P 1985 1016000

Macleod's reputation for fairness in applying the law, and in successfully quelling the whisky traffic that had devastated native society, won him the respect of native leaders. In 1877 he helped negotiate Treaty No. 7 with the Siksika (Blackfoot), Kainai (Blood), Piikani (Peigan), Tsuu T'ina (Sarcee) and Stoney peoples. This treaty prepared the way for railway construction and nonnative settlement in what is now southern Alberta. Macleod retired from the NWMP in 1876 but returned as its commissioner from 1877–80. In his final years, Macleod served as a judge of the Supreme Court of the North-West Territories, and in that capacity he was a member of the governing territorial council in Regina. He died in 1894 in Calgary, where he is buried.

When the Macleod branch of the Calgary and Edmonton Railway arrived and the town was incorporated in 1892, its name was simplified to Macleod. The original name was restored in 1952, and the Fort Museum was built in 1956–57. Both the original fort site and the town hall (the former territorial courthouse) are National Historic Sites.

Colonel Macleod commanded the North-West Mounted Police fort that is named for him. He suggested the name Calgary for the fort at the Bow River, and the road from Calgary to Fort Macleod became known as Macleod Trail. Calgary Public Library PC1101

Fort McMurray

Urban Service area within the regional municiplaity of Wood Buffalo on Highway 63, approximately 378 kilometres northeast of Edmonton

Built in 1870 on the site of an earlier North West Company post, Fort McMurray began as a Hudson's Bay Company post established by Factor H. John Moberly (1835–1931) and named by him for his superior, Inspecting Chief Factor William McMurray (1824–1877). With the establishment of the Great Canadian Oil Sands project in 1964, Fort McMurray was incorporated as a new town. It was one of several communities incorporated between 1956–1967 under the New Town Act. Oil discoveries led to the creation of instant boomtowns, and the New Town Act was intended to smooth the development of local government and infrastructure.[96] In the 1970s Fort McMurray absorbed the hamlet of Waterways, once the terminal point of the Alberta and Great Waterways Railway, which connected Edmonton with Waterways in 1922. Fort McMurray was incorporated as a city in 1980, but later became an Urban Service area within the regional municipality of Wood Buffalo.

Fort Saskatchewan

City on highways 15 and 21, approximately 35 kilometres northeast of Edmonton

In 1875 the newly arrived North-West Mounted Police (NWMP) built two new posts in what is now Alberta: one on the Bow River (the future site of Calgary) and another on the North Saskatchewan River, where Fort Edmonton, the Hudson's Bay Company (HBC) trading post, was already well established. The chief factor of the HBC's Saskatchewan district, Richard Hardisty (for whom the town of Hardisty was named), hoped the NWMP would build its police post close to Fort Edmonton. But the Mounties chose a site 32 kilometres downstream, where the terrain seemed more inviting for the transcontinental railway that was already being planned. When it was finally built a decade later, the Canadian Pacific Railway followed a southern route through Calgary, and Edmonton—not Fort Saskatchewan—emerged as Alberta's northern metropolis. Fort Saskatchewan was incorporated as a village in 1899, as a town in 1904 and as a city in 1985. Its origin as a police post is perpetuated through the Fort Saskatchewan Correctional Centre, a provincial penitentiary and formerly the site of executions. The last man hanged at Fort Saskatchewan was 23-year-old Robert Raymond Cook on November 15, 1960.

Fort Vermilion

Hamlet on Highway 88, approximately 67 kilometres east southeast of High Level

Author Will Ferguson, a native of Fort Vermilion and its most famous son, observes that his hometown is "closer to the Arctic Circle than the American border." Historic Fort Vermilion was a major North West Company post when it was built in 1788 and became a Hudson's Bay Company post when the two rival companies merged in 1821. The fort moved several times during its existence. In 1929, in one of Alberta's most celebrated incidents, famed pilot W.R. "Wop" May—who a decade earlier had been pursued by the Red Baron—braved a blizzard to fly diphtheria antitoxin to remote Fort Vermilion on the Peace River. Prime Minister Brian Mulroney and Alberta Premier Don Getty attended Fort Vermilion's bicentennial celebrations in 1988, and Mulroney unveiled a Historic Sites and

Monuments Board plaque. The source of the name is the red clay found along the Peace River.

Fox Creek

Town on Highway 43, approximately 75 kilometres west northwest of Whitecourt

Fox Creek developed in response to a sour gas discovery and was incorporated as a new town in 1967. It was one of several communities incorporated between 1956–1967 under the New Town Act. Oil discoveries led to the creation of instant boomtowns, and the New Town Act was intended to smooth the development of local government and infrastructure.97

Fox Creek bills itself as "Canada's Centennial Community." The creek for which the town is named was itself named for the animal. Fox Creek was incorporated as a town in 1983.

Gadsby

Village north of Highway 12, approximately 25 kilometres east of Stettler

Toronto reporter Henry Franklin Gadsby was evidently the namesake for the post office opened here in 1909. Gadsby became a village in 1910.98

Gainford

Hamlet on Highway 16, approximately 43 kilometres north northeast of Drayton Valley

When its post office opened in 1910, the existing settlement of Seba was renamed for Gainford, a centre in Durham, England.

Galahad

Village on Secondary Highway 861, approximately 33 kilometres north of Castor

The post office at this location, opened in 1906, was first known as Loveland. Postal authorities gave it the present name in 1916, probably in reference to Sir Galahad, one of the mythical Knights of the Round Table. In Arthurian legend, Galahad was the son of Sir Lancelot and succeeded in finding the Holy Grail. Galahad became a village in 1918.

Gem

Hamlet west of Secondary Highway 862, approximately 134 kilometres east of Calgary

Gem was a touching name for a new home precious to its settlers. The Gem post office opened in 1914.

William Reynolds Gibbons and his family settled in the Sturgeon Valley in 1894. Canadian National Railways built its station on what had been his homestead. Provincial Archives of Alberta B.7967

Gibbons

Town on Highway 28A, approximately 30 kilometres north of Edmonton

When Canadian National Railways (CNR) renamed the town of Battenberg in 1920, it honoured the late William Reynolds Gibbons (1855–1916). In 1894, after sojourning in Ontario and Edmonton, English-born Gibbons moved north, settling along the Athabasca Trail in the area known as Sturgeon Valley. A decade later, residents signed a petition to establish a local post office but neglected to give it a name. Postmaster Henry Astley obliged, and from 1903–06 the community was known as Astleyville. Once Astley moved away, citizens petitioned for another name—preferably Sturgeon Valley or Sturgeon Bridge, because the community lay along the Sturgeon River. The post office named the town Battenberg. The present designation was the result of railway development. The CNR wanted to buy Gibbons' homestead, which lay along their right-of-way, but he resisted their overtures until nearly the end of his life. Gibbons is buried in Emmanuel Anglican Cemetery in nearby Namao.

Girouxville

Village on Secondary Highway 744, approximately nine kilometres west of Falher

French Canadian residents at Fowler, a siding established by the Edmonton, Dunvegan and British Columbia Railway in 1915, persuaded the railway to change the name of the community to Girouxville after Father Henri Giroux (1869–1956).[99] As a colonization agent for the Congregation of Oblates of Mary Immaculate, Giroux persuaded a number of francophone settlers from Quebec and the northeastern United States to move to this district, beginning in 1912. Girouxville was relocated to its present location in 1928; the original townsite, about five kilometres to the west, was renamed Dréau, after early missionary Father Jean Dréau. Girouxville became a village in 1951. Father Giroux is buried in Girouxville's Oblate cemetery.

Gleichen

Hamlet on Secondary Highway 547, approximately 65 kilometres east southeast of Calgary

According to legend, when the first Canadian Pacific Railway (CPR) train pulled in at the 12th Siding west of Medicine Hat in 1883, a group of VIP passengers stepped onto the platform to inspect the locale just outside the Blackfoot Reserve. One of these men was Count Albert Gleichen (1863–1937), an investor in the CPR. Gleichen, who pronounced his name "Glaikhen," was said to have been taken with the area's beauty. Another member of the group—Augustus Nanton, an investment promoter with CPR connections (and for whom the town of Nanton was named)—suggested on the spot that the siding be named for the count. This kind of story—a group of dignitaries naming a railway point on the spot—is typical of toponymic mythology. The name was more likely chosen by a railway executive or a committee.

"Gleichen was named after a German Count who came through here in 1884," wrote Gleichen postmaster D.B. McNeill two decades later, in response to a query from the chief geographer of the Department of the Interior. "We cannot find out on what business he was here nor whether he is dead or alive at the present time."[100] Such is the level of immortality that a toponym confers. Gleichen's main commercial thoroughfare was named Crowfoot Street, for the 19th century Blackfoot chief who guided his people from independence to life on the reserve. A siding east of Gleichen was also named Crowfoot. Gleichen became a village in 1899 but has since reverted to hamlet status.

Gleichen's main street was named for Crowfoot, head chief of the Siksika (Blackfoot) who guided his people from their traditional lifestyle to settlement on the reserve. Glenbow Archives NA-29-1

Glendon

Village on Secondary Highway 882, approximately 28 kilometres west of Bonnyville

This village was named for the mother of J.P. Spencer, who became Glendon's first postmaster in 1912 and held the post until 1917. Incorporated as a village in 1956, Glendon boasts the world's largest pyrogy, a 7.62 metre tall fibre glass and steel sculpture of a pyrogy on a fork, unveiled in 1993. It is located in Pyrogy Park, just off Pyrogy Drive.

Glenevis

Hamlet south of Highway 43, approximately 37 kilometres south southwest of Barrhead

Pioneer postmaster John A. McLeod named this post office for the Glennevis, Cape Breton Island, Nova Scotia hometown of his wife, Annie. One of the 'n's was dropped.

Glenwood

Village north of Secondary Highway 505, approximately 61 kilometres southwest of Lethbridge

This Mormon agricultural village was named for Edward Glen Wood (died 1933), the son of prominent local Mormon Edward James Wood. The original intention was to name the settlement Edwood, but the elder Wood declined in favour of his son. Glenwood was known as Glenwoodville until 1979. The Woods are buried in the Cardston Cemetery.

Goodfare

Hamlet on Secondary Highway 671, approximately 55 kilometres west of Grande Prairie

This optimistic name was adopted by the post office when it opened in 1919.

Goose Lake

Hamlet north of Highway 55, approximately 31 kilometres southeast of Lac La Biche

This hamlet is set amidst many lakes, none of them named Goose. The post office opened in 1932. Alberta has at least two lakes by this name, one east of Edmonton and another east of Hanna. The hamlet is named for the bird.

Grande Cache

Town on Highway 40, approximately 115 kilometres northwest of Hinton

Fur traders historically cached goods they could not carry in a hiding place, or cache, where they remained safe for later retrieval. On one occasion, Hudson's Bay Company trader Ignace Giasson was loaded down with more furs than he could handle, and stored them in a large such hiding place—in French, a *grande cache*. Besides this town, the name also applies to Grande Cache Ford, Grande Cache Lake and Grande Cache Valley. Grande Cache was incorporated as a new town in 1966, and as a town in 1983.[101]

Grande Prairie

City on Highway 40, approximately 150 kilometres southwest of Peace River

In the early 1800s, the prairie districts in the Peace River country were known collectively as the Grand Prairie. By mid-century the term was used exclusively for that prairie lying west of the Smoky River between the Wapiti River and the Saddle Hills. When the Hudson's Bay Company established a trading post off La Glace Lake in 1880, it was called Grand Prairie. Much of the Grand Prairie was subdivided for homesteading in 1909 and experienced its first major land rush in 1910. That summer, the Argonauts Company subdivided a new townsite, Grande Prairie City, along a proposed Canadian Northern Railway (CNoR) route. The CNoR never came, but a trail connected Grande Prairie to the railway centre of Edson, and in 1916 the Edmonton, Dunvegan and British Columbia Railway arrived. Grande Prairie was incorporated as a village in 1914, as a town in 1919, and as a city in 1957.

Granum

Town on Secondary Highway 519, approximately 50 kilometres northwest of Lethbridge

Granum was originally known as Leavings, as the point on the Calgary–Fort Benton Trail that left the banks of Willow Creek. Its location in a fertile wheat-growing district prompted future provincial treasurer Malcolm McKenzie, who represented the area in the legislature, to suggest a new name: *Granum*, the Latin word for "grain." The Leavings post office was renamed Granum in 1907. Granum became a village in 1908 and a town in 1910.

Grassland

Hamlet on Highway 55, approximately 40 kilometres east northeast of Athabasca

This hamlet's descriptive name was adopted by the post office when it opened in 1927.

Grassy Lake

Hamlet on Highway 3, approximately 80 kilometres east of Lethbridge

The name comes from the Blackfoot *moyi-kimi*, "grassy waters," but it refers to the grassy prairies themselves, and not to a body of water. Seen from a distance, long grass waving in the wind can resemble open water. This former village reverted to a hamlet in 1996. According to lore, the names of Grassy Lake and Bow Island were accidentally transposed.

Green Court

Hamlet on highways 18 and 43, approximately 10 kilometres northwest of Mayerthorpe

Original postmaster Hamilton Baily, who held the post from 1908–1937, reportedly suggested the name to recall the grounds of King's School, Canterbury, Kent, England, where he had once taught.

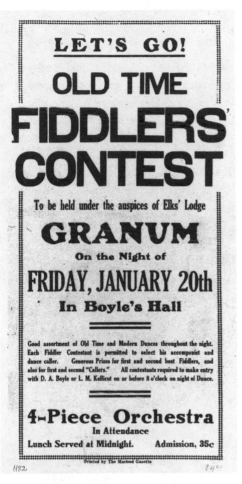

Poster advertising old time fiddler's contest, Granum, circa 1928. GLENBOW ARCHIVES NA-3356-1

Greenshields

Hamlet east of Highway 41, approximately eight kilometres southeast of Wainwright

When the main line of the Grand Trunk Pacific Railway entered the province in 1908, this station was named for one of its directors, Montreal businessman Edward Black Greenshields. The existing post office, Holmstead, was renamed Greenshields in 1909. A onetime president of the Montreal Board of Trade, Greenshields also served as Governor of McGill University and as a councillor of the Montreal Art Association. He wrote *Landscape Painting and Modern Dutch Artists*.

Grimshaw

Town on Highway 2A, approximately 20 kilometres west of Peace River

Born in Kingston, Ontario, Dr. Matthew E. Grimshaw (died 1929) settled in the Peace River district in 1914, set up a medical practice and won election to the Peace River Crossing village council. He was village commissioner when Peace River became a town in 1919 and served as Peace River's second mayor, a position he held until 1922. The Central Canada Railway, for which Grimshaw reportedly served as medical officer, was extended west of Peace River in 1921 and the new siding was named for him. Dr. Grimshaw died in Fairview, where he had only recently set up a new practice. He is buried in the Waterhole Cemetery.[102] His wife, Doris Grimshaw, was a graduate nurse and also taught music and drama to children. Their daughter, also Doris, was the stepmother of actor David Carradine, famed as the star of the 1970s television series *Kung Fu*. Grimshaw became a village in 1930 and a town in 1953. As the southernmost point of the Mackenzie Highway, which leads to Fort Simpson, North-West Territories, Grimshaw is known as Mile 0.

Grouard

Hamlet on Secondary Highway 750, approximately 24 kilometres northeast of High Prairie

In the 19th century, Roman Catholic missionary activity in what is now Alberta was largely the work of the Oblates of Mary Immaculate, an order founded in France in 1816. The order's first foreign mission was Canada, and Oblate missionaries reached what is now western Canada in 1845. One such missionary was Father Émile-Jean-Marie Grouard (1840–1931), who left France in 1862, spent most of his life in what became northern Alberta and became a bishop in 1891. Grouard Mission north of this hamlet was named for him, as was Grouard Street in Chicoutimi, Quebec. Bishop Grouard is buried in Grouard. The present hamlet was originally called Stoney Point, translated from the Cree. The post office opened in 1903 as Lesser Slave Lake, and in 1909 the name was changed to honour Bishop Grouard. Grouard once boomed as an inland port on Lesser Slave Lake, but declined when it was bypassed by the Edmonton, Dunvegan and British Columbia Railway.

Bishop Émile-Jean-Marie Grouard, of the Oblates of Mary Immaculate, left France at the age of 22 and spent most of his life in what is now northern Alberta. MISSIONARY OBLATES, GRANDIN ARCHIVES OB.8450 (DETAIL)

Grovedale

Hamlet on Secondary Highway 666, approximately 17 kilometres south southwest of Grande Prairie

This hamlet's descriptive name was adopted by the post office in 1939.

Gunn

Hamlet on Highway 43, approximately 32 kilometres northwest of Stony Plain

Just as it served his television detective counterpart, Henry Mancini's well-known theme music might have suited Alberta's Sheriff Peter Gunn (1864–1927). In 1883, while still in his teens, Gunn left his native Scotland to work for the Hudson's Bay Company in what is now northern Alberta. Over the next quarter century, Gunn headed the company's posts at Dunvegan, Fort St. John, Grouard and Lac Ste. Anne. He became Lac Ste. Anne's first Member of the Legislative Assembly in 1905 and remained in the legislature for a dozen years. In the last decade of his life, Gunn served as sheriff of the Athabasca and Peace River districts. Memories of his early career must have flooded back to him in

1925, when an astonishing discovery was made on the bank of the Peace River at Dunvegan. A buried box of refuse from the Dunvegan post yielded company journals dating from 1839–41 and 1853–55, as well as a letter to Gunn himself, written in 1896 by Dunvegan's chief trader and finally delivered nearly three decades late. Gunn gave the material to the province, and it is now housed at the Provincial Archives of Alberta.

Guy

Hamlet east of Highway 49, approximately 23 kilometres southwest of McLennan

As with many other Alberta centres, this hamlet was named for a missionary of the Oblates of Mary Immaculate, a Roman Catholic order that played a large role in Alberta's missionary field. Bishop Joseph Guy (1883–1951) was born in Montreal and ordained in Ottawa. He served as Apostolic Vicar of Grouard during the 1930s, after which he became Bishop of Gravelbourg, Saskatchewan. Bishop Guy was appointed director of the Oblate Commission for native missions in 1943. He is buried in Richelieu, Quebec.

Gwynne

Hamlet on Highway 13, approximately 11 kilometres east northeast of Wetaskiwin

In 1902, when pioneer homesteader Charles Rodberg (known in his native Belgium as Chevalier Charles Rodberg de Walden) opened a store and post office in the area known as Rodberg's Flat or Rodberg's Crossing, it took the name of his oldest child, Diana. He opened a stopping house the following year. The Canadian Pacific Railway (CPR) arrived in 1905, and the community was renamed to honour the wife of a prominent railway personality. Julia Maude Schreiber (nee Gwynne) was the second wife of Sir Collingwood Schreiber (1831–1918), a railway builder, former chief engineer of the CPR and former federal deputy minister of railways and canals. Julia was president of the Ottawa Ladies' golf club and vice-regent of the Daughters of the Empire in Ottawa.

Hairy Hill

Hamlet south of Highway 45, approximately 18 kilometres northwest of Two Hills

When bison were plentiful in this district, each spring they rubbed themselves against a nearby hill to shed their heavy winter coats, leaving mats of hair on the ground. The post office adopted this descriptive name in 1907. Hairy Hill became a village in 1946 but later reverted to hamlet status.

Half Moon Lake

Hamlet east of Secondary Highway 824, approximately 28 kilometres east of Edmonton

Established in 1987, this resort hamlet is named for the adjacent oxbow lake of the same name.

Halkirk

Village on Highway 12, approximately 19 kilometres northwest of Castor

When the Canadian Pacific Railway (CPR) laid out this townsite on its new Lacombe–Consort line in 1909, one of the first property owners was blacksmith John Ainsworth. The CPR offered residents a list of possible place names, from which Ainsworth and other settlers selected Halkirk, the name of a village in Caithness-shire, Scotland. (Malcolm Groat, a Scottish émigré for whom Edmonton's Groat Bridge, Groat Estate and Groat Road were named, came from the original Halkirk.) Ainsworth's son, the first child born in the new community, was named John Halkirk Ainsworth. Halkirk was incorporated as a village in 1912.

Hanna

Town on Highway 9, approximately 145 kilometres east southeast of Red Deer

Until the Canadian Northern Railway (CNoR) arrived in 1913, the local post office was known as Copeville, for postmaster G.R. Cope. Here the CNoR established a divisional point named for the railway's third vice-president, David Blythe Hanna (1858–1938). Hanna Road in Toronto is also named for him. In his 1924 memoir, *Trains of Recollection*, Hanna remarked on the quirk of fate that led him to Canada: had his protective Scottish family not hidden a job acceptance letter from him, a teenaged Hanna might have ended up in Ceylon "curing tea for Sir Thomas Lipton."[103] In 1882 the young railway clerk emigrated to Montreal to work for the Grand Trunk Railway. He joined the upstart Canadian Northern Railway in 1896 and later served both of his former employers as the first president of the amalgamated Canadian National Railways. Though Hanna did not mention his namesake town in his memoirs—perhaps out of modesty—the *Hanna Herald* noted his passing 14 years later. In a toponymic coincidence, Hanna lived on Toronto's Cluny Drive. Hanna is buried in Mount Pleasant Cemetery in Toronto. The village of Hanna was incorporated as a village in 1912, and became a town in 1914.

David B. Hanna, first president of Canadian National Railways, as pictured in his 1924 tome Trains of Recollection. Reprinted from D.B. Hanna, *Trains of Recollection* (Toronto: The Macmillan Company of Canada Ltd., 1924).

Hardisty

Town on Secondary Highway 881, approximately 110 kilometres east southeast of Camrose

Senator Richard Charles Hardisty (1831–89) was born in Quebec, educated at Red River and joined the service of the Hudson's Bay Company

(HBC) in 1849. By 1872 he had worked his way up to the position of chief factor, a title his father and grandfather had held. Hardisty made his headquarters at Fort Edmonton, where he administered the company's affairs over a vast territory. By this time, the company's territory—Rupert's Land—had become part of Canada. Hardisty served both as Fort Edmonton's last chief factor and as its first postmaster. He married Eliza McDougall, daughter of pioneer Methodist missionary George McDougall, and was called to the Canadian Senate in 1888. On his death a year later, Hardisty was replaced in the Senate by his niece's husband, James Lougheed (for whom the village of Lougheed was named).

In 1966, Hardisty's long lost papers from his HBC years were discovered in an old house in east Calgary and are now housed at the Glenbow Archives. The Canadian Pacific Railway reached Hardisty by 1906, the year it was incorporated as a village. Hardisty became a town in 1910.

Harmattan

Hamlet south of Highway 27, approximately 14 kilometres east southeast of Sundre

Harmattan is the name of a hot, dry wind in west Africa and became the name of Annie Davis' post office in 1900.

Hartell

Hamlet on Highway 22, approximately 10 kilometres south of Black Diamond

This crossroads was known as Hartell corner long before the hamlet developed, because Welsh-born rancher John Hartell (1862–1947) owned land on two corners and rented the land on the other two. With the development of oilfields in the Black Diamond–Turner Valley district in the 1920s, Hartell subdivided his property in 1929 and launched this hamlet, which quickly emerged as a commercial and shopping centre for the district, but later declined. Hartell offered free land to anyone who would build a store and post office. "He had to ride four miles to get his mail," notes grandson Duke Hartell, who still owns and lives on the family property. "That's why he wanted to get the post office."[104] John Hartell and his wife, Carrie, are buried in Calgary's Union Cemetery.

Harvie Heights

Hamlet on the Trans-Canada Highway (Highway 1), approximately five kilometres northwest of Canmore

In 1930, the control of Alberta's natural resources was transferred from Ottawa to the provincial government, and John Harvie became Alberta's first deputy minister of lands and mines. In 1951 the provincial government set aside this terrace north of the Banff Highway for the construction of vacation homes and on the eve of the deputy minister's retirement named the new resort centre for him.[105]

Hastings Lake

Hamlet north of Highway 14, approximately 17 kilometres west northwest of Tofield

Joseph Burr Tyrrell, geologist and namesake for Drumheller's Royal Tyrrell Museum of Palaeontology, named Hastings Lake for a fellow member of his 1884 Geological Survey party, Tom Hastings. This hamlet is located on the lake's south shore.

Hay Lakes

Village north of Highway 21, approximately 45 kilometres southeast of Edmonton

The name evidently comes from two nearby lakes, Big Hay Lake and Little Hay Lake. The Cree knew one of the lakes as *a-pi-chi-koo-chi-was*, meaning "little swamp." Settlers called the lush grass, such as that found here, "prairie wool." The Hay Lakes post office opened in 1913, and in 1928 the village of Hay Lake was incorporated. It was renamed Hay Lakes in 1932. (The nearby village of New Sarepta was originally known as Little Hay Lakes.)

Haynes

Hamlet north of Highway 11, approximately 30 kilometres east of Red Deer

A post office established in 1900 was named for Isaac Haynes (born 1852), a pioneer who settled along Haynes Creek east of Red Deer. Canadian National Railways built its Brazeau line through Haynes in 1918.

Hays

Hamlet on secondary highways 574 and 825, approximately 80 kilometres west of Medicine Hat

Irrigation specialist David Walker Hays (1878–1958) was born in California, studied at the Nevada School of Mining and Engineering and worked for the United States Reclamation Bureau before coming to Alberta in 1912. From his home in Medicine Hat, Hays managed a farm settlement company that eventually became known as the Canada Land and Irrigation Company, which controlled over 200,000 hectares. Hays retired when the federal government bought the company in 1950. The post office in this hamlet, named to honour him, opened in 1954.

Hayter

Hamlet on Highway 13, approximately 10 kilometres east of Provost

After a long career as a federal civil servant, Hayter Reed became manager of the Canadian Pacific Railway's hotel system. His wife, Kate, did interior design for the company's hotels. National Archives of Canada C-73984

The Canadian Pacific Railway (CPR) named this point for one of its own: Major Hayter Reed, who managed the company's extensive hotel system and whose wife, Kate, designed the hotel's interiors. The Reeds lived in the CPR's lavish Place Viger Hotel in Montreal. A former senior civil servant, Hayter Reed had served as assistant Indian commissioner for Manitoba and the North-West Territories, as a member of the North West Council and as deputy superintendent–general of Indian Affairs from 1893–97. "Hayter was founded in 1909, the same year the railroad went through," observes the hamlet's local history book, *Early Furrows* (1977). "It was named in honour of Mr. Hayter Reid or Mr. Reid Hayter, we don't seem to know for sure which."[106]

Heinsburg

Hamlet off Secondary Highway 893, approximately 28 kilometres southeast of Elk Point

Postmaster John Heins held the post from 1913–20, and his name has remained ever since.

Heisler

Village on Highway 855, approximately 51 kilometres northeast of Stettler

Though he died only two years after this community was formed, the legacy of Martin Heisler (1847–1917) has been long-lived and twofold. Born in Pennsylvania to Bavarian immigrant parents, Heisler married Austrian-born Catherine Meyer and moved to what is now Alberta in 1903. The farmhouse where they raised several children doubled as a stopping house. In 1915 the Canadian Northern Railway established its townsite on land purchased from Heisler, and the company reportedly allowed him to name it. One of his two suggestions was Alma, the name of his deceased adopted daughter; the other was his own name, Heisler.

Heisler died in Camrose and is buried in St. Peter's Roman Catholic Cemetery in Daysland. After his father's death, Jacob Heisler donated land in his honour for a Roman Catholic church and cemetery in Heisler. Originally dedicated as St. Joseph's, it was renamed St. Martin's in 1937—presumably to honour Martin Heisler, though it was coincidentally during the pastorship of Father Daniel Martin.[107] Heisler was a village from 1920–43 and was again incorporated in 1961.

Hemaruka

Hamlet on Secondary Highway 884, approximately 62 kilometres east northeast of Hanna

When it opened in 1912, the post office was originally called Zetland, after a village in Huron County, Ontario. The name changed in 1927 to conform to the new Canadian National Railways (CNR) station, Hemaruka. Albert Edward Warren (1874–circa 1938), general manager of the CNR's central region, had four daughters—Helen, Marjorie, Ruth and Kathleen. Warren fashioned a compound name from the first two letters of each daughter's name. The CNR sold its Hemaruka station in 1969, and it was moved to a nearby farm.

Heritage Pointe

Hamlet east of Highway 2, approximately five kilometres southeast of Calgary

This residential district, golf course and artificial lake is a few minutes' drive from Calgary and was created in the late 1980s. It was named by its developer.

Herronton

Hamlet north of Highway 23, approximately 56 kilometres southeast of Calgary

"Honest John" Herron (1853–1936) came west in 1874 with the North-West Mounted Police, whom he served as a blacksmith. He helped build Fort Macleod that year and was present in 1875 when the Mounties reached the future site of Fort Calgary. Herron later ranched in the Pincher Creek area and sat in the House of Commons as a Conservative from 1904–1911. He used his influence to have a post office established here, and it was named for him in 1912. Herron is buried in Pincher Creek.

High Level

Town on Highway 35, approximately 253 kilometres north of Peace River

The typical explanation for this place name is that it describes the height of land between the Hay and Peace rivers. But former resident Lorna Bell has a different story, told to her by one of the old-timers and once part of the area's common knowledge. Freighters hauling north from Fort Vermilion to Meander River and on to the North-West Territories used to ford the Bushe River near the present site of High Level. One spring in the 1920s, the river flooded and the freighters were stuck. A group of them felled some big trees and built a sturdy little bridge. The river later dropped to its normal level, leaving the bridge high above the water. With tongues firmly in cheek, they began calling it the "High Level Bridge," taking the name of Edmonton's landmark bridge that had been constructed in 1915. By the 1940s the area became known as High Level Crossing. The deeply embedded freighters' trail can still be seen traversing farmers' fields, but the makeshift bridge is long gone and the Mackenzie Highway now crosses the Bushe River at a different location. As evidence of the name's origin, Bell points out that High Level is actually at a low point in the area, not on a height of land.[108] High Level became a new town in 1965. It was one of several communities incorporated between 1956–1967 under the New Town Act. Oil discoveries led to the creation of instant boomtowns, and the New Town Act was intended to smooth the development of local government and infrastructure.[109] High Level became a town in 1983.

High Prairie

Town on Highway 2, approximately 100 kilometres southeast of Peace River

This descriptive name replaced its early form, Prairie River, which had been derived from an aboriginal term of the same meaning. The High Prairie post office opened in 1910, and the Edmonton, Dunvegan and British Columbia Railway established its High Prairie station in 1915. High Prairie became a village in 1945 and a town in 1950.

High River

Town on Highway 2A, approximately 40 kilometres south of Calgary

Named for the Highwood River, itself a translation from the Blackfoot, *spitsí*, for "tall trees," the tops of which could be seen from some distance away.[110] In its original location, High River was known as The Crossing, as the river crossing point on the trail from Calgary to Fort Benton, Montana. It became an important ranching centre with the arrival of the Canadian Pacific Railway in 1892. High River was incorporated as a village in 1901 and as a town in 1906. It is the birthplace of Canada's 16th prime minister, Joe Clark, and is the setting for many of W.O. Mitchell's stories.

The trees along the Highwood River inspired its name in the Blackfoot language, spitsí *("tall trees").* The treetops could be seen for some distance across the prairies. Calgary Public Library PC 189

High River Town Hall, n.d. Calgary Public Library PC 1091

Hilda

Hamlet east of Highway 41, approximately 63 kilometres northeast of Medicine Hat

Little Hilda Koch was the daughter of Samuel Koch, the hamlet's first postmaster from 1910–1917. The Kochs had come from Oklahoma, and in 1923 they moved to California. Hilda Koch-Murray died there half a century later.

Hill Spring
Village on Secondary Highway 800, approximately 70 kilometres south-west of Lethbridge

Known traditionally as Spring Hill, for the water springs on a nearby hill, this Mormon settlement became Hill Spring to avoid duplicating another place name when its post office opened in 1911. Hill Spring became a village in 1961.

Hillcrest Mines
See Crowsnest Pass, Municipality of

Hilliard
Hamlet on Highway 15, approximately 10 kilometres northwest of Mundare

"The . . . station Hilliard was named after one Hilliard McConkey," explained Robert Douglas, secretary of the Geographic Board of Canada in 1926, "whoever that may be."[111] Little is known of McConkey, pioneer settler for whom this post office was named in 1918. The Hilliard Hotel has been moved to Edmonton's Ukrainian Cultural Heritage Village.

Hines Creek
Village on Highway 64, approximately 25 kilometres north northwest of Fairview

The name comes from a nearby creek, itself possibly named for an early Anglican missionary. The community originated in 1930 with the arrival of the Northern Alberta Railways, and became a village in 1952.

Hinton

Town on Highway 16, approximately 70 kilometres north northeast of Jasper

Though his birthplace of Hintonburg, Ontario (named for his father, Robert Hinton), has been subsumed into Ottawa, this pulp-and-paper town at the eastern entrance to Jasper National Park perpetuates the name of William Pitman Hinton (born 1871), general passenger agent of the Grand Trunk Pacific Railway (GTP). The GTP arrived in Hinton in 1910 as part of the company's main line, which reached the coastal terminal of Prince Rupert, British Columbia, in 1914. Hinton later became president and general manager of the GTP's Pacific Coast Steamship Company. Hinton, Alberta, developed a boom and bust cycle, and might hold the record for the townsite that moved the most. Through its changing economic bases—railway construction, coal mining and since 1955, pulp and paper—Hinton has shifted locations some 10 times. Residents protested in 1957 when the provincial government tried to change the name to Drinnan, the name of a community with which Hinton amalgamated at that time.[112] (Drinnan was probably named in honour of R.G. Drinnan, director of Luscar Collieries.)

Grand Trunk Pacific Railway executive William Pitman Hinton, 1906. NATIONAL ARCHIVES OF CANADA PA-214359

Hinton was incorporated as a new town in 1956. It was one of several communities incorporated between 1956–1967 under the New Town Act. Oil discoveries led to the creation of instant boomtowns, and the New Town Act was intended to smooth the development of local government and infrastructure.[113] Hinton became a town in 1958.

Hinton drug store, pool room and ice cream parlour, n.d. The Grand Trunk Pacific Railway reached Hinton in 1910. CALGARY PUBLIC LIBRARY PC60

Hoadley

Hamlet on Highway 20, approximately 70 kilometres west southwest of Wetaskiwin

Okotoks rancher George Hoadley (1866–1955), a British émigré, sat in the Alberta legislature as a Conservative from 1909–20, and served briefly as opposition leader in 1918. He left the Tories for the United Farmers of Alberta, a new party that trounced the governing Liberals in Alberta's 1921 provincial election. Hoadley served as provincial secretary, health minister and minister of agriculture. The Haverigg post office, which opened in 1913, was renamed for Hoadley in 1924. George Hoadley is buried in Vancouver.

Hobbema

Hamlet on Highway 2A, approximately 15 kilometres southwest of Wetaskiwin

According to historian James G. MacGregor, it was Canadian Pacific Railway president William Cornelius Van Horne who provided the name for this station on the Calgary and Edmonton Railway, established in 1891.[114] Myendert Hobbema (1638–1709), a Dutch Baroque landscape painter, was reportedly a favourite of Van Horne. Hobbema developed originally as a Roman Catholic mission and native boarding school.

Holden

Village on Highway 14, approximately 45 kilometres northeast of Camrose

When the Grand Trunk Pacific Railway (GTP) was building its main line from Winnipeg to Edmonton in 1907, GTP Land Commissioner George Urquhart Ryley asked James Bismark Holden (1876–1956), Liberal Member of the Legislative Assembly (MLA) for Vermilion, for permission to name a siding in his constituency for him.[115] Thus Vermilion Valley was renamed Holden. The next siding to the west became Ryley. Born in rural Ontario, Holden worked for a grain firm in Winnipeg before moving to present-day Alberta in 1898. Two years later he married Gertrude Worth, and the couple homesteaded at Vegreville. Holden was elected to Alberta's first legislature in 1906, and when he died half a century later, he was one of only three surviving original MLAs. Holden served as mayor of Vegreville for 24 years between 1914–1945 and is buried in that town. The village of Holden was incorporated in 1909.

Hughenden

Village on Highway 13, approximately 30 kilometres southeast of Hardisty

Railway official Charles E. Stockdill chose the name for this station, established in 1909 on the Canadian Pacific Railway's Saskatoon–Edmonton branch, for the Buckinghamshire estate of Benjamin Disraeli, Lord Beaconsfield (1804–81). As prime minister of Britain (1868, 1874–80), Disraeli championed the cause of empire. He purchased Hughenden Manor, an 18th century house, in 1848, and it remained his country home for the rest of his life. Of the 11 prime ministers who served during Queen Victoria's long reign, Disraeli was her favourite. Protocol prevented the Queen from attending his funeral at Hughenden, but she later visited his grave. Hughenden (accent on the first syllable) was sold after Disraeli's last male heir died in 1936, and in 1949 it became property of the National Trust. Hughenden, Alberta, became a village in 1917. The name is shared with Hughenden Lake.

Hussar

Village on Secondary Highway 561, approximately 47 kilometres south of Drumheller

The German Canadian Farming Company, which established a settlement here in 1910–11, was one of many such corporations that created an ethnic bloc settlement on land acquired from the Canadian Pacific Railway. For these particular settlers—some of whom had been Hussars (members of a light cavalry regiment) in the German army—the timing could hardly have been worse. In 1914, the outbreak of war between the British Empire and its German, Austro-Hungarian and Ottoman counterparts saw some of these colonists attempt to return to their fatherland, where they were still reserve officers. Others who remained behind were interned; the company collapsed and its assets were lost. Still, both the post office and the Canadian Pacific Railway station retained the name, and the village of Hussar was incorporated in 1928.

Huxley

Hamlet on Highway 21, approximately 11 kilometres north of Trochu

Named in 1907 for the British biologist, Darwin associate and zealot of agnosticism, Thomas Henry Huxley (1825–95). The post office opened in 1907.

Hylo

Hamlet on Secondary Highway 663, approximately 20 kilometres southwest of Lac La Biche

Hylo is a term used in the card game faro, played by workers who built the Alberta and Great Waterways Railway through here. The post office opened in 1921.

Hythe

Village on Highway 2, approximately 50 kilometres west northwest of Grande Prairie

In 1911, Henry (Harry) Hartley, his wife, Mary Ellen, and their children left Manitoba to settle in Alberta's Peace River country. The Hartleys established a post office in 1914 and reportedly submitted a list of possible names, including Happy Valley and Hungry Hollow. One of Mary Ellen's suggestions was Hythe, the name of an English port town. Hythe, Alberta, became a village in 1929.

Iddesleigh
Hamlet west of Secondary Highway 884, approximately 89 kilometres northwest of Medicine Hat

Sir Walter Stafford Northcote (1818–87), the Earl of Iddesleigh, was a member of the British parliament who served two contemporary giants of British politics: Liberal Prime Minister William Gladstone (whom Northcote served as private secretary) and Conservative Prime Minister Benjamin Disraeli (under whom Northcote served as Chancellor of the Exchequer). Northcote was governor of the Hudson's Bay Company from 1869–74, and it was reportedly he who convinced the company to accept the sale of Rupert's Land—the company's vast fur domain that constituted much of present-day Canada, including the prairie provinces—for £300,000. Northcote eventually became leader of Britain's Conservative party. Besides this hamlet on the Canadian Pacific Railway's Empress–Bassano branch (the "royal line"), Northcote was also the namesake for Calgary's Northcote Avenue, changed to Fifth Avenue south in 1904. Other place names along this "royal line" that were chosen for their connections to royalty or aristocracy include Duchess, Empress, Millicent, Patricia, Princess and Rosemary.

Imperial Mills
Hamlet on Secondary Highway 881, approximately 30 kilometres northeast of Lac La Biche

The post office opened in 1949, and was named for the sawmill operated by the Imperial Lumber Company.

Indian Cabins
Hamlet on Highway 35, approximately 151 kilometres north of High Level

The name of this hamlet along the Hay River, only 15 kilometres south of the North-West Territories border, is probably descriptive of dwellings that stand in the vicinity. A post office opened in 1953, and the Great Slave Lake Railway, connecting Peace River with Hay River in the North-West Territories, arrived in the early 1960s. The Slavey once called this area *Tsentu* ("dirty water"), which referred to the river's silt.[116]

Indus

Hamlet on Highway 22x, approximately 17 kilometres southeast of Calgary

On a visit to Alberta in 1904, Presbyterian pastor Dr. J.M. Fulton of St. Paul, Minnesota, was so taken with the province that he, along with his brothers, procured 4,000 hectares of farmland in the Langdon district. But the brother who was supposed to manage the operation sold out to J.M. and left. Dr. Fulton had no agricultural experience, but moved his family from the U.S. and became a farmer. When the Canadian Pacific Railway arrived in 1911, it used Dr. Fulton's suggestion, naming the point Indus. Fulton reportedly believed the railway would bring industry to the community and simply shortened the word.

Innisfail

Town on Highway 2, approximately 30 kilometres south southwest of Red Deer

Before the Calgary and Edmonton Railway was completed in 1891, travellers on the five-day Calgary–Edmonton Trail knew this stopping point as Poplar Grove. *Innis Vail* is understood to be Gaelic for "Isle of Destiny," and though the details vary between the stories that explain this choice of name, Ireland is the common element. Early resident Estella Scarlett later recalled that she had suggested the name, adopted by the post office in 1892, to honour her grandmother's home in Ireland. If so, there is no Innisfail in Ireland, and perhaps she meant Innisfallen, an island in Lough Leane. Innisfail became a village in 1899 and a town in 1903.

Innisfree

Village on Highway 16, approximately 37 kilometres southeast of Vegreville

The post office opened in 1905 as Del Norte, but the name changed in 1909 to conform to that of the Canadian Northern Railway station,

Innisfree. Early resident Maude Nodwell later recounted that a visit by Sir Edmund Walker, general manager (and future president) of the Canadian Bank of Commerce, resulted in the present name being adopted. Walker was already a senior official with the bank when he visited Del Norte on a scouting trip to locate sites for bank branches. Walker admired the view at nearby Birch Lake, which reminded him of his home at Innisfree, and indicated that he would build a fine bank branch if Del Norte adopted the name. Del Norte became Innisfree and the bank was built. Senior bank officials actually did make such scouting trips, and the Glenbow Archives in Calgary has a series of photographs documenting Walker's trip, which included Innisfree. His inspiration might have been Innisfree in Ireland, about which William Butler Yeats wrote the poem, "The Lake Isle of Innisfree": "I will arise and go now, and go to Innisfree. . . . And I shall have some peace there." Innisfree became a village in 1911.

Irma

Village on Highway 14, approximately 26 kilometres west northwest of Wainwright

Following the alphabetical sequence on its main line through Alberta, (built in 1908–09), the Grand Trunk Pacific Railway supplied the name Irma for the station between Hawkins and Jarrow. One theory has it that Irma was named for the daughter of William Wainwright, the railway's second vice-president (and for whom the town of Wainwright was named). But Wainwright's daughters were Gladys, Marguerite and Rosabel Hilda. Unless Gladys or Marguerite had Irma for a middle name, a second theory sounds more likely: that Irma was the secretary of a railway official. The community's first baby was the daughter of grain elevator manager Harry Burkholder and his wife, and they named her Irma. The village of Irma was incorporated in 1912.

Iron Springs

Hamlet on Highway 25, approximately 25 kilometres north northeast of Lethbridge

A Canadian Pacific Railway branch line from Kipp reached this location in 1925, and Iron Springs—named for mineral deposits in the nearby Blackspring Ridge—flourished as a commercial centre in the 1920s and 1930s.

Irricana

Village west of Highway 9, approximately 42 kilometres northeast of Calgary

This manufactured name—an amalgam of "irrigation" and "canal"—captured the optimism and promotional enthusiasm that irrigation promised in early 20th century southern Alberta. The post office adopted the name when it opened in 1909, and the village of Irricana was incorporated as a village in 1911. Ironically, no irrigation canal was ever completed in the area.

Irvine

Hamlet on the Trans-Canada Highway (Highway 1), approximately 30 kilometres east southeast of Medicine Hat

In 1875 Quebec-born Acheson Gosford Irvine (1837–1916) joined the newly formed North-West Mounted Police, which he served as assistant commissioner from 1876–80 and as commissioner from 1880–86. (In his capacity as assistant commissioner, Irvine played a role in the naming of Calgary.) Irvine warned that government policies toward natives and Métis could lead to rebellion, and he resigned after the North-West Rebellion of 1885. He later served as warden of Stony Mountain and Kingston penitentiaries. Irvine is situated on the Canadian Pacific Railway main line built in the 1880s.

Islay

Hamlet east of Secondary Highway 893, approximately 22 kilometres east northeast of Vermilion

When its post office opened in June 1905, this hamlet became known briefly as Island Lake, Saskatchewan, as it lay within the Saskatchewan district of the North-West Territories. When provincehood came three months later, it became Island Lake, Alberta. The Canadian Northern Railway arrived that fall, and by 1907 the station, the post office and the newly incorporated village all had a shorter name: Islay. One explanation suggests the hamlet was named for Islay, Ontario, the original home of some of the early settlers—although, judging from the name alone, it seems possible it was condensed from Island Lake. Islay reverted to hamlet status in 1944.

Janet

Hamlet south of Highway 1A, approximately 10 kilometres east of Calgary

Janet, a name of forgotten origin, began as a siding and flag station in 1912.

Janvier

Hamlet east of Secondary Highway 881, approximately 90 kilometres south southeast of Fort McMurray

Located south of the Janvier Indian Reserve No. 194, Janvier takes its name from the Paul Janvier family of the Chipewyan Prairie First Nation.

Jarrow

Hamlet on Highway 14, approximately 38 kilometres west northwest of Wainwright

This hamlet, named for a northern English town on the River Tyne, was part of an alphabetical continuum along this Grand Trunk Pacific Railway branch. Jarrow is situated between Irma and Kinsella. Coincidentally, both of the early names applied to the local post office also began with 'J': Jackson Coulee (for postmaster Edwin Jackson, used until 1909) and Junkins (possibly for the vice-president of Westinghouse, Church, Kerr and Company, in use until 1919).

Jarvie

Hamlet west of Highway 44, approximately 35 kilometres north northwest of Westlock

Jarvis was the name of a surveyor or engineer associated with the Edmonton, Dunvegan and British Columbia Railway, which reached this point around 1913. When the post office opened in 1920, the name was changed to Jarvie to avoid duplicating an existing name.

Jasper

Hamlet on Highway 16, in Jasper National Park, approximately 66 kilometres southwest of Hinton

Jasper House—a North West Company fur post built at Brûlé Lake in

1813 and known originally as Rocky Mountain House—was renamed for Jasper Hawes, believed to have been from Missouri, who took charge of the North West Company post in 1817. It became a Hudson's Bay Company post after the two companies merged in 1821. It was later relocated and was then abandoned in 1884. The name was revived with the establishment in 1907 of Jasper Forest Park (the future Jasper National Park). The Canadian Northern Railway arrived in 1911–12 and named its station Jasper Park, but the rival Grand Trunk Pacific Railway (GTP), which chose the site for a divisional point, named its facility for GTP director E.H. Fitzhugh. The post office was called Fitzhugh when it opened in 1912, but its name changed to Jasper the following year. The name Jasper applies also to Jasper Lake, Jasper National Park and Jasper Park Lodge.

Bungalows at Jasper Park Lodge, built by Canadian National Railways in 1922. The hotel helped develop Jasper as a tourist destination and at one time even had its own post office. Calgary Public Library PC329

Jean Côté

Hamlet east of Secondary Highway 774, approximately 20 kilometres north northwest of Falher

Father Constant Falher (for whom the town of Falher was named) reportedly named this hamlet to honour Quebec-born Jean Leon Côté

(1867–1924), an engineer, Dominion Land Surveyor and provincial politician. Côté's work for the Department of the Interior brought him in 1893 to what is now Alberta, and he worked on the Alaska–Yukon boundary preliminary survey in 1893–95. Côté was elected to the Alberta legislature in 1909 and sat in the government benches as the Liberal member for Grouard until the upset election of 1921, won by the United Farmers of Alberta. Côté served as provincial secretary for three years. He was called to the Senate in 1923, but died the following year.

Jenner

Hamlet on secondary highways 555 and 884, approximately 85 kilometres northwest of Medicine Hat

This former village was named for Dr. Edward Jenner (1749–1823), the British physician who developed the smallpox vaccine in 1796. Perhaps coincidentally, area homesteaders Bill and Archie Stallworthy came from Jenner's home town of Cirencester, Glouchestershire. The Websdale post office, named for postmaster A.E. Websdale in 1911, relocated to Jenner in 1913 and was renamed.

Joffre

Hamlet west of Secondary Highway 815, approximately 19 kilometres east of Red Deer

Marshal Joseph Jacques Césaire Joffre, seated front row fourth to left, at Mount Vernon, April 1917. Joffre commanded the French armies during the early years of World War I. National Archives of Canada PA-051607

The Canadian Northern Railway established and named this station on its Brazeau branch in 1918. At that time World War I still raged, and Marshal Joseph Jacques Césaire Joffre (1852–1931), who had command-ed the French armies from 1914–16, was still a fresh name in the public memory. The post office, established in 1923 and named Blades for orig-inal postmaster R.H. Blades, was renamed Joffre in 1934.

Johnson's Addition

Hamlet on Highway 864, immediately west of Taber

The name of this hamlet was likely provided by its developer.

Josephburg

Hamlet on Secondary Highway 830, approximately 30 kilometres north-east of Edmonton

In the late 1880s, a group of Galician immigrants who homesteaded near Medicine Hat named their settlement Josefsberg, after a village in Galicia. In 1891, drought caused them to relocate farther north (to the site of current hamlet), where they remained and established the Josefsberg Public School District #296 in 1893. The school district's sec-retary–treasurer changed the spelling to its current form.

Joussard

Hamlet north of Highway 2, approximately 75 kilometres west of Slave Lake

Father Henri Célestin Joussard (1851–1932) was a member of the Oblates of Mary Immaculate, a Roman Catholic order that played a large role in Alberta's missionary field. The French-born priest served at a variety of northern missions in what is now Alberta and the North-West Territories, including Joussard (1912–13). In 1909 he became the auxil-iary bishop of Athabasca. The post office at this settlement was named for him when it opened in 1928. Bishop Joussard is buried in Grouard.

Kananaskis

Hamlet on Highway 1A, approximately 17 kilometres east of Canmore

Captain John Palliser, along with other members of his eponymous scientific expedition to the Canadian west in the late 1850s, named many of the features they described. In his report to the British government, Palliser explained his choice of name for the Kananaskis Pass. Kananaskis (from the Cree), Palliser explained, was "an Indian of whom there is a legend, giving an account of his most wonderful recovery from the blow of an axe, which had stunned but failed to kill him, and the river which flows through this gorge also bears his name."[117] Besides the hamlet, Kananaskis is also the name of a lake, range and river.

Kathyrn

Hamlet on Secondary Highway 566, approximately 25 kilometres northeast of Calgary

This unique name is traditionally explained as bad spelling. According to tradition, the Grand Trunk Pacific Railway (GTP) bought this townsite from settler Neil McKay, and the source of the name was his daughter, North Dakota school teacher Kathryn McKay.[118] The sign painter for the new GTP station in 1913 misspelled Kathryn's name.

Kavanagh

Hamlet on Highway 2A, approximately 10 kilometres south of Leduc

This hamlet on the Canadian Pacific Railway's Calgary–Edmonton branch was named in 1911 for Charles Edmund Kavanagh, railway mail service superintendent in Winnipeg. The post office opened in 1925.

Keephills

Hamlet south of Secondary Highway 627, approximately 45 kilometres west of Edmonton

George H. Collins opened this post office in 1909 and evidently suggested its name, traditionally explained as being a town in Buckinghamshire, England. The entire hamlet was moved in 1983 to make way for an open-pit coal mine.

Keg River

Hamlet on Highway 35, approximately 91 kilometres southwest of High Level

The post office at Keg River opened in 1932 and took its name from the river that empties into the Peace River. The Keg's name dates back at least to 1828 and is of uncertain origin. Dr. Mary Percy Jackson (1904–2000), an English-born physician who practiced for 43 years at Keg River, claimed the name derived from the Cree *markak seepee* and describes "something narrow and deep like a keg."[119] However, in his 1908 *Through the Mackenzie Basin: a Narrative of the Athabaska and Peace River Treaty Expedition of 1899*, Charles Mair referred to the name alternatively as "Keg of Rum," suggesting a different origin.

Kelsey

Hamlet south of Highway 13, approximately 27 kilometres southeast of Camrose

In 1901 Moses Smith Kelsey (circa 1847–1927) of Millbank, South Dakota, homesteaded with his family near Driedmeat Creek. The Canadian Northern Railway arrived in 1916 and built its station on a portion of Kelsey's land. He is buried in Melville Cemetery.[120]

Keoma

Hamlet east of Highway 9, approximately 37 kilometres northeast of Calgary

Keoma is believed to be a native term for "far away." Keoma owes its birth to the Canadian Pacific Railway's arrival in 1910.

Killam

Town on Highway 13, approximately 70 kilometres east southeast of Camrose

In 1906, within a year of his appointment as first Chairman of the Railway Commission of Canada, retired jurist Albert Clements Killam (1849–1908) was honoured as the namesake of a townsite on the Canadian Pacific Railway's new Edmonton–Saskatoon branch line. Born in Yarmouth, Nova Scotia, Killam earned a law degree at the

University of Toronto and later practiced in Windsor and Winnipeg. After serving a term in the Manitoba legislature, Killam was elevated to the bench, becoming chief justice of Manitoba in 1899 and a judge of the Supreme Court of Canada in 1903. He was a member of the panel that heard Louis Riel's unsuccessful appeal in 1885. Killam became a village in 1906 and a town in 1965.

Justice Albert Clements Killam, a judge of the Supreme Court of Canada, 1904. He later became the first chief commissioner of the Board of Railway Commissioners for Canada. National Archives of Canada PA-193371

Kimball

Hamlet on Secondary Highway 501, approximately 71 kilometres south-west of Lethbridge

Homesteader Henry Cope Colles opened a post office on his land in 1893, and for the first decade, it was called Colles. One of his successors as postmaster was Orsen H. Kimball, who held the post from 1900–01. However, when the name changed to Kimball in 1903, it was for Herber C. Kimball, another pioneer resident.

Kingman

Hamlet north of Secondary Highway 617, approximately 23 kilometres northeast of Camrose

Postmaster F.W. Kingsbury opened this post office in 1907, but a Kingsbury post office already existed in Quebec, so postal officials assigned an alternate name.

Kinsella

Hamlet on Highway 14, approximately 32 kilometres southeast of Viking

When it built its main line in 1908, the Grand Trunk Pacific Railway established an alphabetical continuum of station names and used the name of the vice-president's private secretary for the 'K' station. The namesake was almost certainly Nicholas Kinsella, whom Montreal city directories between 1900–1910 list first as a Grand Trunk Railway clerk and subsequently as stenographer. The Kinsella post office opened in 1910.

Kinuso

Village north of Highway 2, approximately 40 kilometres west of Slave Lake

Once known as Swan River, this village just south of Lesser Slave Lake was renamed Kinuso, from the Cree word for fish. The Kinuso post office opened in 1915, and the Edmonton, Dunvegan and British Columbia Railway arrived in 1921.

Kipp

Hamlet on Highway 3, approximately seven kilometres northwest of Lethbridge

Only kilometres from this village stood Fort Kipp, a trading post that flourished before the arrival of the North-West Mounted Police in the mid-1870s. Built by two Americans, Joseph Kipp (1847–1913) and Charlie Thomas, in 1870, Fort Kipp stood at the confluence of the Belly and Oldman rivers. The Mounties found it abandoned only a few years later. The present hamlet is a few kilometres east of the fort site.

Kirkcaldy

Hamlet on Highway 23, approximately 87 kilometres southeast of Calgary

Kirkcaldy was created in 1911 by the Canadian Pacific Railway's Kipp–Aldersyde line. Its namesake town in Fife, Scotland, was once the home of economist Adam Smith (1723–90), and it was there that he wrote *The Wealth of Nations*. Scholar and writer Thomas Carlyle (1795–1881) once taught at the original Kirkcaldy.

Kirriemuir
Hamlet south of Highway 12, approximately 47 kilometres south of Provost

About a decade after *Peter Pan* premiered on the London stage in 1904, the name of its author's hometown found its way to the Alberta map. A Canadian Pacific Railway surveyor working on the line thought this area reminiscent of Kirriemuir, a Scottish agricultural town in what is now the county of Tayside. The tracks reached Kirriemuir, Alberta, on Victoria Day, 1914. Scotland's Kirriemuir is both the birthplace and burial place of *Peter Pan* creator Sir James Barrie (1860–1937).

Kirriemuir offers another, indirect link between Alberta and Scotland. Not far from the original Kirriemuir is Glamis Castle, which Shakespeare made famous in fiction as Macbeth's castle. It was actually the home of the Earls of Strathmore and Kinghorne. The 13th Earl—grandfather of the late Queen Mother—was the namesake of Strathmore, Alberta.

Kitscoty
Village on Highway 16, approximately 23 kilometres west northwest of Lloydminster

A cromlech, or megalithic tomb, in Kent, England, is the namesake for this village. Known as Kit's Coty House, the ancient stone structure stands in a cornfield north of Aylesford, between Rochester and Maidstone. (Perhaps it is no coincidence that Maidstone, Saskatchewan, was only a few railway stops to the east of Kitscoty, Alberta.) Theo. H. Currie opened the Kitscoty, Alberta, post office in 1907, and Kitscoty became a village in 1911, following the arrival of the Canadian Northern Railway's main line from Winnipeg to Edmonton.

La Corey
Hamlet on highways 41 and 55, approximately 19 kilometres north of Bonnyville

This name, adopted by the post office in 1917, is of unknown origin.

La Crête

Hamlet west of Secondary Highway 697, approximately 56 kilometres southwest of High Level

The French word *crête*—"crest"—can apply equally to a crest of land or to a rooster's crest. For the Rivard brothers from Quebec, who settled here during World War I, both meanings were applicable to a geographic feature that reminded them of a rooster's crest. The hamlet is named for the feature.

La Glace

Hamlet on Highway 59, approximately 32 kilometres northwest of Grande Prairie

Charles La Glace (circa 1847–1909) was an admired Beaver chief who drowned in what was then called Rat Lake, and was buried near its shore. This post office was named for him in 1917, and Rat Lake was renamed La Glace Lake in the 1950s.

Lac des Arcs

Hamlet on the Trans-Canada Highway (Highway 1), approximately 18 kilometres west of Canmore

This hamlet was created in 1979 and named for the nearby lake.

Lac La Biche

Town on highways 36 and 55, approximately 84 kilometres east of Athabasca

The name of the lake (spelled Lac la Biche, as opposed to the town, Lac La Biche), translated from the French for "lake of the red doe," dates back at least to 1790. David Thompson of the North West Company (NWC) established the first trading post here in 1798, followed within the year by the rival Hudson's Bay Company (HBC) and its Greenwich House, built by Peter Fidler. The two companies amalgamated in 1821 under the HBC name and kept the NWC's designation for the post, Lac La Biche. An Oblate mission was established nearby in 1853. The Alberta and Great Waterways Railway arrived in 1914. Lac La Biche became a village in 1919 and a town in 1951.

Lacombe

Town on Highway 2A, approximately 22 kilometres north northeast of Red Deer

In 1891 the Calgary and Edmonton Railway established a station near Barnett's Stopping House. Despite the local population's predominantly Protestant character, the station was named for Father Albert Lacombe (1827–1916), an Oblate missionary and perhaps the most famous Roman Catholic priest in 19th century Alberta.

Born in Lower Canada (now Quebec), Lacombe arrived at Fort Edmonton in 1852. He established missions at Lac Ste. Anne, St. Albert and St. Paul des Cris (and later, its successor, St. Paul des Métis) before taking charge of a Winnipeg parish in 1872. Lacombe returned to what is now Alberta a decade later, this time serving in southern Alberta. The widely respected priest influenced both native leaders and government officials, and became known as "The Man of the Good Heart." Historian James G. MacGregor credits Lacombe with the naming of Nisku, Ponoka and Wetaskiwin.[121]

A 1904 Board of Trade booster publication locates Lacombe on the globe. The local newspaper, the Lacombe Globe, *had already been in business for a year and was known as the* Western Globe.
Glenbow Library, The District of Lacombe (pamphlet, 1904)

Lafond

Hamlet on Secondary Highway 646, approximately 16 kilometres south-west of St. Paul

After a sojourn in Rhode Island, where his wife, Victorine, died in 1903, Quebec-born Charles Borommé Lafond (1841–1930)—a widower and father of 17—homesteaded in this area with three of his sons; other family members later followed. Lafond served as postmaster from 1907–1918 and was killed in an accident in his home at the age of 90.[122] He is buried in Lafond's St. Bernard Roman Catholic Cemetery.

Lake Louise

Hamlet on the Trans-Canada Highway (Highway 1), in Banff National Park, approximately 60 kilometres northwest of Banff

The construction of the Canadian Pacific Railway (CPR) through what is now southern Alberta in 1883 produced Holt City, a temporary construction camp named for railway contractor Sir Herbert Holt. The CPR later placed a station on the spot and named it Laggan, after a Scottish hamlet. The name was likely chosen by CPR Land Commissioner John MacTavish, who favoured using Scottish place names along the line. The adjacent lake had been named in 1884 for Princess Louise Caroline Alberta (1848–1939), daughter of Queen Victoria and the source of the province's name. The CPR changed Laggan station to Lake Louise around 1914, making it clear to tourists bound for the lake that here was the place to detrain. Laggan post office was also renamed Lake Louise in 1914.

Lamont

Town on Highway 15, approximately 50 kilometres northeast of Edmonton

In 1958, in a typical occurrence of toponymic mythology, the *Edmonton Journal* observed that Lamont was "named after Frank Lamont, a section foreman on the railway." Established in 1905–06, this townsite on the Canadian Northern Railway's main line from Winnipeg to Edmonton was named for John Henderson Lamont (1865–1936), who was at that time the attorney general of Saskatchewan, the first person to hold that post. A Toronto lawyer, Lamont moved to Prince Albert in

Lake Louise as seen from the Chalet Lake Louise near Laggan, n.d. Laggan was renamed Lake Louise around 1914. CALGARY PUBLIC LIBRARY PC1245

The Canadian Pacific Railway's Chalet Lake Louise, circa 1907. It was built piecemeal from 1894–1912. All but the new concrete wing burned in 1924, and the present Chateau Lake Louise replaced it. CALGARY PUBLIC LIBRARY PC204

1899 and sat briefly in the House of Commons before joining Saskatchewan's first provincial cabinet. He later served as a judge on the Supreme Court of Saskatchewan and in 1927 was appointed to the Supreme Court of Canada. Lamont became a village in 1910 and a town in 1968.

Honourable John Henderson Lamont, first attorney general of Saskatchewan, was appointed to the Supreme Court of Canada in 1927. NATIONAL ARCHIVES OF CANADA PA-088429

Lamoureux

Hamlet off Highway 15, across the North Saskatchewan River from Fort Saskatchewan

Spelled variously as Lamoureux and L'Amoureux, this post office opened in 1896, and its postmasters have included Theophile Lamoureux (1898–1902) and Philadore L'Amoureux (briefly in 1921). Brothers Joseph and François Lamoureux settled in this district in 1872.

Landry Heights

Hamlet on Highway 40, approximately 12 kilometres south of Grande Prairie

Dale Landry's farm was subdivided in 1977, and the hamlet that took its place perpetuates his name.

Lanfine

Hamlet south of Highway 9, approximately 146 kilometres east of Drumheller

In 1911 Scottish émigrés William Davidson and partner, Nisbet, started a store. The following year Davidson became postmaster and Nisbet his assistant. Both had come from what is now East Ayrshire, south of Glasgow. Between Davidson's native Newmilns and Nisbet's hometown of Darvel stood the private estate of Lanfine House. Postal authorities approved their suggestion to name the post office after it.[123]

Langdon

Hamlet on Secondary Highway 797, approximately 18 kilometres east of Calgary

In Canadian mythology, there is perhaps no greater national project than the construction of the Canadian Pacific Railway. But Americans played no small role: two of the company's earliest presidents, William Cornelius Van Horne and Thomas George Shaughnessy, were from the United States. So too were contractors Langdon and Shepard of St. Paul, Minnesota, who in 1882–83 built the line from Brandon, Manitoba, to the Rocky Mountains. In their honour, the first two stations east of Calgary were named Langdon and Shepard (see Shepard). According to lore, a man named John (or Jim) Langdon was killed on the tracks only a year after turning the settlement's first sod. History shows the real Langdon had a happier fate. Robert Bruce Langdon (1826–95) had a long career building bridges, canals, flour mills and railways, and served as a Minnesota state senator (1873–78 and 1881–85). The village of Langdon, Minnesota, is also named for him. Langdon is buried in Minneapolis.

Lavoy

Hamlet on Highway 16, approximately 14 kilometres east southeast of Vegreville

This former village began in 1903 as Dinwoodie, named for its first postmaster, farmer Richard Dinwoodie, who held the post until his death in 1906. That year the post office was renamed for pioneer settler and stopping-house keeper Joseph Lavoy.

Leavitt

Hamlet on Highway 5, approximately 80 kilometres southwest of Lethbridge

Mormon settler Thomas Rowell Leavitt (1834–91) was born in eastern Canada, but settled in the United States with his parents while he was a child. Leavitt and his family left Utah as a result of new laws against polygamy and settled north of the border in Alberta.[124] The Leavitt post office opened in 1900. Its postmasters have included William Leavitt (1901–10 and 1918–21) and Emily Leavitt (1944–48 and 1952–62). A cairn was dedicated to Thomas R. Leavitt in 1994.

Leduc

City on Highway 2, approximately 32 kilometres south of Edmonton

The very mention of certain cities around the world conjures images of an event or a concept as much as it does the city itself: Munich (the sacrifice of Czechoslovakia in 1938), Oslo (the Middle East peace process) and Versailles (the treaty that ended World War I). For Albertans, Leduc refers not only to a city but to a sea change in the province's history. On February 13, 1947, Imperial Oil's stunning discovery west of Leduc heralded a sustained era of prosperity and thrust the province onto the national stage. Black Gold Drive, a major thoroughfare, emphasizes the association.

Leduc was named for Father Hippolyte Leduc (1842–1918), a French-born Catholic priest from the order of the Oblates of Mary Immaculate. Ordained in Ottawa in 1864, Leduc came west to minister in Edmonton and St. Albert in 1867. He served as Superior in both Edmonton and Calgary, and is interred in the crypt at the St. Albert Roman Catholic church. In 1884 Father Leduc and Father Albert Lacombe (for whom the town of Lacombe was named) acquired the land that became Rouleauville, a Roman Catholic village south of Calgary that was annexed by the city in 1907. Leduc became a village in 1899, a town in 1906 and a city in 1983. The city's Telford Lake was named for Robert T. Telford (1860–1933), Leduc's original farmer, postmaster, mayor and Member of the Legislative Assembly (and for whom the hamlet of Telfordville was named).

Leedale

Hamlet west of Secondary Highway 766, approximately 17 kilometres southwest of Rimbey

Originally known as Wittenberg, the post office was renamed in 1917 for William Henry Lee, who served as postmaster from 1914–16 and 1921–25.

Plains, trains and automobiles in Leduc, 1921. The Curtiss JN4, *owned by Lethbridge Aircraft Company, has been superimposed.* Glenbow Archives NA-1644-93

Legal

Village on Secondary Highway 651, approximately 28 kilometres south southwest of Westlock

Bishop Emile Joseph Légal, Oblates of Mary Immaculate, was the first Roman Catholic archbishop of Edmonton. Missionary Oblates, Grandin Archives Ob.8450 (DETAIL)

The first archbishop of Edmonton, Emile Joseph Légal (1849–1920), was born in France and came to what is now Alberta in 1881 as a missionary of the Oblate order. He was consecrated bishop of St. Albert in 1902 and became archbishop of Edmonton a decade later. A post office by this name opened in 1900. Legal became a village in 1914 and a town in 1998.

Leslieville

Hamlet on secondary highways 598 and 761, approximately 17 kilometres west of Eckville

John and Martha Reilly were among the earliest settlers in this district in 1905, and within two years their pioneer status was recognized when the post office was named for their Toronto-born son, Leslie Howard (1885–1965).

Lethbridge

City on highways 3, 4 and 5, approximately 180 kilometres southeast of Calgary

William Lethbridge of London, a partner in W.H. Smith and Son, invested in the North Western Coal and Navigation Company and served as its first president. He never set foot in Lethbridge. Sir Alexander Galt Museum and Archives P 1965 2008000

Apart from William Lethbridge himself, two names that are inseparable from the history of Alberta's "windy city" are Sir Alexander Tilloch Galt (1817–93) and his son, Elliott Torrance Galt (1850–1928). Sir Alexander was Canada's high commissioner to Britain in the 1880s, and Elliott was an assistant Indian commissioner in Canada's newly acquired North-West Territories (NWT). Elliott reported on coal deposits being developed along the Belly River, in what would later become southern Alberta. One of Sir Alexander's official responsibilities was to promote the development of the NWT and its resources. His public and private endeavours converged in the North Western Coal and Navigation Company, which Sir Alexander established and for which he recruited investors in London. One such investor was William Lethbridge (1825–1901), a partner in W.H. Smith and Son, a London bookseller. Lethbridge became the company's first president in 1882. The coal mining settlement that formed in the valley bottom became known as the Coal Banks. (Aboriginal terms for the area included "black rocks," "steep banks," "medicine stone" and "where they slaughtered the Crees.")[125]

Residents began calling the settlement Lethbridge by the time it was relocated to prairie level in 1885. A Lethbridge already existed in Ontario (there is another in Newfoundland), so postal authorities ignored local usage and, in October 1885, named it Coalhurst. Residents reciprocated by ignoring the post office designation. Two weeks later, the postal authorities relented and made Lethbridge the official name. The Galts named some of the streets after their British investors,

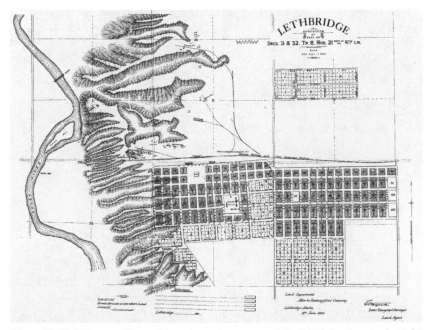

Map of Lethbridge, 1890. Many of its early streets were named for British investors in the Galts' business interests. Sir Alexander Galt Museum and Archives P 1981 1055000

including Courtland Street (now 6th Avenue S.) for William Lethbridge's English country estate in Devon, Crabb Street (now 6th Street S.) for Edward Crabb and Round Street (now 5th Street S.) for Edmund Round. Smith Street (now 4th Street S.) was named for bookseller W.H. Smith. (The nearby town of Coaldale was named for Elliott's Lethbridge residence, Coal Dale.) William Lethbridge never visited his namesake town, and his death passed unnoticed in the *Lethbridge News*. Decades later, Lethbridge teacher Albert Candy—whose mother, as a girl, had worked in William Lethbridge's household—researched Lethbridge's life and visited his grave at South Tauton, South Devon.

The Canadian Pacific Railway built Lethbridge's High Level Bridge in 1907–09. Calgary Public Library PC1224

Lindbergh

Hamlet north of Secondary Highway 646, approximately 15 kilometres east of Elk Point

In May 1927 American aviator Charles Lindbergh (1902–74) made history with his pioneering nonstop solo flight from New York to Paris. Weeks later, in celebration of Canada's Diamond Jubilee of Confederation, Lindbergh again flew the *Spirit of St. Louis*, this time to Ottawa to bring greetings to Prime Minister W.L. Mackenzie King from President Calvin Coolidge. Lindbergh and his American military escort planes circled Parliament Hill's new Victory Tower (renamed the Peace Tower in 1933). Tragically, one of the escort planes crashed at the landing field, killing its pilot.

Lindbergh's trans-Atlantic flight made him an instant hero, and around the world, airfields, hotels, parks, schools and streets were named for him. Canadian National Railways President Sir Henry Thornton gave Lindbergh a lifetime railway pass and named this station for him in 1927.[126] A decade later, in the prelude to World War II, Lindbergh lost popularity with his "America First" isolationist position, and his hometown of Little Falls, Minnesota, removed his name from its water tower. However, Lindbergh, Alberta, remained on the map, and the aviator's heroic reputation was eventually restored.

Charles Lindbergh and the Spirit of St. Louis *in Ottawa, July 1, 1927. Canadian National Railways President Sir Henry Thornton named a station for Colonel Lindbergh after his famous trans-Atlantic flight.* National Archives of Canada PA-062329

Linden

Village on Secondary Highway 806, approximately 32 kilometres southwest of Three Hills

Holdeman Mennonites settled in this area around 1904, and the school they established was named Linden. A post office opened under this name in 1949, and Linden was incorporated as a village in 1963. The origin of the name is forgotten, but it may have been the name of one of Linden's pioneers. Linden is also a name used for the lime tree, as well as an herb derived from it.

Linn Valley

Hamlet on Highway 11A, approximately 1.6 kilometres northwest of Red Deer

Established as a hamlet in 1980, Linn Valley takes the family name of an early farmer on this quarter section. When the first subdivision plan was registered in 1960, the proposed name had been Valleyview, a name already in use by an Alberta town.

Lisburn

Hamlet on Highway 43, approximately 26 kilometres southeast of Mayerthorpe

The Canadian Northern Railway arrived in 1915 and apparently named its station for a town in Antrim, Northern Ireland, southwest of Belfast. The Merebeck post office was renamed Lisburn in 1916.

Little Buffalo

Hamlet south of Secondary Highway 986, approximately 75 kilometres northeast of Peace River

Known as L'Hirondelle until 1981, Little Buffalo is named for the nearby lake, itself a name of uncertain origin. Joseph L'Hirondelle, who settled along the lake in 1913, was of Iroquois ancestry and came west as part of the fur trade.

Little Smoky

Hamlet south of Highway 2A, approximately 25 kilometres west of High Prairie

This community originated with the opening of the Edson Trail in 1911, and served as a ferry point across the Little Smoky River for which it is named.

Lloydminster

City on highways 16 and 17, approximately 235 kilometres east of Edmonton

But for the disorganization and alleged incompetence of Reverend Isaac Montgomery Barr (1849–1937), founder of the Barr Colony, Alberta's "Border City" might have been called Barrview instead of Lloydminster.[127] In 1902—inspired by that icon of empire Cecil Rhodes—Ontario-born Barr and a fellow Anglican clergyman from Canada, Reverend George Exton Lloyd (1865–1940), recruited nearly 2,000 middle-class Britons to form the All-British Colony in Canada's North-West Territories. Barr's plans started going awry during the ocean voyage, and Lloyd comforted the overcrowded passengers while Barr remained in his cabin doing "paperwork."[128] There was no love lost between Lloyd, a teetotaler, and Barr, a tippler.

Bishop George E. Lloyd with Barr colonists, Saskatoon, Saskatchewan. <small>GLENBOW ARCHIVES NA-118-26</small>

Soon after the group arrived at the colony site, a combination of hardships—illness, bad food, exorbitant expenses, too few horses and the absence of lumber—moved the colonists to oust Barr and to choose Lloyd as their leader. Members decided overwhelmingly to name the colony's town after Lloyd. Literally, the name means "Lloyd's monastery." Lloyd went on to become Anglican bishop of

Saskatchewan and is buried in Victoria. Barr settled in Australia, where he is buried.

In 1905 the two-year-old village of Lloydminster was divided by the boundary between the new provinces of Alberta and Saskatchewan. Lloydminster, Saskatchewan, became a town in 1907, while its Alberta counterpart remained a village. The two municipalities were amalgamated in 1930 as a town, and in 1958 the town was incorporated as a city. Residents and visitors casually cross the interprovincial boundary, defined within the city limits by Fiftieth Avenue (Meridian Road), which runs along the Fourth Meridian.

Lodgepole

Hamlet on secondary highways 620 and 753, approximately 27 kilometres southwest of Drayton Valley

The name is descriptive of the area's lodgepole pine trees. Lodgepole was incorporated as a new town in 1956. It was one of several communities incorporated between 1956–1967 under the New Town Act. Oil discoveries led to the creation of instant boomtowns, and the New Town Act was intended to smooth the development of local government and infrastructure.[129] Lodgepole has since reverted to hamlet status.

Lomond

Village on Secondary Highway 845, approximately 72 kilometres northeast of Lethbridge

G.R. Plumb opened the area's first post office in 1910, and it was known as Brunetta. With the arrival of the Canadian Pacific Railway in 1914, the post office shifted to the new townsite and was renamed Lomond, presumably for Loch Lomond in Scotland. Lomond became a village in 1916.

Long Lake

Hamlet east of Secondary Highway 831, approximately 45 kilometres southeast of Athabasca

This hamlet is named for the nearby, descriptively named lake. The name is shared with Long Lake Provincial Park.

Longview

Village on Highway 22, approximately 17 kilometres south southeast of Turner Valley

Ontario schoolteacher Thomas Long homesteaded with his brother Oliver at Big Hill, a short distance east of the present village. The name Longview derives from the brothers' family name and the view from the post office, opened in 1908 by Samuel McBee. The post office later moved to its present location, and Big Hill is now known as Longview Hill. When a crude oil discovery revived the Turner Valley oilfields in 1936, bustling Longview became known as Little New York. The nearby community of Royalties was called Little Chicago and another local settlement became Little Philadelphia.

A crude oil discovery in 1936 transformed Longview into booming Little New York. Nearby Royalties was called Little Chicago, and another nearby settlement was called Little Philadelphia.

Looma

Hamlet on Highway 21, approximately 25 kilometres southeast of Edmonton

The post office that opened under this name in 1920 took part of the name of an earlier post office, Looma Vista, which operated between

1908–1913. The name Looma Vista had first been used by the local school district and might have been descriptive. The *Concise Oxford Dictionary* defines *loom* as "a vague often exaggerated first appearance of land at sea" and *vista* as "a long narrow view as between rows of trees."

Loon Lake

Hamlet west of Highway 88, approximately 145 kilometres north north-west of Slave Lake

This hamlet was named for nearby Loon Lake, whose name was inspired by the birds that frequent the lake.

Lottie Lake

Hamlet on highways 28 and 36, approximately 20 kilometres west north-west of St. Paul

Established in the 1980s, this hamlet is situated on the eastern shore of Lottie Lake and shares its name. Its origin is a mystery.

Lougheed

Village on Highway 13, approximately 10 kilometres southeast of Sedgewick

When it comes to immortality through toponymy, a senator trumps a postmaster. The post office was originally named Holmstown, after postmasters Gus and Adolph Leedholm, members of a pioneering Swedish–American family. When the Canadian Pacific Railway (CPR) arrived in 1906, Holmstown was renamed for Alberta Senator James A. Lougheed (1854–1925), Conservative leader in the upper house. (The railway named the next station to the east for Lougheed's immediate predecessor, who was also his wife's uncle, Senator Richard Hardisty.) Ontario-born Lougheed earned his law degree at Osgoode Hall, and in 1883 moved to Calgary, where he became the CPR's legal counsel. Lougheed entered the federal cabinet in 1911, and in 1917 he was knighted for his World War I service as head of the Military Hospitals Commission. Two months after Lougheed's death, Wind Mountain in Banff National Park was renamed Mount Lougheed in his honour. The senator's grandson, Peter Lougheed, served as premier of Alberta from 1971–85. Though named for a partisan Conservative, Lougheed ironically was once situated in a municipal district named for a Liberal prime minister of Britain (Herbert H. Asquith, who governed from 1908–16). Lougheed was incorporated as a village in 1911.

Sir James Alexander Lougheed, circa 1890s. Lougheed was called to the Senate in 1889 on the death of his wife's uncle, Senator Richard Hardisty. Both have towns named for them. Glenbow Archives NA-3232-7

Lousana

Hamlet east of Highway 21, approximately 10 kilometres southeast of Red Deer

William Henry Biggs (died 1919)—known to all as Judge Biggs— hailed from Hermann, Missouri, and settled here with his wife in 1904. Biggs acquired several quarters of land, brought 300 head of longhorns from Missouri and began ranching. When the Grand Trunk Pacific Railway arrived around 1912, Biggs sold a portion of his land for townsite purposes and reportedly suggested naming it for the city of Louisiana, Missouri. Postal authorities demurred but accepted Lousana as an alternative.

Lowland Heights

Hamlet north of Secondary Highway 785, immediately northeast of Pincher Creek

Pincher Creek flows through these lowlands, but both north and south of the creek banks—about 15 metres back from the water—the land rises, giving this hamlet its apparently contradictory name. This point was once known as Goforth Crossing.

Loyalist

Hamlet south of Highway 12, approximately 36 kilometres east southeast of Coronation

The coronation of King George V, on June 22, 1911, displayed all of the pomp and ceremony that the still-mighty British Empire could muster. The Canadian Pacific Railway showed its patriotism through the choice of station names along its new Lacombe–Kerrobert branch in Alberta, including Fleet, Consort, Coronation, Throne, Veteran and Loyalist, and possibly also Federal and Monitor.[130] In this context, *Loyalist* means "a person who adheres to his sovereign."[131] The name is shared with Loyalist Creek. The post office here was known as Vallejo from 1909–13.

Lundbreck

Hamlet south of Highway 3, approximately six kilometres west northwest of Cowley

When the side of Turtle Mountain collapsed onto the town of Frank, Alberta, in 1903, it killed 76 people (by official count) and disrupted service on the Canadian Pacific Railway's Crow's Nest branch. It took railway contractor John Breckenridge (1861–1913) only 16 days to rebuild the over three kilometres of ruined track. The Scottish-born contractor had previously worked on the Northern Pacific Railroad in Washington State, and he later built part of the Canadian Northern Railway between Edmonton and the Pacific coast. In 1902 Breckenridge established the

Railway contractor John Breckenridge and his partner, Peter Lund, formed the Breckenridge and Lund Coal Company. The hamlet of Lundbreck was named for them.
Courtesy of John and Rebecca Breckenridge

Crow's Nest Pass Lumber Company with partner Peter Lund. The two men formed the Breckenridge and Lund Coal Company in 1903, and before long they opened a coal mine a short distance from Cowley. The settlement that developed was named for the two partners. Nearby Lundbreck Falls shares this manufactured name. Breckenridge is buried in a large prominent grave in Calgary's Union Cemetery, next to Senator James A. Lougheed (for whom the village of Lougheed was named).

Lyalta

Hamlet east of Highway 9, approximately 28 kilometres east of Calgary

This hamlet was originally known as Lyall, but the name had to be changed because there was another Lyall in the province. Harry A. Parsons, of the Lyall Trading Company, suggested a combination of the original name and the name of the province.

MacKay

Hamlet on Secondary Highway 751, approximately 45 kilometres southwest of Mayerthorpe

The Grand Trunk Pacific Railway named this hamlet on its main line in 1911, evidently for William Duncan MacKay (1882–1959), a Chip Lake–area lumberman who later became a railway tie and lumber inspector. Born in Pictou County, MacKay married fellow Nova Scotian Jessie Catherine Fraser in 1925, and the newlywed MacKays settled west of Chip Lake, where they opened a store. Jessie became MacKay's first postmistress in 1928 and held the position until her death in 1960. Bill and Jessie are buried in the Anglican cemetery a short distance to the north.

Madden

Hamlet on Secondary Highway 574, approximately 46 kilometres north northwest of Calgary

The son of an esteemed professor, college-educated Bernard Anthony ("Barney") Madden left his genteel life in Ireland for Canada's ranching frontier around 1880. He took part of his ranch pay in Percheron horses and eventually became a rancher and Percheron breeder in his own right. Barney and his French wife, Marie, brought refinement to their loghouse, which they decorated with oil paintings and where they had French china for everyday use. Though childless, the Maddens paid for many orphans to attend boarding school, and on holidays they brought these children to their ranch. The Maddens spent the winters of their twilight years in Palm Springs, California, and it was there that they reportedly died in the 1920s. The post office in this area, opened in 1931, was named for them.

Magrath

Town on highways 5 and 62, approximately 30 kilometres south of Lethbridge

Had the choice been left to Charles Alexander Magrath (1860–1949), this town would have been named Brandley, for Theodore Brandley of the village of Stirling.[132] In 1878 a young Magrath left his native Ontario for the North-West Territories, where he worked as a topographical surveyor for the federal government. Seven years later, he entered the payroll of Sir Alexander T. Galt, a powerful member of the Conservative party who had extensive coal, land and railway interests in southern Alberta. Before long Magrath became land commissioner of Galt's North-Western Coal and Navigation Company, and in 1899 he married Galt's daughter, Mabel.

To attract agricultural settlers to this dry region and thereby profit from the Galt interests, Magrath and others envisioned a massive irrigation scheme along the St. Mary and Milk rivers. They received support from the federal government and obtained a partnership with southern Alberta's Mormon community, which had experience with dryland farming. Mormon leader Charles Ora Card (for whom the town of Cardston was named) turned the project's first sod in 1898, and the following year, Magrath surveyed and laid out townsites for two new Mormon settlements at either end of the irrigation project: Magrath and Stirling. Magrath became a village in 1901 and a town in 1908.

C.A. Magrath enjoyed political success as the first mayor of Lethbridge (1891), as a member of the North-West Territories legislature (1891–1902, including a cabinet post as minister without portfolio) and as a Conservative Member of Parliament (1908–11). He later returned to Ontario, where he served on the International Joint Commission

(1911–36) and held a number of important posts, including Canadian fuel controller (1917–20) and chairman of the Ontario Hydro-Electric Power Commission (1925–31). In Lethbridge, Magrath is commemorated by a major thoroughfare, Mayor Magrath Drive. The Historic Sites and Monuments Board of Canada unveiled a memorial to Magrath at Lethbridge's City Hall in 1952.

Surveyor, irrigation promoter and politician Charles A. Magrath became the first mayor of Lethbridge in 1891. Besides his namesake town, Magrath is immortalized by Mayor Magrath Drive in Lethbridge. GLENBOW ARCHIVES NA-433-3 (DETAIL)

Mallaig

Hamlet north of Highway 22A, approximately 25 kilometres north northwest of St. Paul

Mallaig was established in 1928 with the arrival of Canadian National Railways line that extended to Cold Lake. It was named for a Scottish port town.

Manning

Town on Highway 35, approximately 73 kilometres north northwest of Peace River

In 1947 hotel developers Howard Singleton and Pat Craig opened the Aurora Hotel, a modern structure on the Mackenzie Highway in the Notikewan River valley. The two promoters had also surveyed and subdivided a townsite, but their preferred name of Aurora was already in use by a post office in Ontario. At a public meeting that fall, residents of the new northern community approved the name Manning, to honour Ernest Charles Manning (1908–96), the premier of Alberta and the second Social Credit party leader to hold the post. Manning post office opened in 1947. Manning became a village in 1951 and a town in 1957.

On the death of Premier William Aberhart in 1943, Manning became premier and hosted the weekly radio program, "Canada's National Back to the Bible Hour." Manning held office at the time of the Leduc oil discovery in 1947, and his quarter century in power was marked by prosperity. He was called to the Canadian Senate in 1970, where he served until 1983. Manning was the first person to receive the Alberta Order of Excellence. His son, Preston Manning, became the founding leader of the Reform Party of Canada in 1987 and became opposition leader in the House of Commons in 1997.

Alberta Premier Ernest C. Manning addressing students of Red Deer Public School District, 1955. The town of Manning was named for him during his term as premier. Red Deer Archives MG 88 DT 1

Mannville

Village on Highway 16, approximately 22 kilometres west of Vermilion

Like his partner William Mackenzie, Donald Mann (1853–1934) rose from gruff railway contractor to national stature and knighthood by developing the Lake Manitoba Railway and Canal Company into the transcontinental Canadian Northern Railway (CNoR). Though highly spiritual, Mann dropped out of divinity school and worked in lumber camps and as a railway construction foreman. As a railway contractor, Mann worked in western Canada, the United States, China and South America. The CNoR's Winnipeg land agents named this village, on the main line between Lloydminster and Edmonton, for Mann. It was incorporated as a village in 1907.

Both Mackenzie and Mann were knighted for their accomplishments in 1911, but in 1918 the Canadian government nationalized the faltering Canadian Northern, and it was later incorporated into Canadian National Railways.

Sir Donald Mann and his partner, Sir William Mackenzie, built the transcontinental Canadian Northern Railway. The faltering company was later nationalized and incorporated into Canadian National Railways.
WWW.CANADIANHERITAGE.CA ID#20152, NATIONAL ARCHIVES OF CANADA

Manola

Hamlet north of Secondary Highway 654, approximately 11 kilometres east southeast of Barrhead

Once known as the California Settlement, Manola was reportedly named at the suggestion of its first postmistress, Mrs. James A. McPhee, in 1907. According to the story, Mrs. McPhee made three suggestions, each for place names in her native California. Since Eureka and Orlando would have created post office duplication, Manola was selected. The problem with the story is that Manola appears nowhere in David Durham's authoritative *California's Geographic Names*. However, the McPhees' second daughter's second name was Manola, and that might be the explanation.[133] The Edmonton, Dunvegan and British Columbia Railway reached Manola in 1927.

Manyberries

Hamlet on Highway 61, approximately 72 kilometres south of Medicine Hat

Manyberries is a descriptive name, referring to the chokecherries and saskatoons that native peoples historically gathered in this area. Manyberries Creek shares the name. The Manyberries post office opened in 1911, and the Canadian Pacific Railway arrived in 1916.

Marie Reine

Hamlet on Secondary Highway 774, approximately 28 kilometres south of Peace River

Marie Reine is a French name for Mary, mother of Jesus, that characterizes her as "queen." The post office opened here in 1955.

Markerville

Hamlet south of Secondary Highway 592, approximately 19 kilometres northwest of Innisfail

For Christian Peter Marker (1868–1949), a youthful job at a creamery in his native Jutland, Denmark, began a career that spanned 50 years and two continents. He emigrated to Canada in 1890 and in 1897 moved to Calgary as the superintendent of dairying for the district of Alberta, North-West Territories. In 1906 he became the provincial dairy commissioner, a post he held for nearly 30 years, and in 1921 he became head of the University of Alberta Department of Dairying. Marker firmly believed that a strong dairy industry would release farmers from dependence on the grain economy. He developed new methods of buttermaking that eventually became standard in Canadian creameries, and once he quipped, "I've learned from dairying on which side my bread is buttered."[134] Marker is buried in the Edmonton Cemetery.

Through Marker's efforts, a government creamery was established in 1899 at Tindastoll, an Icelandic settlement founded in 1888 and named for a mountain in Iceland. Grateful residents adopted his name for their community, and in 1902 the new post office of Markerville opened. A nearby creek retains the name Tindastoll.

Marlboro

Hamlet on Highway 16, approximately 25 kilometres southwest of Edson

The name of this hamlet describes the area's marl deposits, used in cement manufacturing here. The post office opened in 1912.

Marten Beach

Hamlet west of Highway 88, on the eastern shore of Lesser Slave Lake

This hamlet adjacent to Lesser Slave Lake Provincial Park takes its name from Marten Lakes, which themselves were named for Marten Mountain. The name possibly comes from the valuable fur-bearing mammal.

Marwayne

Village on Highway 45, approximately 33 kilometres northwest of Lloydminster

"The pleasing name of [this] small town," the *Edmonton Journal* once noted, "is a combination of the first syllables of Marfleet and Wainfleet, the former being the name of the pioneer family, the latter that of their native town in Lincolnshire, England."[135] Even before leaving England, W. Creasey Marfleet had named his new farm Marwayne and had his calling cards printed, erroneously locating Marwayne in Saskatchewan.[136] Marfleet served as postmaster from 1906–21 and was succeeded by his son Fred Marfleet (1922–50) and by Agnes Marfleet (1950). Incorporated in 1952, this village is the namesake for Marwayne Creek.

Mayerthorpe

Town on Highway 43, approximately 116 kilometres west northwest of Edmonton

Robert Ingersoll Mayer (circa 1881–1937), a civil engineer for the Chicago Northwestern Railroad who hailed originally from Indianapolis, moved to Alberta with his wife, Emma, in 1908. They homesteaded along the Little Paddle River northwest of Edmonton and accepted the invitation of Peter Gunn, Member of the Legislative

Assembly (and for whom the hamlet of Gunn was named), to operate the post office. Gunn first proposed the name Mayerville for the post office, and when that was rejected he changed it to Mayerthorpe, adding a suffix understood to mean village or hamlet (or else the name of a local teacher). With the approach of the Canadian Northern Railway in 1919, settler Leo Oscar Crockett (circa 1884–1965), a U.S. navy veteran, subdivided and promoted the townsite of Little Paddle about five kilometres east of the Mayers' post office. Crockett resisted

Robert Ingersoll Mayer on a survey crew, 1908. He later served as postmaster of Mayerthorpe.
Provincial Archives of Alberta A.5019 (detail)

the call to rename the settlement "Crockett," and when the Mayers' post office closed in 1921 and a new one opened in the townsite, Little Paddle became Mayerthorpe.[137] Bob Mayer moved to Edmonton in 1922 and worked there as a railway bridgeman until his death.[138] Crockett remained in Mayerthorpe, where his namesake son later became mayor. Both Mayer and Crockett are buried in Edmonton. Mayerthorpe was incorporated as a village in 1927 and as a town in 1961.

McLaughlin

Hamlet south of Secondary Highway 614, approximately 33 kilometres south southwest of Lloydminster

When the delightfully named Lorenzo Loveless opened this post office in June 1908, it was named for pioneer settlers John M. and Thomas McLaughlin.

McLennan

Town on Highway 2, approximately 135 kilometres northeast of Grande Prairie

Derailed train on the Edmonton, Dunvegan and British Columbia Railway (which many dubbed "Exceedingly Dangerous and Badly Constructed") near McLennan. The town was named for Dr. John K. McLennan, an executive (and future vice-president) of this railway. Provincial Archives of Alberta A.10,177

In 1915, as its rails approached the Peace River country, the Edmonton, Dunvegan and British Columbia Railway (ED&BC) reached the shore of Round Lake (now Lake Kimiwan). Bypassing the existing settlements of Grouard and Round Lake, the ED&BC established the new divisional point of McLennan. Round Lake residents quickly packed up and resettled in McLennan. Despite its Scottish name, many of McLennan's settlers were French Canadians. The townsite was named for Dr. John K. McLennan, the railway company's secretary-treasurer, purchasing agent and future vice-president. After earning a medical degree in Winnipeg, McLennan moved to California where he practiced until J.D. McArthur recruited him for the administration of the ED&BC. When the Canadian Pacific Railway took over the line in 1920, McLennan and his family returned to California. McLennan was incorporated as a village in 1944 and as a town in 1948.

Meander River

Hamlet on Highway 35, approximately 67 kilometres north northwest of High Level

This hamlet is descriptively named for the river nearby. The post office opened in 1954.

Meanook

Hamlet east of Highway 2, approximately 16 kilometres south of Athabasca

The Canadian Northern Railway's Athabasca branch arrived in 1912, and used the Cree term meaning "good camping place" for its station.[139]

Mearns

Hamlet east of Highway 44, approximately 14 kilometres northwest of Morinville

This Scottish place name, an alternative name for Kincardineshire, Scotland, might have been the source for this Edmonton, Dunvegan and British Columbia Railway's station, built in 1912.

Medicine Hat

City on the Trans-Canada Highway (Highway 1), approximately 150 kilometres east northeast of Lethbridge

Medicine Hat's colourful name is steeped in legend, and its exact origins are a mystery. Historian Marcel Dirk has written an entire book on the subject. One theory has it that a hill east of the city, identified as Medicine Hat on an 1883 map, was so named because it looked like a native medicine man's headdress. Others have said that a native chief saw an apparition of a man wearing a medicine man's headdress and rising from the South Saskatchewan River or that a medicine man gave his hat to a brave who rescued a woman from the river or that during a battle against the Blackfoot, a Cree medicine man lost his headdress in the river or that, after a group of white settlers had been killed, a medicine man took the hat of one of the victims. In the Blackfoot language the name was *sawáwms*, "holy headdress."¹⁴⁰

Natural gas shaft near Medicine Hat, circa 1913. Because of its gas reserves, Rudyard Kipling declared the city had "all hell for a basement." CALGARY PUBLIC LIBRARY PC785

As a place name, Medicine Hat was used as early as 1882, when it appeared in the annual report of the North-West Mounted Police. Medicine Hat was incorporated as a village in 1894, as a town in 1898 and as a city in 1906. By 1910 some thought the name embarrassing and suggested it be changed to Gasburg (reflecting the area's extensive natural gas resources) or Smithville (to honour Canadian Pacific Railway executive Donald A. Smith, whose title was Lord Strathcona).¹⁴¹

Advocates of the old name turned for support to Rudyard Kipling, who had visited four years earlier (and noted of the gas field that Medicine Hat had "all hell for a basement"). "Believe me, the very name is an asset," said Kipling.

> It has the qualities of uniqueness, individuality, assertion and power. Above all, it is the lawful, original, sweat-and-dust-won name of the city, and to change it would be to risk the luck of the city to disgust and dishearten old-timers, not in the city alone, but the world over, and to advertise abroad the city's lack of faith in itself.[142]

Kipling added that a city that sold out its name might as well be called Judasville.

Descriptive street names in the vicinity of Medicine Hat's Clay Industry Interpretive Centre recall aspects of the city's industrial history: Elevator Street, Factory Street, Foundry Street, Medalta Avenue, Mill Street, Pottery Street, Smelter Avenue, Steel Street and Tractor Avenue.

Alberta Clay Products Plant, Medicine Hat, n.d. The city became famous for its pottery industry, which inspired the names of Pottery Street and Medalta Avenue (for Medalta Potteries). Calgary Public Library PC532

Meeting Creek

Hamlet west of Highway 56, approximately 20 kilometres northeast of Bashaw

During buffalo hunts, the nearby namesake creek was once a meeting point between the Cree to the north and the Blackfoot-speaking peoples to the south. A post office by this name opened in 1905, and was briefly renamed Edenville in 1911–12.

Metiskow

Hamlet south of Highway 13, approximately 27 kilometres west northwest of Provost

This hamlet's name is descriptive—at least it was in 1910, when the post office was established—from the Cree *metosi skaw*, meaning "many trees."

Michichi

Hamlet on Secondary Highway 849, approximately 43 kilometres west southwest of Hanna

The Cree term for "hand" or "little hand" supplies the name for Michichi Creek, whose five branches evoke the five digits on a human hand. The hamlet is named for the creek. In 1930 Canadian National Railways changed the spelling of its station (Mecheche) to conform to the post office and the municipality of Michichi.[143]

Milk River

Town on Highway 4, approximately 80 kilometres southeast of Lethbridge

"The waters of the river possess a peculiar whiteness being about the colour of a cup of tea with the admixture of a tablespoon of milk," wrote explorers Meriwether Lewis and William Clark, who had been commissioned by U.S. President Thomas Jefferson in 1801 to explore the west. "From the colour of its waters we call it Milk River."[144] As part of the Missouri basin, this area was once claimed by Spain, and nine flags have flown over it. The Alberta Railway and Irrigation Company named its station for the river, and the post office opened in 1908.

Millarville

Hamlet west of Highway 22, approximately 24 kilometres southwest of Calgary

Like many other veterans of the North-West Mounted Police, Scottish-born Malcolm Tanner Millar (1860–1937) remained in the west, and in 1886 he and his wife, Helen Shaw (1863–1943), settled at Sheep Creek and took up ranching. Malcolm operated a post office and trading post from 1892–1911, and the Millar ranchhouse became a well-known stopping place for travellers on the Calgary–Macleod Trail.

Poster advertising Calgary–Millarville mail stage, circa 1906. GLENBOW ARCHIVES NA-2567-1

Millet

Town on Highway 2A, approximately 15 kilometres north northwest of Wetaskiwin

Two different stories account for the naming of Millet, created through the construction of the Calgary and Edmonton Railway (C&E) in 1890–91. The first has it that Sir William Cornelius Van Horne, presi-

Malcolm and Helen Millar and their daughters in a California cart, Millarville, circa 1904. Malcolm remained in the west after his service in the North-West Mounted Police, and the family ranchhouse became a familiar stopping place. GLENBOW ARCHIVES NA-2520-2

dent of the Canadian Pacific Railway (CPR) that operated the C&E, admired the works of the French artist Jean François Millet. (The naming of Hobbema, for 17th century Dutch artist Myendert Hobbema, might lend support to this theory.) The second version credits the name to Father Albert Lacombe (for whom the town of Lacombe was named), to whom tradition ascribes the naming of several C&E stations.[145] Lacombe had known and travelled with a fur trader named August (or John) Millet.

Millicent

Hamlet north of Secondary Highway 544, approximately 104 kilometres northwest of Medicine Hat

This hamlet is named for Millicent Fanny St. Clair-Erskine (1867–1955), an editor and writer. Her husband was Cromartie Sutherland-Leveson-Gower, the 4th Duke of Sutherland (1851–1913), a British aristocrat with substantial land holdings in the Brooks area. Their daughter, Lady Rosemary Millicent Leveson-Gower (1893–1930), was the namesake for another point on the Canadian Pacific Railway's Empress–Bassano branch, Rosemary.

Milo

Village on Secondary Highway 542, approximately 91 kilometres southeast of Calgary

In 1907 Ontario-born Milo Munroe (circa 1865–1928) homesteaded north of Vulcan and opened a post office in his farmhouse the following year. Despite his brief tenure as postmaster, this railway village retains Munroe's first name. The Canadian Pacific Railway bypassed the original Milo settlement when it arrived in 1924, and the railway company laid out the present village at that time. Milo was incorporated in 1931. Milo Munroe died in Calgary.

Minburn

Village on Highway 16, approximately 34 kilometres west of Vermilion

When the Canadian Northern Railway (CNoR) built its Edmonton–Lloydminster line in 1905, it named this station for Miss Mina Burns of Ottawa. According to lore, Mina wrote magazine articles about the Canadian west and was said to have been the girlfriend of a CNoR official. But periodical guides from the time yield no articles under that byline. Mina attended Ottawa Collegiate and Ottawa Normal School, and taught in Ottawa schools for over 40 years. She helped organize the Ontario Women Teachers' Federation and once served as its president.[146] If Mina was the girlfriend of a railway official, they evidently never married. She died in 1960 and is buried in Ottawa's Beechwood Cemetery. Minburn became a village in 1919.

Mirror

Village on Highway 50, approximately 17 kilometres south southwest of Bashaw

Through its subsidiary land company, the Grand Trunk Pacific Railway (GTP) laid out this townsite as a future railway divisional point. London's *Daily Mirror,* for which the townsite was named, wrote glowingly of the future city and noted that its streets and avenues were named for members of the newspaper's staff. The GTP arranged a special train from Winnipeg (via Saskatoon and Edmonton) for the auction of lots held July 11, 1911. Auctioneer (and future Manitoba premier) Rodmond

P. Roblin conducted the two-day event, which saw 577 lots sold for a total price of over a quarter-million dollars. Like so many other settlements, Mirror failed to emerge as a city, and landowners in Britain, the United States and around the world found that they owned unserviced lots that most never saw again. Many were reclaimed through nonpayment of taxes.[147] Mirror was incorporated as a village in 1912.

Future Manitoba Premier Rodmond P. Roblin conducts the two-day auction of Mirror's townsite lots in 1911. GLENBOW ARCHIVES NA-1922-8

Monarch

Hamlet on Highway 3A, approximately 20 kilometres northwest of Lethbridge

Evidently named in a fit of patriotism, Monarch would have evoked King Edward VII, the sovereign when this hamlet and its post office were established in 1908. Its streets had such names as Alexandra (the Queen Consort), Empress, Prince, Princess and Victoria.

Monitor

Hamlet on Highway 12, approximately 46 kilometres south southwest of Provost

As part of the Lacombe–Kerrobert line, the Canadian Pacific Railway

(CPR) might have named Monitor to honour King George V's coronation in 1911. Other stations on the line, including Fleet, Consort, Coronation, Throne, Veteran and Loyalist, and possibly Federal, were named that year to honour the event.[148] By one explanation, *monitor* referred to "a heavily armed shallow-draft warship" (as defined by the *Concise Oxford Dictionary),* evoking the power of the British navy—or it referred to the king himself, as "one who admonishes or warns of faults, and informs of duty."[149] The former explanation is unsatisfying, because the generic name came from an American vessel, the USS *Monitor.* Another explanation entirely is that a settler named Jack Deadmarsh suggested the name to honour an English town. The post office, opened in 1911 as Sounding Lake, was renamed Monitor in 1913.

Moon River Estates

Hamlet south of Highway 3, approximately 16 kilometres east of Fort Macleod

Established as a hamlet in 1984, Moon River Estates was named by its developer.

Morinville

Town on Highway 2, approximately 32 kilometres north northwest of Edmonton

As a colonization agent, Abbé Jean-Baptiste Morin brought many French-speaking settlers from Quebec to Alberta. Missionary Oblates, Grandin Archives Ob.3814

Established in 1891 as a French Canadian settlement, Morinville is named for Abbé Jean-Baptiste Morin (1852–1911), a colonization agent who brought many settlers from Quebec to new French-speaking communities in Alberta. His promotional pamphlet, *Le Nord-ouest Canadien et ses Resources Agricoles*, was published in 1894. Morinville became a town in 1911.

Morningside

Hamlet on Highway 2A, approximately 12 kilometres south southwest of Ponoka

Peter Gzowski's *Morningside Papers* books might make no mention of this central Alberta hamlet but the radio and television host did visit the province several times and likely knew of this hamlet that shared a name with his popular radio program. The station on the Calgary and Edmonton Railway was established in 1891 and named for a suburb of Edinburgh, Scotland.

Morrin

Village north of Highway 27, approximately 36 kilometres east of Three Hills

Flowering bluebell, beard's tongue and crocus led pioneers to name this settlement Blooming Prairie. There is no clear explanation why the Canadian Northern Railway renamed it Morrin when the Munson–Stettler branch was built here in 1911. Local lore offers three explanations: Morrin was the engineer who brought the first train through, that the name was changed to satisfy the "bloomin' English" and that the name implied there was "more in" this district than in others. CNoR records suggest the namesake might have been Dr. Joseph Morrin (1792–1861), a Scottish-born physician and staunch Presbyterian whose benevolence established Morrin College, a Presbyterian institution in Quebec City. Morrin, Alberta, never had a Presbyterian church, though the Union Church, built in 1911, served Methodists, Presbyterians and other denominations long before the United Church of Canada was formed in 1925. Morrin's United Church was built in 1953.

Mossleigh

Hamlet on Highway 24, approximately 55 kilometres southeast of Calgary

Joseph Higginbotham Saxon Moss (1859–1914) hailed from Bedford Leigh, Lincolnshire, which should explain the origin of both components of the name—"Moss" and "leigh." According to the family's account, however, Leigh was Moss' mother's family name. As a child, Moss emigrated to Quebec with his parents, and in 1879 he came west with a survey party, befriending surveyor Charles Magrath (who later became the first mayor of Lethbridge and for whom the town of Magrath was named). He worked as a freighter during the North-West Rebellion of 1885 and later worked for Montana-based I.G. Baker & Co. Moss' wife, Elizabeth, reportedly provided Mossleigh as the name for the local school district, which she served as secretary-treasurer until her death in 1911. The name was later used for the hamlet.[150]

Mountain View

Hamlet on Highway 5, approximately 84 kilometres southwest of Lethbridge

Mountain View is a simple, descriptive name. The post office opened in 1894.

Mulhurst Bay

Hamlet on the northeast shore of Pigeon Lake, accessible from Highway 13 west, then 795 north, 43 kilometres northwest of Wetaskiwin

Ontario-born George Wellington Mulligan homesteaded in this area in 1903 and opened the first post office in 1912. Mulhurst comprises the first syllable of Mulligan's name, and the suffix *hurst,* means "grove" or "small wood." Mulhurst became Mulhurst Bay in 1992.

Mundare

Town on Highway 15, approximately 77 kilometres east of Edmonton

In 1907, only a year after Mundare (originally spelled Mundaire) had been established by the Canadian Northern Railway, neither D.B. Hanna nor G.U. Ryley (senior railway officials for whom Hanna and

Ryley were named) could remember the source of the name.[151] Varying accounts relate the name to a French missionary named Father Mundaire, to early station agent William Mundare or to the word for "monastery" in the mother tongue of the settlers—Ukrainian. (There was a Basilian monastery nearby.) Mundare became a village in 1907 and a town in 1951.

Municipality of Crowsnest Pass
See Crowsnest Pass, Municipality of

Munson
Village west of Highway 9, approximately 40 kilometres east southeast of Three Hills

To the urban observer, this tiny farming village must seem the antithesis to urban bustle. But its namesake, lawyer John Henry Munson, K.C. (1859–1918), kept his offices at that epitome of prairie metropolitanism: Winnipeg's corner of Portage and Main. Munson was counsel for the Canadian Northern Railway, which established a station here on its Saskatoon–Calgary line in 1911. Munson is buried in his hometown of Cobourg, Ontario, and the site of his Winnipeg home on Wellington Crescent is now called Munson Park. The CN Building, where he once worked, still stands at Winnipeg's busiest intersection.

Musidora
Hamlet on Highway 45, approximately 12 kilometres east of Two Hills

The traditional explanation for this name is that Edvert Robarge (died 1928), who carried the mail between Beauvallon and Duvernay, suggested this post office name, after his hometown in France. Musidora's post office opened in 1909.

Myrnam
Village on Highway 45, approximately 35 kilometres east southeast of Two Hills

The post office that Paul Melnyk opened in 1908 took a Ukrainian word meaning "peace to us" as its name. Myrnam is part of a Ukrainian Canadian bloc of settlement north and east of Edmonton. The Canadian Pacific Railway built its Willingdon line through here in 1927, and Myrnam became a village in 1930.

Namaka

Hamlet south of the Trans-Canada Highway (Highway 1), approximately 45 kilometres east of Calgary

Namaka is a derivation of the Blackfoot name for the Bow River. Retired General Thomas Bland Strange (1831–1925), who had helped organize the Canadian artillery and later fought in the North-West Rebellion of 1885, established a ranch here by this name. The Canadian Pacific Railway proposed naming its station "Strange," but the General requested that it take the name of his ranch so that his visitors would know were to detrain. The Namaka post office opened in 1908. Namaka Lake shares the name.

Namao

Hamlet on Highway 37, approximately 17 kilometres north of Edmonton

This hamlet on the Sturgeon River takes the Cree name for sturgeon. The Namao post office opened in 1892.

Nampa

Village on Highway 2, approximately 24 kilometres south southeast of Peace River

Homesteader Robert Perry "Pa" Christian (1869–1951) came originally from Missouri and owned the land traversed by the Central Canada Railway in 1916. In addition to his store, Christian operated the railway's pumphouse, and when he became postmaster in 1921, the office was named Tank. It was renamed Nampa in 1924, but in response to a query that year from the secretary of the Geographic Board of Canada, the postmaster was unable to explain the name. "I understand it is an Indian name meaning 'Small Village,'" Christian wrote, adding that there was "a town in Idaho by this same name."[152]

Nanton

Town on Highway 2, approximately 65 kilometres south of Calgary

Besides the two Alberta communities named for him, at least in part, Sir Augustus Meredith Nanton (1860–1925) is the namesake for streets in a dozen places in central and southern Alberta. (Even his ancestral home in Toronto—a mansion called Rosedale—became the name of a district in that city.) Nanton left his native Toronto in 1883 and spent the next four decades in Winnipeg as a partner in the investment and brokerage firm of Osler, Hammond and Nanton, promoting investment in, and development of, the prairie west. The firm administered the Calgary and Edmonton Land Company, an arm of the Calgary and Edmonton Railway (C&E), which was operated by the Canadian Pacific Railway (CPR). In that capacity, Nanton's firm handled land sales and located townsites along the line built between South Edmonton (Strathcona) and Fort Macleod from 1890–92. Streets in a dozen or so of those townsites still bear the names of these three partners. (The hamlet of Ohaton is named for all of them.) One community on the line—known unofficially as Mosquito Creek, in the heart of ranching country south of Calgary—was named Nanton when the Macleod branch of the C&E arrived in 1892. Nanton became a director of several corporations, including the CPR and the Hudson's Bay

Business street in Nanton, n.d. Before the Calgary and Edmonton Railway arrived in 1892, the community here was known as Mosquito Creek. CALGARY PUBLIC LIBRARY PC1483

Company, and was knighted in 1917 for his work as president of the Manitoba Patriotic Fund during World War I. He became president of the Dominion Bank in 1924. When he died less than a year later, flags on office buildings across the country were lowered to half-mast. Nanton is buried in Winnipeg.

Neerlandia

Hamlet on Secondary Highway 769, approximately 23 kilometres north of Barrhead

Original postmaster Alb. Minne Mast was among a group of four Dutch families who settled here in 1912. Additional settlers from the Netherlands strengthened the district's early Dutch character, which is reflected in the hamlet's name.

Nestow

Hamlet on Highway 2, approximately 19 kilometres northeast of Westlock

Nestow is Cree for "brother-in-law," but why this hamlet was so named is unknown. The post office opened in 1908.

Nevis

Hamlet on Highway 12, approximately 23 kilometres west of Stettler

This hamlet is named for the Ben Nevis Coal Mine, itself named for Ben Nevis in Inverness-shire, the highest mountain in Britain. The post office opened in 1911.

New Brigden

Hamlet east of Highway 41, approximately 40 kilometres north of Oyen

Named for Brigden, Ontario, the home of early settlers. The post office opened in 1912.

New Dayton

Hamlet on Highway 4, approximately 45 kilometres southeast of Lethbridge

David E. Hunter, late of Dayton, Ohio, subdivided this townsite in 1906 and promoted it to American settlers. He named it for his hometown.

New Norway
Village on Highway 21, approximately 18 kilometres south southwest of Camrose

In his response to a 1906 query about the origin of this name, postmaster Joseph Neveu replied plainly, "New Norway has been called by the above name through being mostly settled by Norwegian people."[153] New Norway became a village in 1910.

New Sarepta
Village north of Highway 21, approximately 40 kilometres southeast of Edmonton

Zarephath, a Biblical city now known as Sarafand, Lebanon, was called Sarepta in the King James version of the Bible. Sarepta was also the name of a town in Russia settled by Volga Germans in the 18th century. Varying accounts identify both places as the source for New Sarepta, Alberta, a settlement known until 1905 as Little Hay Lakes. It was named by Moravian Bishop Clement Hoyler, who thought a Biblical name would "raise no objection" among the settlers of many nationalities.[154] It was called "New Sarepta" to distinguish it from Sarepta post office in Ontario. New Sarepta was incorporated as a village in 1960.

New Sarepta became widely known through the work of Yardley Jones, whose 1960s editorial cartoons in the *Edmonton Journal* often made reference to the village. A calendar from a New Sarepta business, such as the New Sarepta Tire and Girdle Company, hung in the background no matter what the subject of the cartoon. To Jones, New Sarepta must have seemed a city-dweller's archetypical small town. Jones visited New Sarepta in 1963 and was greeted enthusiastically by its mayor and villagers.[155]

Newbrook
Hamlet on Secondary Highway 661, approximately 40 kilometres northwest of Smoky Lake

According to *Place-Names of Alberta* (1928), the original post office established in 1917 was located on a creek that had been discovered in 1914 when the trail to the new settlement was cut. In another account, a group of railway officials—sitting in an Edmonton drug store with a map spread out before them—named this and other railway locations. In that story, Newbrook was a local homesteader.[156]

Nightingale
Hamlet on Secondary Highway 564, approximately 50 kilometres east northeast of Calgary

In the summer of 1910, settlers at the English Colony northeast of Strathmore were already planning a meeting to choose a permanent place name when they heard that Florence Nightingale (1820–1910) had died. Nightingale was the most famous nurse in the world, and her dedication to the wounded during the Crimean War (1854–56) was still within living memory. Like "the lady with the lamp," the settlers were all from Great Britain, and they decided to perpetuate her memory by naming their colony, established by the Canadian Pacific Railway, for her.

Nisku
Hamlet on Highway 2, approximately eight kilometres north of Leduc

In its 1928 publication *Place-Names of Alberta*, the Geographic Board of Canada identified Nisku, a name adopted in 1908, as Cree for "goose." However, "nisku" is also a Polish word meaning "low," and according to his descendants, it was Stanislaus Sarnecki (circa 1860–1930) who came up with the name. When he arrived in 1897, Sarnecki was reportedly the second Polish immigrant in what is now Alberta and the first to arrive without a sojourn in a third country. Sarnecki and his wife, Victoria, settled five kilometres west of present-day Nisku, and he wrote to his kinsmen about the wonderful homestead land available in the new country. Some 20 families came after reading Stanislaus' correspondence. Stanislaus described a nearby slough—a landmark point for travellers, still visible at the Nisku junction on Highway 2—by the Polish term, and the name stuck. The Sarneckis are buried in a Polish churchyard west of Nisku.[157] The Edmonton International Airport is located at Nisku. There is a centre in present-day Poland named Nisko.

Niton Junction

Hamlet on Highway 16, approximately 45 kilometres east of Edson

This playful name comes from the nearby former hamlet of Niton and is explained traditionally as the backwards spelling of "not in"—presumably the message left when the station agent was away. The Grand Trunk Pacific Railway established its Niton station in 1911. Another explanation, frequently used and difficult to verify, is that Niton was the name of a railway contractor.

Nobleford

Village on Secondary Highway 519, approximately 22 kilometres northwest of Lethbridge

If ever there was proof that lightning can strike twice, it is in the story of Charles Sherwood Noble (1873–1957), inventor and manufacturer of the Noble Blade Cultivator. In 1897 Noble left his native Iowa to farm in North Dakota. To avoid competition from other prospective homesteaders, he got off the train at Knox, North Dakota, simply because no one else did. After lightning killed his horses and hail ruined his crops in 1902, Noble moved on to Alberta. A failed stint in real estate and farm implement sales brought him back to farming. He built up a 2,000-hectare operation with some 40 employees. The settlement of Noble grew up on his property, and in 1910 the post office opened under that name. However, in 1913 the name changed to Nobleford, traditionally explained because there was already a Noble in Ontario. With the arrival of the Canadian Pacific Railway in 1918, Nobleford became a village.

During World War I, Noble expanded his holdings massively to meet increased demand for food production. But in 1922 a depressed market, drought and debt cost him his 14,000-hectare operation, regarded to have been the largest wheat farm in the British Empire. He took a job as a bank sales agent, but within a year returned to the land, at first renting—and then buying—portions of his former holdings. Soil drift during the Dirty Thirties inspired the inventor in Noble and allowed him to recover his lost wealth. He adapted a concept he had seen in California—a sugar beet harvester that cut subsurface growth without knocking down the plant—to develop a cultivator blade that did not turn the soil. Noble's blade left the stubble of the previous crop in place, and the stubble anchored the soil, preventing drift. He established Noble Cultivators Ltd. and constructed a factory in Nobleford. By the time of his death, Noble had earned an honourary doctorate, an MBE (Member of the Order of the British Empire) and a place in the history books. "Dr. Noble may not quite rank with McCormick and his reaper, or John Deere and his mould-board plow," eulogized the *Calgary Albertan*, "but he was the same kind of man as they."[158]

Charles S. Noble, inventor of the Noble Blade Cultivator, turns the sod for a new factory at Nobleford, 1950.

Nordegg

Hamlet on Highway 11, approximately 155 kilometres northwest of Red Deer

Born in Germany as Martin Cohen (or Cohn), Martin Nordegg (1868–1948) studied engineering and photochemistry at the Berlin

Technical Institute and managed a printing plant in Berlin before emigrating to Canada in 1906. The bold entrepreneur met the prime minister, Sir Wilfrid Laurier, before moving west in 1907. He explored for coal in the Alberta foothills and discovered the Nordegg coal basin. In partnership with William Mackenzie of the Canadian Northern Railway, he established Brazeau Collieries to develop it. Nordegg planned a model company town and gave it the name he had adopted for himself in 1909. In 1912 Nordegg brought his daughter, Marcelle, to visit the town he created. "[A] dog's barking welcomed us," Nordegg wrote his daughter in a memoir later published as *To The Town That Bears Your Name,* "and, riding through a dense grove of spruce trees, we suddenly spotted the first house in the town that bears your name. Did you heart beat like mine?"[159] The Canadian Northern Railway reached Nordegg in 1914, but the outbreak of World War I that year marked Nordegg himself as an enemy alien. He was advised to leave the country, and eventually he lost control of the collieries. The railway station was renamed Brazeau, although the post office and the hamlet's residents continued to call it Nordegg. Martin Nordegg returned to

Martin Nordegg established Brazeau Collieries and planned a model company town. He wrote a memoir to his daughter of their trip to Nordegg, titled To The Town That Bears Your Name. *His own memoir was published posthumously as* The Possibilities of Canada Are Truly Great: Memoirs 1906–1924 *(1971).* National Archives of Canada C-035065

Canada in 1920 and visited the community in 1927. When Nazi Germany annexed Austria in 1938, Nordegg—who was Jewish—travelled to Vienna to help his friends and their relatives to emigrate, and during World War II he and his wife offered financial assistance to hundreds of refugees from Germany.[160]

The postwar conversion to diesel locomotives spelled the end of Brazeau Collieries, and the last mine closed in 1955. A Nordegg historical society was formed in 1984, and a decade later the mine site became a provincial historic site. The Nordegg River and Martin Creek were also named for Martin Nordegg.

Communist Party of Canada leader Tim Buck welcomed in Nordegg, 1935. Buck was a popular figure among many coal miners, and a radical town council in Blairmore named a street after him.
GLENBOW ARCHIVES NA-2635-93

North Cooking Lake

Hamlet on Secondary Highway 630, approximately 40 kilometres east southeast of Edmonton

Translated from the Cree *opi mi now wa sioo*, Cooking Lake east of Edmonton was historically a camping spot used by natives. This hamlet, where a post office opened in 1912, is located on the north shore.

North Star

Hamlet on Highway 35, approximately seven kilometres south of Manning

The post office at this northern settlement opened in 1929 and takes the descriptive name of the star Polaris.

Notikewin

Hamlet on Highway 35, approximately six kilometres north of Manning

In 1919 the original post office name was Battle River Prairie, referring to the nearby Battle River. Because the river's name duplicated another within the province, the river was renamed in 1915, using a variation on the native name, *Notenaygewn*.

Ohaton

Hamlet on Highway 13, approximately 13 kilometres east southeast of Camrose

Osler, Hammond and Nanton are common street names in a dozen or so communities in central and southern Alberta, including Bowden, Carstairs, Crossfield, Didsbury and Innisfail. These are among the townsites that were developed and sold by the Winnipeg investment and brokerage firm of Osler, Hammond and Nanton, which administered the Calgary and Edmonton Land Company, the real estate arm of the Calgary and Edmonton Railway (C&E). Ohaton is a manufactured name that honours all three partners. Sir Edmund Boyd Osler (1845–1924) served as president of the Dominion Bank, as a director of the Canadian Pacific Railway (CPR), which operated the C&E, and as a Conservative Member of Parliament for West Toronto (1896–1917). He is also the namesake for Osler, Saskatchewan. Herbert Carlyle Hammond (1844–1909) was a Toronto philanthropist and financier. Sir Augustus Meredith Nanton is the namesake of Nanton. The CPR reached Ohaton in 1906, and the post office opened that year.

Okotoks

Town on Highway 2A, approximately 90 kilometres south of Calgary

The Blackfoot word *okotok* ("rock") is the source of this town's name and refers to the massive glacial erratic located eight kilometres west of town. The name was first used for the post office in 1884, but in 1891—when the Macleod branch of the Calgary and Edmonton Railway (C&E) arrived—the name changed to Dewdney. Sir Edgar Dewdney (1835–1916) served as Indian commissioner for the North-West Territories (1879–88) and as the territories' lieutenant-governor (1881–88), and turned the first sod for the C&E in 1890. The name Okotoks resurfaced in 1897.

The name Okotoks derives from the Blackfoot okotok, *meaning "rock." The term refers to the huge glacial erratic eight kilometres west of town.* Courtesy of Shannon Lee Rae

Olds

Town on Highway 2A, approximately 58 kilometres south southwest of Red Deer

In 1891 the Calgary and Edmonton Railway (C&E) reached the Lone Pine district, an area along the Calgary–Edmonton Trail best known for the Lone Pine Stopping House. The Canadian Pacific Railway (CPR), which leased and operated the C&E, abandoned this colourful name and dubbed its station Sixth Siding, marking its location along the rail line north from Calgary. The new settlement was briefly called Hay City, reflecting its superb grazing lands. The railway company proposed the name Shannon—for Irish-born CPR contractor David Shannon, who was present at the CPR's last spike ceremony in 1885, and whose homestead became the Hay City townsite. But Shannon declined, so the company named its station after another CPR veteran, George Olds (born 1832). As a young man, Olds left his native Gloucestershire, England and became a railway man in Canada and the U.S. He served the CPR as general traffic manager from 1886–96 and later lived briefly in the settlement that bears his name. Olds was reportedly buried in Airdrie, but the cemetery was later moved and there is no record of his interment. Olds was incorporated as a village in 1896 and as a town on Dominion Day, 1905.

George Olds, general traffic manager of the Canadian Pacific Railway from 1886–1896, circa 1890. He lived in Olds briefly. Canadian Pacific Railway Archives NS.19996

Onoway

Village east of Highway 43, approximately 50 kilometres west northwest of Edmonton

This settlement was originally meant to be named Beaupré for its first postmaster, William Philip Beaupré (1852–1936). But the name had already been taken, and the post office became Onoway. One explanation given is that it was the native equivalent to Beaupré, meaning "good, rich or lush meadow." Another explanation, however, is that the name is a misspelling of *Onaway*—meaning "awake"—which the narrator shouts in Henry Wadsworth Longfellow's epic poem "Hiawatha." According to family lore, the name was chosen by Virginia-born Madison Martin, who also named the hamlet of Opal.[161]

Opal

Hamlet west of Highway 28, approximately 50 kilometres north northeast of Edmonton

This hamlet in the Ukrainian block east of Edmonton was originally named Rutherford, presumably for Alberta's first premier, Alexander G. Rutherford. By the time the post office opened in 1912, Rutherford's political star had fallen in a railway scandal and the post office was named for Opal May Martin, daughter of Madison Martin, an early homesteader. Opal's son, William George Morrow (1917–80), became a justice of the North-West Territories' Territorial Court, the Supreme Court of Alberta and the Court of Appeal of Alberta.

Orion

Hamlet on Highway 61, approximately 65 kilometres south of Medicine Hat

The post office known originally as Needmore became Orion when the Canadian Pacific Railway arrived in 1916. Local residents reportedly suggested the new name for the constellation and its associated Greek mythological figure. Street names on the original subdivision plan included Aenopion and Diana streets, and Chios, Merope and Rigel avenues. In one version of the Greek myth, the giant hunter Orion went to Chios Island, where he asked King Aenopion for permission to marry his daughter Merope. The king promised Merope's hand if Orion killed all the beasts in the kingdom, but reneged after Orion had completed the task. In a different version, Orion fell in love with Artemis, but she accidentally killed him. Diana is the Roman equivalent of Artemis. Rigel is a star in the constellation Orion.

Orton

Hamlet south of Highway 3, approximately 32 kilometres west of Lethbridge

Though many suggested place names were rejected as duplicates of older Canadian centres, Orton somehow slipped by. (There is an older

Orton near Guelph, Ontario.) The post office here was named in 1907 for pioneer settler Josiah Orr, who served as the area's first postmaster (1907–15) and its last (1924–26).

Oyen
Town on Highway 41, approximately 156 kilometres east of Drumheller

Around 1887 a teenaged Andrew Anderson Oyen (1870–1937) left his native Norway for the United States, where he eventually ended up in Spokane, Washington. In 1908 Oyen walked from Spokane to the future townsite of Oyen, where he homesteaded. Brothers Simon and Melkor (Mike) Oyen later joined him and took up farming nearby. Some thought this community might be named Bishopberg, for pioneer merchant Billy Bishop, but when the post office opened in 1912, it was named for the pioneer Norwegian settler who "never turned a wayfarer from his door."[162] A lifelong bachelor, Andy Oyen is buried in Oyen Cemetery. Oyen became a village in 1913 and a town in 1965.

Paddle Prairie
Hamlet east of Highway 35, approximately 76 kilometres south southwest of High Level

Historically this was a swampy area, but when it dried out, the Beaver and Slavey people who lived here moved farther north. Early settlers discovered their abandoned canoes and paddles hanging from trees. "Prairie" is an important element in place names in bush country. Naturally occurring meadows, often along rivers, were important to people with cattle and horses to feed. The Paddle Prairie post office opened in 1934. The name is shared by the Paddle Prairie Metis Settlement to the north.

Paradise Valley
Village east of Secondary Highway 897, approximately 35 kilometres southwest of Lloydminster

Frank Henton was one of many American settlers who came to this district in 1907, and reportedly it was he who suggested the name. This community began to develop with the arrival of the railway. It became a village in 1964.

Parkland

Hamlet on Highway 2, approximately 75 kilometres south of Calgary

In partnership with his father-in-law, politician W.J. Parkhill of Midland, Ontario, Bailey Powell surveyed and promoted the townsite of Parkland around 1904. The name was originally meant to be Parkhill, but it had to change to avoid confusion with Parkhill, Ontario. Powell proclaimed that the new community would become "a second Chicago," but Parkland failed to develop and its promoters lost ownership of most of their property.[163] Calgary librarian Georgina Thomson (1892–1963) grew up on a homestead near Parkland, and her 1963 book *Crocus and Meadowlark Country* captures Parkland's history and her happy childhood there.

Patricia

Hamlet north of Secondary Highway 544, approximately 98 kilometres northwest of Medicine Hat

The Canadian Pacific Railway established this station in 1912 as part of its "royal line" from Empress to Bassano and named it for Princess Patricia of Connaught (Lady Patricia Ramsay, 1886–1972), a grand-daughter of Queen Victoria. At the time the station was named, the Princess' father, the Duke of Connaught, was governor-general of Canada. Other place names along this line, chosen for their connections to royalty or aristocracy, include Empress, Duchess (named for Patricia's mother), Iddesleigh, Millicent, Princess (also named for Patricia, but now too small to be a hamlet) and Rosemary.

In 1914 the Princess became honourary Colonel of the Princess Patricia's Canadian Light Infantry, a position she held for the rest of her life.

Peace River

Town on Highway 2, approximately 152 kilometres northeast of Grande Prairie

Princess Patricia of Connaught, Colonel-in-Chief of Princess Patricia's Canadian Light Infantry, inspects the regiment in England, 1919. NATIONAL ARCHIVES OF CANADA PA-139714

The Peace River—the Mighty Peace—flows into the province from Fort St. John, British Columbia, and cuts across northern Alberta to Wood Buffalo National Park, where it empties into the Slave River, itself a tributary of the Mackenzie, which flows north to the Beaufort Sea. The Peace River figures large in the history of the fur trade, and it was near the site of present-day Peace River, at its confluence with the Little Smoky River, that fur trader Alexander Mackenzie of the North West Company established Fort Fork in 1792. The Peace River lends its name to the town as well as to the district—a latter-day frontier, transformed by railways and settlers in the first three decades of the 20th century—and to the pioneer trail by which it was accessed before the rails arrived. The river takes its name from the Peace Point, near Lake Athabasca, where around 1792 the Beaver and Knisteneux (Cree) settled a dispute.

The Peace River Crossing post office opened in 1905, and in 1914 part of what had become known as Peace River Landing Settlement was incorporated as the village of Peace River Crossing. The name was simplified to Peace River in 1916, and in 1919 Peace River became a town. The Central Canada Railway reached Peace River in 1916.

Ferry at Peace River Crossing, 1909. En route to Grande Prairie in 1909, D.C. Cranston and his outfit cross the Peace River by ferry at the appropriately named Peace River Crossing. The community's name was simplified to Peace River in 1916. GLENBOW ARCHIVES NA-488-3

Peerless Lake

Hamlet on Secondary Highway 686, approximately 156 kilometres north of Slave Lake

This hamlet was named for the adjacent lake, itself named in 1912 for its unrivalled beauty.

Peers

Hamlet on Highway 32, approximately 30 kilometres northeast of Edson

In its tradition of naming railway points in alphabetical order, the Grand Trunk Pacific Railway chose this name in 1911 to honour Sir Charles Peers Davidson (1841–1929), Chief Justice of the Superior Court of Quebec from 1912–1915. During World War I, Davidson was a member of commissions related to purchasing and other wartime matters.

Pelican Point

Hamlet south of Highway 53, approximately 12 kilometres southeast of Bashaw

This descriptive name, in use as early as the 1930s, referred to a point near shallow water where pelicans gathered. The feature was officially named in 1979, and this hamlet shares the name.

Penhold

Town on Highway 2A, approximately 15 kilometres south of Red Deer

Both the post office and the Calgary and Edmonton Railway (C&E) station adopted this name in 1891. It was likely selected by Osler, Hammond and Nanton, the firm that administered the C&E's real estate subsidiary and named many of the townsites along the line. In response to a government query in 1905 about the name's origin, the postmaster replied, "The name Penhold, as a number of other names along the C&E Railway, is Scotch being the name of a hamlet in one of the counties of Scotland."[164] If this is true, then the original Penhold is too small a hamlet to appear on the map, or its name has changed. Other stories told about the name are that it refers to animal pens near the railway station or that a railway official dropped his pen and it stuck in the map—hence "pen hold." Penhold was incorporated as a village in 1904 and as a town in 1980.

Peoria

Hamlet east of Highway 733, approximately 35 kilometres northeast of Grande Prairie

Peoria, Illinois—the hometown of feminist pioneer Betty Friedan, the launching point of Abraham Lincoln's political career and a farm machinery manufacturing centre—is the probable namesake for this northern hamlet, where a post office opened in 1928.

Perryvale

Hamlet east of Highway 2, approximately 30 kilometres southwest of Athabasca

Yorkshire-born Thomas Lewis (1860–1946) worked as a shepherd and stonemason before emigrating to Canada along with his wife, Elizabeth, and their children in 1888. After homesteading at Gibbons, the Lewises moved north to the Athabasca Trail, where they took over the Spring Creek Stopping Place (a short distance east of modern Perryvale) in 1907. Until the railway arrived in 1913, stagecoaches operating between Edmonton and Athabasca stopped at the Lewises for meals, to change horses and to drop off the mail. Thomas was appointed postmaster in 1913, but the post office took the name Perryvale instead of the locally used Lewiston—possibly because there was already a Lewiston in Nova Scotia. The name evidently came from the district's other pioneer family, the Whiteleys. William Eusby Whiteley (1861–1941) and his wife, Martha, also came from England and operated a stopping house, and William succeeded Thomas Lewis as postmaster in 1916. Perryvale is reportedly named for William's brother in London, Charles Perry Whiteley.[165] *Vale*, meaning valley, evokes the hamlet's setting.

Pibroch

Hamlet west of Highway 44, approximately 12 kilometres north northwest of Westlock

Pibroch, a type of bagpipe music, became the name of the post office when it opened at this Scottish settlement in 1910. The Edmonton, Dunvegan and British Columbia Railway named its station Debney, for engineer Philip Debney, but the name Pibroch stuck.

Pickardville

Hamlet west of Highway 44, approximately 10 kilometres south of Westlock

William Pickard (died 1933) homesteaded just east of the present hamlet in 1906 and opened the Pickardville post office the following year. He remained its postmaster until 1914.

Picture Butte

Town on secondary highways 519 and 813, approximately 20 kilometres north of Lethbridge

This once-descriptive name has been rendered anachronistic through road and street construction that has nearly eliminated the "beautiful hill" for which the town was named. The Siksika (Blackfoot) called his feature *anatskim-ikway* ("the beautiful hill") or *ist-sanatshimek-ay* ("that beautiful hill that can be seen from afar").[166] A Canadian Pacific Railway branch line arrived in 1925. Picture Butte was incorporated as a village in 1943 and as a town in 1960.

Pigeon Lake, Village at

Hamlet on Highway 13, approximately 35 kilometres west of Wetaskiwin

Established as a subdivision in 1997, the name of this hamlet on the south shore of Pigeon Lake was supplied by its developer. The lake itself was named by 1858. Pigeon Lake Creek, Pigeon Lake Reserve #138A and Pigeon Lake Provincial Park share the name.

Pincher Creek

Town on Highway 6, approximately 85 kilometres west southwest of Lethbridge

Various accounts differ in their details, but a single event explains this name: a pair of pincers, a tool used for gripping, left behind near a

Schofield and Hyde's general store, Pincher Creek, 1885. James Schofield opened Pincher Creek's first store in 1883 and became its first postmaster in 1884. His partner, Harry Hyde, became Pincher Creek's first banker and succeeded Schofield as postmaster. GLENBOW ARCHIVES NA-1602-8

creek. Prior to 1880, when the name appears in surveyors' reports, a member of a surveying party or a group of prospectors left a pair of pincers at the creek now known as Pincher Creek. In one version, the item was quickly retrieved; in another, the rusty pincers were discovered years later by the North-West Mounted Police. According to a third story, the men were captured by natives, and searchers found the pincers in the men's final campsite. The word *pincer* became *pincher,* describing the tool's function, and the creek's name was adopted by the post office in 1884. Pincher Creek became a village in 1898 and a town in 1906.

Pincher Station

Hamlet on Highway 3, approximately 84 kilometres west southwest of Lethbridge

The Canadian Pacific Railway (CPR) never reached Pincher Creek, so the nearest station, approximately five kilometres to the north, became Pincher Station. To promote the townsite, the CPR originally referred to Pincher Station as Pincher City.

Pine Lake

Hamlet on Secondary Highway 816, approximately 28 kilometres southeast of Red Deer

The hamlet takes its name from the adjacent lake, once known as Ghost Pine Lake. According to a native legend, the howling of the dead who fell in battle can be heard through the pine trees at night. The Pine Lake post office opened in 1895.

Pine Sands

Hamlet north of Highway 37, approximately 32 kilometres northwest of St. Albert

The name of this hamlet on the south shore of Sandy Lake is evidently descriptive.

Pinedale

Hamlet north of Highway 16, approximately 22 kilometres east of Edson

The origin of this hamlet's name is unknown, but may simply be descriptive. The post office opened in 1931.

Pipestone

Hamlet east of Secondary Highway 795, approximately 30 kilometres west northwest of Wetaskiwin

The name refers to the argilite stone used by natives to make pipes.

Plamondon

Hamlet on Secondary Highway 858, approximately 25 kilometres west northwest of Lac La Biche

This former village was named for homesteader Joseph Plamondon (1861–1923), its first postmaster (1909–14). The original name, Plamondonville, was shortened in 1915. Though his family's Quebec roots dated back to the 17th century, Plamondon himself came from Michigan. He is buried in Plamondon's St. Isidore Roman Catholic Cemetery. Plamondon became a village in 1965, but later reverted to hamlet status.

Pollockville

Hamlet on Secondary Highway 876, approximately 87 kilometres south-east of Drumheller

Rancher Robert Pollock (1873–1941) became the first postmaster in 1910 and held the post until his death. Ida Maude Pollock succeeded him and remained postmistress until 1949.

Ponoka

Town on Highway 2A, approximately 37 kilometres south southwest of Wetaskiwin

Early residents hoped that Siding 14 on the Calgary and Edmonton

Railway, constructed in 1891, would become Yescabba. But the townsite and station became Ponoka, from the Blackfoot *ponokaii* ("elk"). For many Albertans, Ponoka has become synonymous with the psychiatric hospital established near the town in 1911. Ponoka was incorporated as a village in 1900 and as a town in 1904.

Poplar Ridge

Hamlet west of Highway 22, approximately 1.6 kilometres west of Drayton Valley

This hamlet's name describes the plentiful poplar trees in the area.

Priddis

Hamlet on Highway 22, approximately 28 kilometres southwest of Calgary

After an initial visit to the district in the 1880s, looking after a survey party's horses, Ontario-born Charles Priddis came back to the Fish Creek area to homestead. He remained for the rest of his life. Though he never married, Priddis strongly supported the local school: the first classes were held in his house, and Priddis donated land for the construction of a schoolhouse. He served as the area's first postmaster, (1894–97). Priddis Creek shares the name.

Priddis Greens

Hamlet on Highway 22, approximately 14 kilometres southwest of Calgary

This descriptively named hamlet is a housing development near Priddis Creek. The name was likely provided by the developer.

Provost

Town on Highway 13, approximately 105 kilometres south southwest of Lloydminster

Among its other meanings found in the *Concise Oxford Dictionary*, *provost* means "the head of a municipal corporation or burgh." It is the Scottish equivalent of "mayor," and Provost's street names are also Scottish in character. The Canadian Pacific Railway named this station in 1907. Provost became a village in 1910 and a town in 1952.

Purple Springs

Hamlet on Highway 3, approximately 67 kilometres east of Lethbridge

The name is taken from a coulee nearby, itself descriptively named for its springs and the purple flowers that grew there.

Queenstown

Hamlet west of Secondary Highway 842, approximately 85 kilometres southeast of Calgary

The name is traditionally explained as the choice of a surveyor named Captain Dawson, who used the name of his hometown of Queenstown (now Cobh), Ireland, and promoted the location to settlers. Perhaps this was Simon James Dawson (1820–1902), a surveyor and civil engineer born in Banffshire, Scotland. In the 1850s Dawson surveyed in the area between Lake Superior and Red River (in what is now southern Manitoba), and his work resulted a decade later in the Dawson Route, an all-Canadian passage to Red River that remained in use until the transcontinental Canadian Pacific Railway (CPR) was completed. His connection to Queenstown (either one of them) remains unknown. The Queenstown post office opened in 1908. (The original Queenstown, incidentally, was the final port of call for the *Titanic*.) The CPR's Suffield branch arrived in 1925.

Radway

Hamlet south of Highway 28, approximately 15 kilometres north northeast of Redwater

Born in Berlin, Wisconsin, homesteader and merchant Orlando Samuel Radway (1858–1925) moved to what is now Alberta in 1894, and in 1908 Orlando, his wife, Melvina, and their children settled in the present Radway district. Orlando travelled frequently to Fort Saskatchewan to get mail and supplies, and in 1910 he opened the Radway Centre post office. He retired as postmaster in 1918 and, in 1925, "he finished a meal, pushed back his chair and died quietly of a heart attack."[167] Canadian National Railways evidently simplified the name to Radway when it arrived in 1918–19, and the post office followed suit in 1928.

Rainbow Lake

Town on Highway 58, approximately 132 kilometres west of High Level

Incorporated as a new town in 1967—two years after a major oil discovery in the area—this town near the province's northwest corner was named for nearby Rainbow Lake, itself named either because of its shape or else for Rainbow Fournier, an area trapper in the late 1800s. In the Beaver, Cree and Slavey languages, the names for this feature translate as "Long Lake."

Rainbow Lake was one of several communities incorporated between 1956–1967 under the New Town Act. Oil discoveries led to the creation of instant boomtowns, and the New Town Act was intended to smooth the development of local government and infrastructure.[168]

Rainier

Hamlet west of Highway 36, approximately 90 kilometres northeast of Lethbridge

Settlers poured into this dry southern country in the years following World War I, once the Canadian Pacific Railway had developed an irrigation infrastructure. Many came from the American northwest, and it was evidently their presence that influenced the name—the same as it had for Mount Rainier and the town of Rainier in Washington state. Captain George Vancouver named the mountain after Rear Admiral Peter Rainier.

Ralston

Hamlet on Secondary Highway 884, approximately 40 kilometres northwest of Medicine Hat

Lawyer, Liberal politician and World War I veteran James Layton Ralston (1881–1948) served as Prime Minister W.L. Mackenzie King's defence minister (1926–30 and 1940–44), with a brief stint as finance minister (1939–40). Colonel Ralston's support for overseas conscription during World War II brought him into conflict with King, who is credited with Canada's most famous equivocation: "Conscription if necessary, but not necessarily conscription." Ralston was established by the Defence Research Board (DRB) in 1949 to house personnel of the

Suffield research establishment. It was named at the suggestion of G.W. Dunn of the DRB. Ralston is adjacent to the board's Suffield Experimental Station.

Ranfurly

Hamlet on Highway 16, approximately 27 kilometres east southeast of Vegreville

Through the Ranfurly Shield, symbolic of rugby championship in New Zealand, Sir Uchter John Mark Knox (1856–1933), 5th Earl of Ranfurly, is probably better remembered in the South Pacific than he is in his native Scotland or in Ranfurly, Alberta. (Many Canadians probably recall Lord Stanley or Earl Grey for their sports trophies to the same extent.) Ranfurly served as governor of New Zealand from 1897–1904. The Canadian Northern Railway established and named this townsite in 1905. The village of Ranfurly was incorporated in 1929 and dissolved in 1946.

Raymond

Town on Highway 52, approximately 25 kilometres south of Lethbridge

Long before a "bubbling crude" turned poor mountaineer Jed Clampett into a Beverly Hillbilly, Jesse Knight and his family in Utah lived "poor as church mice" until Jesse discovered gold and struck it rich.[169] "Uncle Jesse" became a prominent member of the Church of Jesus Christ of Latter-day Saints, and his son Oscar Raymond (Ray) Knight (1872–1947) attended Brigham Young University in Provo. In 1901 Jesse, along with sons Raymond and William, bought a township and a half of land near Cardston, an important Mormon settlement. They established massive ranching and sugar beet operations and built a pioneer sugar factory. Settlers from Utah flocked to the townsite that Jesse donated and named for Raymond. According to one source, Jesse stipulated that the town could never have a liquor store, or else the deed would be rescinded and the land would return to the Knight family.[170] Cattle prices plummeted after World War I and the Knights lost their lands and sugar factory to the banks. Ray continued to work as a ranch manager. He was an accomplished calf and steer roper and once performed for the Prince of Wales (the future King Edward VIII). The

Raymond Stampede, first held in 1902 (a full decade before its more famous Calgary counterpart), was Ray Knight's brainchild and was reportedly one of the first such events held in Canada.

Rancher Jesse Knight, pictured here, donated this townsite and named it for his son Raymond. The Raymond Stampede was Ray Knight's brainchild. COURTESY OF JESSE KNIGHT

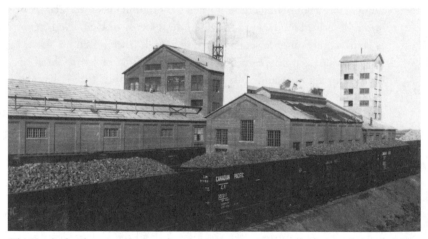

The Knight family owned the Canadian Sugar Factory at Raymond. Natives who worked there referred to the town as eetiyah-pinowukop, *Blackfoot for "where we make sugar."* CALGARY PUBLIC LIBRARY PC63

Red Deer

City on highways 2, 2A and 11, 150 kilometres south of Edmonton and 145 kilometres north of Calgary

Ross Street, Red Deer, pre-World War I. Ross Street was named for James Ross (1848–1913), a Canadian Pacific Railway construction manager involved in development of the Calgary and Edmonton Railway in 1890–91. The same view taken a few years later would show the cenotaph with its soldier figure facing the railway station, heading for home—Red Deer. CALGARY PUBLIC LIBRARY PC1086

The glacier-fed Red Deer River flows across central Alberta—and through the city that bears its name—before joining the South Saskatchewan River just across the provincial boundary from Empress, Alberta. Red Deer's Waskasoo Creek and Waskasoo Park perpetuate the river's original Cree name, *was-ka-sioo*, meaning "Elk River." The area's plentiful elk reminded early explorers or fur traders of the red deer of their native Scotland. In 1882, Red Deer Crossing emerged as an important stopping place along the Calgary–Edmonton Trail. With the outbreak of Louis Riel's North-West Rebellion in 1885, Robert McClellan's stopping house at Red Deer Crossing was commandeered, fortified and garrisoned by a detachment of the 65th Mount Royal Rifles of the Alberta Field Force. It was commanded by Lieutenant J.E. Bedard Normandeau and became known as Fort Normandeau. The name Normandeau now applies to a northern suburb of Red Deer, where the alliterative street names include Nordegg Crescent. The Town of Deerford, surveyed and planned for the crossing site in the 1880s, was never realized. With the construction of the Calgary and Edmonton

Railway in 1891 the settlement moved to its present site seven kilometres downstream, on land donated by Methodist minister and colonization agent Reverend Leonard Gaetz (1841–1907). Gaetz Avenue and Gaetz Lake are named in his honour. Red Deer was established as an "unincorporated town"(equivalent to a village) in 1894, as a town in 1901 and as a city in 1913.

City of Red Deer debenture issued during World War I to help cover the city's growing debt. RED DEER ARCHIVES RG 11-2 BOX 2 FILE 5

Red Earth Creek

Hamlet east of Highway 88, approximately 143 kilometres north northeast of Slave Lake

This hamlet shares the name of a nearby creek, so called because of the red ochre along its banks. The post office opened in 1970.

Red Willow

Hamlet on Secondary Highway 850, approximately 17 kilometres north northeast of Stettler

Descriptive of red willows that grow in the area. The post office originally opened on another site in 1903 and from 1912–15 was known as Coralynn.

Redcliff

Town on the Trans-Canada Highway (Highway 1), approximately 10 kilometres northwest of Medicine Hat

This descriptive name was inspired by the red shale cliffs of the South Saskatchewan River. Incorporated as a village in 1910 and as a town in 1912, Redcliff is practically within sight of Medicine Hat.

Busses manufactured by the Redcliff Motor Company with the name "Redcliff" in stylized lettering on the grill. MEDICINE HAT ARCHIVES MUSEUM & ART GALLERY 154.2.5

Redland

Hamlet west of Secondary Highway 840, approximately 30 kilometres southwest of Drumheller

Redland is a descriptive name referring to the colour of the soil. The post office opened in 1914.

Redwater

Town on Highway 28, approximately 45 kilometres north northeast of Edmonton

Red ochre creates the distinct colour of the nearby Redwater River, for which this town is named. Explorer David Thompson identified it in his 1814 map as the Vermilion River, but it is not connected to the river that bears that name today. The post office was established in 1909, and Redwater moved to its present site when the Canadian Northern Railway arrived in 1918–19. The hamlet grew slowly until 1948, when the discovery of oil propelled Redwater to village status in 1949 and town status in 1950.

Reno

Hamlet east of Highway 2, approximately 32 kilometres southeast of Peace River

Possibly named for Reno, Nevada, itself named after Major-General Jesse Lee Reno, Union soldier killed in the American civil war. The Central Canada Railway established its station here in 1915.

Ribstone

Hamlet on secondary highways 610 and 899, approximately 44 kilometres east southeast of Wainwright

This hamlet was named for nearby Ribstone Creek, itself named long ago for a stone that looks like a person's ribs. The post office opened in 1914.

Rich Valley

Hamlet on Highway 33, approximately 30 kilometres south of Barrhead

The post office at Onion Prairie, as this fertile area was originally known, was descriptively named Rich Valley in 1907 at the suggestion of postmaster Erik Carlin's daughter.

Richdale

Hamlet on Highway 9, approximately 23 kilometres east of Hanna

Tradition says this name describes the area's soil quality, but it may be no coincidence that the first postmaster, from 1910–11, was Fred A. Richardson. Richdale became a village in 1914, but later reverted to hamlet status.

Ridgevalley

Hamlet south of Highway 43, approximately 60 kilometres east of Grande Prairie

Evidently a descriptive name, originally used by the school district in 1931. Ridgevalley became a hamlet in 1992.

Rimbey

Town on highways 20 and 53, approximately 48 kilometres northeast of Red Deer

The Rimbey brothers—Ben (1861–1946), Sam (1868–1952) and Jim (1865–1930)—left their Illinois home for Kansas, where they sojourned before moving in 1900 to what is now Alberta. The brothers and their families, along with their nephew Oscar Rimbey, homesteaded along the Blindman River, and their settlement became known as Kansas Ridge. James M. Cox opened a post office on Sam's homestead in 1903,

Samuel Rimbey around 1890, before he moved to Alberta from Kansas. Rimbey, along with his brothers, his nephew and their families, settled along the Blindman River in 1900.
Courtesy of Don Rimbey

and postal authorities reportedly rejected the name Kansas Ridge, but accepted Rimbey.[171] Jim Rimbey and his wife, Eva, moved back to the United States after a short time, but Ben and Louisa Rimbey, and Sam and Mary Rimbey, remained for the rest of their lives and are buried in the town that shares their name. Rimbey became a village in 1919 and a town in 1948.

Rivercourse

Hamlet on Secondary Highway 614, approximately 29 kilometres south of Lloydminster

The name Rivercourse dates back to the 1907 opening of the River Course post office, and the name is traditionally explained by the proximity of Blackfoot Coulee. The local centennial history book posed an alternate theory in 1967: that John Walker, who collected the mail before the post office opened, had suggested the name River's Court for an estate by that name in England.[172]

Riverview

Hamlet south of Secondary Highway 646, approximately 20 kilometres east southeast of Elk Point

This simple, descriptive name evokes the hamlet's view of the North Saskatchewan River.

Rivière Qui Barre

Hamlet on Highway 44, approximately 12 kilometres west southwest of Morinville

Lumbermen descriptively named the nearby river, in French, because it was too shallow for log drives. Xavier Cyre opened the post office here in 1895.

Robb

Hamlet on Highway 47, approximately 54 kilometres southwest of Edson

Scottish-born Peter Addison "Baldy" Robb (1887–1954) came to Canada as a child with his parents. As a young man he settled at Wolf Creek near Edson, where he took up ranching, freighting, guiding hunting parties and prospecting for coal. Robb freighted for the Grand Trunk Pacific Railway (GTP) when it pushed its main line past Wolf Creek on its way to the Pacific coast. Robb and his fellow prospectors made significant coal discoveries, and the area was developed when the GTP built its Coal Branch in 1912. The district took the railway branch line's name and came to include a number of coal mining towns, including Cadomin, Luscar, Mercoal, Mountain Park and Robb. The Coal Branch flourished for years, but declined in the 1950s with the advent of diesel locomotives.

Originally called Minehead, Robb was renamed in 1912 at the suggestion of William Rae, the area's Member of the Legislative Assembly. (The post office was named Balkan when it opened in 1922, for the Balkan Coal Company, but was renamed Robb in 1923.)

Aside from his coal interests, Robb was active in political campaigning—first for the Conservative party and later for the Liberals—and became an influential local figure. He eventually settled in Edmonton with his wife, Winifred.[173]

Rochester

Hamlet on Secondary Highway 661, approximately 30 kilometres north northeast of Westlock

Herbert Rochester was the secretary to Malcolm H. McLeod, the chief engineer and surveyor (and later general manager) of the Canadian Northern Railway (CNoR). Rochester's name was the CNoR's second choice for its townsite on the Tawatinaw River, laid out along the company's branch line built from Edmonton to Athabasca in 1913. Residents objected to the company's original suggestion—Ideal Flat.

Rochfort Bridge

Hamlet on Highway 43, approximately 10 kilometres southeast of Mayerthorpe

In its original location nearby, this settlement was called Wanekville, after postmaster Rudolph Wanek. In 1920 the office moved nearer the Paddle River, where Canadian National Railways (CNR) had built a massive wooden trestle bridge. The new post office was named for the area's first settler, Gustavus Cowper Rochfort (circa 1870–1934), who succeeded Wanek as postmaster in 1923. According to one account, postal authorities rejected "Rochfort" as too similar to Rockyford, but accepted the name once "Bridge" was added. One wonders if the alteration was inspired only by the nearby CNR trestle or if the town of Rochfort Bridge in County Westmeath, Ireland, was also a consideration. (Had the renaming tradition continued, Rochfort Bridge might have been named for its third postmaster, Grafton Thomas Dance.)

A veteran of the Boer War and World War I, Rochfort was remembered as "the best of all story-tellers." His father-in-law called him "that mad Irishman."[174] Rochfort and his family later moved to British Columbia.

Rocky Mountain House
Town on highways 11 and 22, approximately 75 kilometres west of Red Deer

The coalfields of Nordegg, some 85 kilometres west of this point, attracted both the Canadian Northern (CNoR) and Alberta Central railways to build lines through here from 1912–14. For its station name at this point, the CNoR revived an old name that had been out of use for more than three decades. Two old, ruined chimneys recalled Rocky Mountain House, a North West Company fur trade post that traced its origins to 1799. (The post was named for the Rocky Mountains.) The rival Hudson's Bay Company built its own Acton House, but after the two companies merged in 1821, only Rocky Mountain House remained in use. The chimneys are from the last of several Rocky Mountain House posts, this one built in 1864 and abandoned in 1875. The fort site, some distance upstream from the town, is now within the boundaries of Rocky Mountain House National Historic Site. Modern Rocky Mountain House became a village in 1913 and a town in 1939.

Rocky Rapids
Hamlet east of Highway 22, approximately nine kilometres north of Drayton Valley

This hamlet was descriptively named for the rapids in the nearby North Saskatchewan River. W.E. Jeffery opened this post office in 1909 and reportedly chose its name.

Chimneys at the ruins of Rocky Mountain House, a Hudson's Bay Company fort. The Historic Sites Commission's cairn is seen in the background. CALGARY PUBLIC LIBRARY PC1475

Rockyford

Village on Highway 21, approximately 42 kilometres southwest of Drumheller

This village's descriptive name, refers to a rocky point a short distance south of modern Rockyford, where native people historically forded Serviceberry Creek. The post office opened in 1914, and Rockyford was incorporated as a village in 1919.

Rolling Hills

Hamlet on Secondary Highway 875, approximately 75 kilometres west northwest of Medicine Hat

This descriptively named hamlet was populated in the 1930s, when the federal and provincial governments relocated drought-stricken farmers from devastated areas.

Rolly View

*Hamlet on Secondary Highway 623, approximately 13 kilometres east of
Leduc*

When this post office opened in 1939, it adopted the descriptive name
of the local school district. Rolly View became a hamlet in 1980.

Rosalind

*Village on secondary highways 609 and 854, approximately 15 kilometres
southwest of Daysland*

When this post office first opened in 1905, its was named for an amalgamation of East Lynne and Montrose, two local school districts. The
name of East Lynne was taken from the title of Ellen Wood's popular
Victorian novel *East Lynne* (1861). Rosalind was incorporated as a village
in 1966.

Rosebud

*Hamlet on Secondary Highway 840, approximately 25 kilometres south-
west of Drumheller*

The Siksika (Blackfoot) knew this area as *akokiniskway*, or "many rose-
buds," and the name adheres both to the Rosebud River and to this
hamlet. Before 1896 it was known as Grierson, for postmaster James
Grierson. The wild rose is Alberta's provincial flower.

Rosemary

*Village west of Secondary Highway 550, approximately 148 kilometres
southeast of Calgary*

Lady Rosemary Millicent Leveson-Gower (1893–1930) was the daughter
of the 4th Duke of Sutherland, who owned extensive property near
Brooks, and the wife of William Humble Eric Ward, the 3rd Earl of
Dudley. She was killed in an airplane crash in 1930. Rosemary is situat-
ed on the Canadian Pacific Railway's "royal line," where railway points
are named for royalty and nobility. Nearby Millicent was named for
Lady Rosemary Millicent's mother, Millicent Fanny St. Clair-Erskine.
Other place names along the line include Bassano, Empress, Iddesleigh,

Patricia and Princess. Rosemary's post office opened in 1919, and it became a village in 1951.

Welcome sign, 2002. COURTESY OF JOHN OLSON

Rosyth

Hamlet on Highway 13, approximately seven kilometres southeast of Hardisty

The Canadian Pacific Railway established its station here in 1909–10, and the post office opened in 1911. Both were named for Rosyth, a Scottish naval base northwest of Edinburgh.

Round Hill

Hamlet on Secondary Highway 834, approximately 22 kilometres northeast of Camrose

The name refers to a round-shaped hill to the west. The post office opened in 1904.

Rowley

Hamlet east of Secondary Highway 839, approximately 35 kilometres east northeast of Three Hills

When the Canadian Northern Railway located its stations along the new Edmonton–Camrose–Calgary line, it paid tribute to one of its chief creditors—the Canadian Bank of Commerce. Charles Walsh Rowley (1869–1944) worked for the bank from 1887–1932, when he retired as assistant general manager. Born in Yarmouth, Nova Scotia, Rowley worked in Ontario and British Columbia before his 1902 transfer to Calgary, where he opened and managed the bank's first branch in the city. He threw himself wholeheartedly into the city's life, supporting local colleges and the Young Men's Christian Association, joining the exclusive Ranchman's Club, and serving as president of the Board of Trade and the local Canadian Club. Rowley was transferred to Winnipeg in 1911, and in 1925 both Rowley and Reginald Arthur Rumsey—whose namesake hamlet lies about 12 kilometres from Rowley—became assistant general managers in Toronto. During his tenure, Rowley's signature appeared on the bank's $10 notes, which were legal Canadian tender. Like David B. Hanna (namesake for nearby Hanna) Rowley is buried in Toronto's Mount Pleasant Cemetery.

Charles Walsh Rowley, onetime Calgary bank manager and president of the Board of Trade. Courtesy of CIBC Archives

Rumsey

Hamlet on Secondary Highway 839, approximately 26 kilometres east of Trochu

The Wanderlust has lured me to the seven lonely seas,
  Has dumped me on the tailing-piles of dearth,
The Wanderlust has haled me from the morris chair of ease,
  Has hurled me to the ends of all the earth.

Robert Service, whose poetry captured the spirit of the Klondike, could well have found a model for "The Wanderlust" in peripatetic banker Reginald Arthur Rumsey (1875–1947). While he might well have been motivated more by career advancement than by the sense of adventure, Rumsey served the Canadian Bank of Commerce in New Orleans and New York in the 1890s, then—from 1899–1902, in the wake of the Klondike gold rush—in Dawson City and Whitehorse in the Yukon and in Skagway, Alaska.

"He was a veteran of the 'Trail of '98' era of the Yukon gold rush, where he came to know Robert Service," observed the Canadian Press when Rumsey died.[175] The difficulty with this story: by the time Service reached the Klondike, Rumsey was already gone. The bank transferred him to Innisfail in 1903, and the following year, when Service first moved to the Yukon, Rumsey was living in Moose Jaw, Saskatchewan.

Besides the supposed Rumsey connection, another legend links Robert Service to southern Alberta: Sam McGee (1867–1940), a road contractor who spent time prospecting for gold in the Klondike, is buried in nearby Beiseker. According to lore, Service met McGee in a northern bank, liked his name and asked if he could use it in a poem. *The Cremation of Sam McGee* became Service's best-known work, and urns of Sam McGee's "ashes" became a Yukon tourist souvenir. Sam McGee bought one himself.

In 1904 Rumsey became the first person in Moose Jaw to own an automobile—a one-cylinder Cadillac worth $800.[176] The same car was reportedly the first to arrive in Saskatoon when one of Rumsey's friends drove it there. Rumsey was transferred to Winnipeg in 1905 and returned to his native Ontario in 1911 as chief inspector in Toronto. In 1925 both Rumsey and Charles Walsh Rowley (namesake for nearby Rowley) were appointed assistant general managers in Toronto. In that capacity, Rumsey's signature appeared on the bank's $50 and $100 bills, which were legal Canadian tender. Rumsey retired in 1936 and is buried in the Necropolis Cemetery in Toronto. In naming this station for Rumsey, the Canadian Northern Railway honoured one of its chief creditors, the Canadian Bank of Commerce. The village of Rumsey was incorporated in 1919 and dissolved in 1994.

Rumsey's community hall was built in 1946. COURTESY OF MORRIS SANDERS

Rycroft

Village on highways 2 and 49, approximately eight kilometres south southeast of Spirit River

This community has its roots with the Spirit River post office established in 1905, and it shares a common origin with the nearby town of that name. Today's Rycroft and Spirit River parted ways when the Edmonton, Dunvegan and British Columbia Railway (ED&BC) arrived in 1916. The Spirit River post office relocated to the ED&BC's

Red and White Store in Rumsey, 1946. Red and White Stores were once a common sight in smaller Alberta centres. Courtesy of Shirley Corenblum

new Rycroft siding, while the railway's new Spirit River station to the west became the site of a new post office, appropriately named Spirit River Station. In 1920 the post office harmonized its names with those of the railway—sort of. Spirit River Station became the new Spirit River, while the old Spirit River was renamed Roycroft.

Why Roycroft? Namesake Robert Henry Rycroft (1872–1944) was alive and well and still living in the district. *Roycroft* was simply a spelling error. But by the early 1930s the Rycrofts had moved away, and both postal authorities and the local business community tried to persuade Northern Alberta Railways (successor to the ED&BC) to change its station's name to Rycroft. But the railway argued that its spelling was correct, citing the Geographic Board of Canada's *Place-Names of Alberta* (1928) as its authority.[177] The post office became Rycroft in 1931.

Born in Honolulu to English parents, R.H. Rycroft owned a Hawaiian sugar and coffee plantation when he met Helen Thommesen of Norway in 1906. They married five years later, honeymooned in British Columbia (where he saw snow for the first time) and took up ranching in the Peace River district. Robert became secretary-treasurer of the municipality, a trustee on the school board and a justice of the peace. His name was drawn from a hat. The Rycrofts left the area in 1925, settling in Dunvegan, Smoky Heights, then Teepee Creek, near Sexsmith. Robert died in 1944, the year Rycroft became a village.[178]

Ryley

Village on Highway 14, approximately 19 kilometres southeast of Tofield

After nearly a quarter century's service for the federal government, including the post of chief clerk of the Dominion Lands Branch, George Urquhart Ryley (born 1852) joined the Grand Trunk Pacific Railway (GTP) in 1905, becoming its land commissioner and chief townsite agent. As such he had a hand in naming many new centres along the line. The GTP established this station on its main line in 1908, and Ryley was incorporated as a village in 1910.

Saddle Lake

Hamlet on Secondary Highway 652 in the Saddle Lake First Nation Reserve, 26 kilometres west of St. Paul

Like the creek that flows through it and the First Nation reserve in which it is situated, this hamlet takes its name from nearby Saddle Lake. The name's origin is uncertain. Saddle Lake's post office first opened in 1893. Its most famous son was farmer Ralph G. Steinhauer (1905–87), Alberta's lieutenant-governor from 1974–79 and the first native person in Canada to hold a vice-regal position.

St. Albert

City on Highway 2, immediately northwest of Edmonton

When pioneer Catholic missionary Father Albert Lacombe (for whom the town of Lacombe was named) arrived in what is now Alberta in 1853, he took up residence at Lac Ste. Anne, a remote mission where he ministered to the Cree and learned their language. As the years passed he dreamed of forming a new mission near the Sturgeon River, some 14 kilometres northwest of Fort Edmonton. At a particular hilltop overlooking the Sturgeon, Lacombe believed he could preach to the Blackfoot as well as the Cree, tend to a growing number of Catholics, and develop a self-sustaining agricultural settlement for the Métis of the area. When Bishop Alexandre Taché visited Lac Ste. Anne in the winter of 1860–61, Lacombe brought his superior to inspect the hilltop location. *"Mon Père*, the site is indeed magnificent,"* Bishop Taché enthused. "I choose it for the new mission, and I want it to be called St. Albert, in honour of your patron."[179] Father Lacombe's patron saint was a 13th century German scholar and philosopher who had taught St. Thomas Aquinas.

Father Lacombe's log chapel, which was built on the exact spot Bishop Taché chose for it, still stands. Around it developed a Métis settlement that eventually grew into a village. Incorporated in 1899, the village of St. Albert became a town in 1904 and a city in 1977.[180] To the southeast, St. Albert's city limits are contiguous with the outskirts of Edmonton.

St. Edouard

Hamlet south of Highway 28, approximately 12 kilometres east of St. Paul

The area's two pioneer settlers were Edouard Côté and Edouard Labrie, and St. Edouard was presumably their patron saint. The post office opened in 1909.

St. Isidore

Hamlet south of Secondary Highway 688, approximately 11 kilometres east southeast of Peace River

St. Isidore (1090–1130) is the patron saint both of Madrid, Spain, and of all farmers. Postal authorities approved this post office name in 1964, even though the name had already been used in New Brunswick.[181] St. Isidore was the name saint of Msgr. Isidore Clut, a missionary of the Oblate order at this French Canadian settlement.

St. Lina

Hamlet east of Highway 867, approximately 35 kilometres north northwest of St. Paul

In 1911 the Mageau brothers—Lectande, Emile and Hormidas—brought their families from Ontario and settled northwest of St. Paul, Alberta. Lectande and his wife, Adele, opened a store, and Lectande became its first postmaster. The Mageaus sent a list of suggested names to the postal authorities, whose choice was St. Lina—proposed because Lina had been the name of a character in a book the Mageaus had lately read.[182] The Mageaus later moved to Mallaig, where Lectande again served as postmaster.

St. Michael

Hamlet north of Secondary Highway 637, approximately 13 kilometres northeast of Lamont

St. Michael, one of the seven archangels, became the name of a church built at this location. The post office took this name in 1923.

St. Paul

Town on Highway 28, approximately 115 kilometres east northeast of Edmonton

Modern St. Paul dates back to 1896, when it was founded by Father Albert Lacombe (for whom the town of Lacombe was named) as the mission of St. Paul des Métis and administered by Father J. Adéodat Thérien (for whom the hamlet of Therien was named). Both men were members of the Oblates of Mary Immaculate, a Roman Catholic missionary order that played a large role in Alberta's missionary field. St. Paul des Métis was located in the same area as the mission of St. Paul

Street in St. Paul des Métis (now St. Paul), n.d. The community began as a Roman Catholic mission in 1896 and adopted its present name in 1929. CALGARY PUBLIC LIBRARY PC487

des Cris, which had been established in 1866 but abandoned in 1874. The post office opened in 1899, and in 1912 St. Paul des Métis became a village. The name—which presumably honours the New Testament figure—was simplified to its present form in 1929. St. Paul became a town in 1936.

St. Vincent

Hamlet on Secondary Highway 881, approximately 18 kilometres north of St. Paul

Known to early trappers as *La Croupe au Chien* ("Dog's Rump"), this settlement became Denisville (for the patron saint of France) when its post office opened in 1911. It was renamed for nearby Vincent Lake in 1918. By one account, surveyor A.F. Cotton named the lake for his son Vincent.[183]

Sandy Lake

Hamlet on Secondary Highway 813, approximately 110 kilometres northeast of Slave Lake

This northern hamlet lies on the western shore of the descriptively named Sandy Lake.

Sangudo

Village on Secondary Highway 757, approximately 18 kilometres east southeast of Mayerthorpe

This settlement was originally known as Deep Creek, but its post office became Sangudo when it opened in 1912. One enduring theory, since dismissed as fiction, is that it was an acronym created by early settlers:

S Scott and Sutton, early settlers
A Albers, the first postmaster
N Nanton, hometown of Albers' wife
G Gusal, a pioneer
U United, characterizing the community
D Deep Creek, the original name and a nearby feature
O Orangeville, the first school

In 1977 Cecil Albers—son of original postmaster W.H. Albers—offered a more likely explanation: the name was a composite of two syllables chosen randomly from place names in the post office manual. This is compatible with a 1926 version of the story, which states that the name was a composite of two American place names, formed as a compromise to satisfy two groups of American settlers.[184]

Scandia

Hamlet west of Highway 36, approximately 83 kilometres northeast of Lethbridge

This name likely refers to Scandinavia, the original home of most of Scandia's settlers. There are other Scandias in Minnesota and Washington state; in Canada, Kindersley, Saskatchewan was originally known as Scandia. The post office at Scandia, Alberta, opened in 1924.

Schuler

Hamlet east of Highway 41, approximately 55 kilometres northeast of Medicine Hat

This hamlet was named for the first postmaster, Norman Banks (Tim) Schuler, who held the post from 1910–24. Nearby Schuler Lake shares the name.

Scotfield

Hamlet on Highway 9, approximately 42 kilometres east of Hanna

Scotfield was named for William John Scott, on whose land the hamlet is located. The post office opened in 1914.

Sedalia

Hamlet west of Highway 41, approximately 38 kilometres north northwest of Oyen

The post office opened by Elmer E. Coleman in 1911 took the name of Sedalia, Missouri, hometown of American musician Scott Joplin and of some of this hamlet's early residents.

Sedgewick

Town on Highway 13, approximately 80 kilometres east southeast of Camrose

Supreme Court of Canada justice Robert Sedgewick (1848–1906) died the same year the Canadian Pacific Railway built this branch line between Hardisty and Camrose. Sedgewick was born in Aberdeen, Scotland, but grew up in Nova Scotia and graduated from Dalhousie in 1867. He helped establish the Dalhousie Law School in 1883 and served as one of its first professors. As deputy minister of justice from 1888–1893, Sedgewick had a hand in creating the nation's first criminal code. Sedgewick was incorporated as a village in 1907 and as a town in 1966.

Justice Robert Sedgewick of the Supreme Court of Canada, 1905. Sedgewick helped establish the Dalhousie Law School. NATIONAL ARCHIVES OF CANADA E-94497

Seebe

Hamlet on the Trans-Canada Highway (Highway 1), approximately 21 kilometres east of Canmore

From the Cree *si-pi*, referring to the Bow River. Although this was not traditional Cree territory, the Cree language was the *lingua franca* of the fur trade.

Seven Persons

Hamlet on Highway 3, approximately 20 kilometres southwest of Medicine Hat

This hamlet is named for nearby Seven Persons Creek, a colourful name of uncertain origin. It likely refers to a battle between Blood and Cree, in which seven people were killed. The post office opened in 1903.

Sexsmith

Town on Highway 2, approximately 15 kilometres north of Grande Prairie

Sexsmith was named after David Carpenter Sexsmith (1871–1942), an Ontario Klondiker who first traveled through the district in 1898. After moving to Edmonton, Sexsmith returned in 1911 with his wife, Cliffe, and together acquired eight quarters of land. When the government established a post office in 1913, it chose a stopping place run by Kate Johnston, but named it for the earlier pioneer, who now ran another stopping place to the north at Beaver Dam.

When the Edmonton, Dunvegan and British Columbia Railway surveyed its grade in 1915, it bypassed the Sexsmith stopping place and subdivided a townsite five kilometres northwest. The new townsite, acquired from land owned by Benny and Hannah Foster, was first called Benville. But the Sexsmith post office was moved to Benville and brought with it the original name. The Sexsmith family later settled in Kelowna, B.C. Sexsmith, Alberta became a village in 1929 and a town in 1979.

Shaughnessy

Hamlet on Highway 25, approximately 18 kilometres north of Lethbridge

Besides his role as president of the Canadian Pacific Railway (CPR) from 1898–1918, U.S.-born Thomas George Shaughnessy (1853–1923) was president of the Cadillac Coal Company, whose mine site is now occupied by the hamlet of Shaughnessy. In 1916, during his tenure as CPR president, he became Baron Shaughnessy.

Sheerness

Hamlet on Secondary Highway 577, approximately 71 kilometres east of Drumheller

This coal mining hamlet was probably named for Sheerness, Kent, England. Its post office opened in 1910.

Shepard

Hamlet on Shepard Road, approximately one kilometre east of Calgary

From 1882–1883, Minnesota railway contractors Langdon and Shepard built the transcontinental line of the Canadian Pacific Railway (CPR) between Brandon, Manitoba, and the Rocky Mountains. The CPR named two stations directly east of Calgary—Langdon and Shepard—for its prairie contractors (see Shepard). The original Shepard station is gone, but its 1910 replacement was moved to Calgary's Heritage Park Historical Village in 1970.

Sherwood Park

Urban Service area within Stratchcona County on highways 14, 16 and 21, immediately east of Edmonton

Once reported to be the largest hamlet in the world, Sherwood Park would be a sizable Alberta city if its nearly 50,000 residents so chose. Founded in 1955 by developer John Hook Campbell (and originally known as Campbelltown), Sherwood Park was likely named by the developer to evoke the image of a forested idyll. The Robin Hood Association for the Handicapped draws its name from the association with Sherwood Forest in England.

Shouldice

Hamlet east of Secondary Highway 547, approximately 78 kilometres southeast of Calgary

Rancher and farmer James Shouldice (1850–1925) hailed from Ontario and moved west in 1901. He leased part of the Namaka Ranch, purchased another ranch (this future townsite) in 1911 and acquired the Critchley ranch west of Calgary in 1912. He donated part of the Critchley land—today's Shouldice Park—to the city of Calgary. The Shouldice post office opened the year of his death.

Sibbald

Hamlet on Highway 9, approximately 177 kilometres east of Drumheller

In 1911 the rails of the Canadian Northern Railway's branch line from Alsask, Saskatchewan, to Hanna, Alberta, reached the settlement of Madden just west of the Saskatchewan border. There was already another Madden in the province, so another name had to be chosen. According to legend, when the first passenger train stopped here briefly in 1913, the first person to debark was John Sibbald, a noted railway construction engineer.[186]

Skiff

Hamlet on Highway 61, approximately 80 kilometres southeast of Lethbridge

In an act of whimsy, this inland farming community was named for a type of small boat. The motif was continued with Bow Avenue, Stern Avenue, Rudder Street and Tiller Street. The post office opened in 1918. Skiff appears as a street name in the original plan for the village of Foremost.

Slave Lake

Town on highways 2 and 88, approximately 190 kilometres southeast of Peace River

The present name comes from nearby Lesser Slave Lake, itself derived from the Cree epithet for the area's earlier inhabitants, whom the Cree considered not so much "slaves" as "strangers." The post office established in 1908 was originally called Sawridge, for the descriptively named Sawridge Hill nearby. (It remains the name of the Sawridge First Nation, two Sawridge reserves and Sawridge Creek). The settlement was relocated and adopted its present name when the Edmonton,

Dunvegan and British Columbia Railway arrived in 1921. Slave Lake became a village in 1961 and a town in 1965.

Smith

Hamlet on Highway 2A, approximately 70 kilometres northwest of Athabasca

Named as it is for railway magnate Valentine Whitman Rathbone Smith (born 1878), this hamlet at the confluence of the Athabasca and Lesser Slave rivers had plenty of options for a dramatic name. Mirror Landing, as it was first known, was originally located on the north bank. Steamboat transportation and railway construction transformed it into a free-wheeling boomtown complete with bootleggers, gamblers and prostitutes.[187] In 1913 it was temporarily renamed Port Cornwall (for railway promoter James K. Cornwall), but when the community moved to the new railway townsite on the south bank, it was named for the general manager of the Edmonton, Dunvegan and British Columbia Railway (ED&BC). Valentine, Whitman or Rathbone would have been fine choices, but officials unimaginatively selected the manager's family name. An Oshawa-born civil engineer, Rathbone Smith moved west and helped build the Grand Trunk Pacific Railway, whose staff dubbed him "Trombone Smith" or "T-bone Smith."[188] Between 1913–1920, Smith served as general manager and chief engineer of three Alberta railways: the Alberta and Great Waterways, the Canada Central and the ED&BC.

Smoky Lake

Town on Highway 28, approximately 88 kilometres northeast of Edmonton

Smoky Lake is a translation from the Cree *kaskapatau sakahigan*, referring to a smoky appearance above the water that blurred the view of the opposite side. The Smoky Lake post office opened in 1909, and Canadian National Railways arrived in 1919. Smoky Lake became a village in 1923 and a town in 1962.

South Cooking Lake

Hamlet on Highway 14, approximately 29 kilometres west of Edmonton

Translated from the Cree *opi mi now wa sioo*, Cooking Lake east of Edmonton was historically a camping spot used by natives. This hamlet is located on the north shore.

Spedden

Hamlet on highways 28 and 36, approximately 33 kilometres west northwest of St. Paul

The origin of this name is uncertain, but it has been said that it either commemorates Robert Shedden, who died in 1849 searching for the remains of the Franklin expedition, or that a surveyor named Speddin died while the railway was under construction, and the hamlet is named for him. The original post office that opened in 1917, was called Cache Lake, but the name changed to correspond with the Canadian National Railways station, established in 1920.

Spirit River

Town on Highway 49, approximately 65 kilometres north of Grande Prairie

The name comes from the river, translated from the Cree *chepi-sepe* or *chepi-sipi* and refers to native legends associated with the river. The first Spirit River post office opened in 1905, but relocated to what is now Rycroft when the Edmonton, Dunvegan and British Columbia Railway arrived in 1916. Spirit River was incorporated as a village that year, and it became a town in 1951. Its post office was named Spirit River Station from 1916–1920.

Spring Coulee

Hamlet on Highway 5, approximately 45 kilometres southwest of Lethbridge

This hamlet named for a nearby coulee dates to 1902, when its post office opened. The descriptively named coulee was later renamed Pinepound Creek.

Spring Lake

Village south of Highway 16A, approximately 10 kilometres west of Stony Plain

Originally established in 1959 as the summer village of Edmonton Beach, Spring Lake was incorporated as a village in 1999 and renamed for the adjacent lake. The post office opened in 1926.

Springbrook
Hamlet west of Highway 2A, approximately six and a half kilometres southwest of Red Deer

This hamlet was developed on the former site of Canadian Forces Base (CFB) Penhold, first established during World War II as the Royal Canadian Air Force (RCAF) Manning Depot, a training centre for the British Commonwealth Air Training Plan. It was revived in 1951 as a North Atlantic Treaty Organization (NATO) Flying Training School. In 1990 CFB Penhold was reduced to a detachment of CFB Edmonton and finally decommissioned in 1995. The Permanent Married Quarters had been named Mynarski Park, for Pilot Officer Andrew Mynarski, awarded a posthumous Victoria Cross during World War II. Springbrook is a descriptive name, referring to the headwaters of Waskasoo Creek.

Spruce Grove
City on Highway 16, approximately 27 kilometres west of Edmonton

Ontario-born John Allan McPherson (1855–1944) came west in 1881 as a freighter, then homesteaded west of Edmonton in partnership with his friend Alexander McNabb. The area was dotted with groves of spruce trees, including a fine stand near McPherson's house. Most of these groves were removed when settlers broke the land for farming. McNabb opened the Spruce Grove post office on their farm in July 1894. After McNabb's death, McPherson married his friend's widow, Christine. When the Grand Trunk Pacific Railway reached Spruce Grove in 1908, the settlement moved a little over a kilometre to the west. McPherson became Spruce Grove's first Member of the Legislative Assembly in 1905 and represented the constituency as a Liberal for two terms. He later became the sheriff of Red Deer and finally settled in Vancouver. The village of Spruce Grove, incorporated in 1907, was dissolved in 1916 and re-formed in 1954. It became a town in 1970 and reached city status in 1986.

Spruceview

Hamlet on Highway 54, approximately 25 kilometres west northwest of Innisfail

Both the local school district, established in 1912, and Knud Knudson's homestead were named Spruce View. The hamlet adapted the name, which is evidently descriptive.

Stand Off

Hamlet on Highway 2, approximately 43 kilometres southwest of Lethbridge

Like Fort Whoop-Up, Robber's Roost, Slide-Out and Whisky Gap, this name inherited from American whisky traders reflects both dramatic and desperate times. Stand Off perpetuates the name of Fort Stand Off, an American whisky post built in 1871. The outlaws who built it had "stood off" a Montana sheriff who pursued them north to the Milk River, but he retreated when they pointed out that Canadian territory was beyond the American lawman's jurisdiction. The North-West Mounted Police adopted the name for their new post in 1882.

Standard

Village on Secondary Highway 840, approximately 43 kilometres south southwest of Drumheller

Like the hamlet of Ensign, this village is evidently named for a flag: the *Dannebrog,* the royal standard of Denmark. The Canadian Pacific Railway (CPR) facilitated the development of a Danish American colony on a 8,500-hectare land reserve in this district. This was part of the CPR's strategy to market its 10 million hectares of land in prairie Canada, which had been a grant from the federal government as an incentive to build the transcontinental in the 1880s. Colonists had first wanted to name the settlement Dana or Danaview, but the name had already been used by Dana, Saskatchewan. Standard became a village in 1922.

Stanmore

Hamlet on Highway 9, approximately 29 kilometres southeast of Hanna

The Canadian Northern Railway arrived here in 1912, and the post office opened the following year. Like the original Edmonton, Stanmore's namesake is in Middlesex, England, now part of greater London.

Star

Hamlet on Secondary Highway 831, approximately seven kilometres north of Lamont

Originally called Beaver Creek Crossing, postmaster Ed Knowlton named this post office in the 1890s for his daughter Edna. His successor recognized the possible confusion with Eden and Edina, and by 1899 requested a name change. Suggested alternatives included Beaver Knoll, Kitchener and Mulock, but all were rejected as being identical or nearly identical to existing place names. Local residents wanted the name Sifton, but a post office in Manitoba already had that name. Despite local objections, the name proffered by Reverend Arthur Whiteside, resident minister from 1896–97, was adopted in 1899: Star.[189]

Stavely

Town on Highway 2, approximately 78 kilometres northwest of Lethbridge

In 1882 British Member of Parliament and judge advocate of the Fleet Alexander Staveley Hill, Q.C. (1825–1905) took advantage of the Canadian government's large-scale ranching leases and established the Oxley Ranch in southern Alberta. He wrote *From Home to Home: Autumn Wanderings in the North-West, in the Years 1881, 1882, 1883, 1884,* which was published in London in 1885. Stavely was incorporated as a village in 1903 and as a town in 1912.

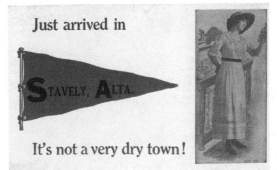

Novelty postcard from Stavely, n.d. Calgary Public Library PC 252

FROM HOME TO HOME:

AUTUMN WANDERINGS IN THE NORTH-WEST,

IN THE YEARS 1881, 1882, 1883, 1884.

BY

ALEX. STAVELEY HILL, D.C.L., Q.C., M.P.

ILLUSTRATED FROM SKETCHES BY MRS. STAVELEY HILL
AND PHOTOGRAPHS BY A. S. H.

"Survey our empire and behold our home."

SECOND EDITION.

LONDON:
SAMPSON LOW, MARSTON, SEARLE, & RIVINGTON,
CROWN BUILDINGS, 188 FLEET STREET.
1885.

Frontispiece of Alexander Staveley Hill's 1885 book, From Home to Home.

Around 1917 Hill's son wrote from England to Canadian postal and railway authorities, requesting that the missing 'e' be restored to the name Staveley. The secretary of the local Board of Trade wrote to the younger Hill, suggesting that if he pay to build a covered skating rink, the town would change the spelling of its name. Hill declined, and postmaster James Rea suggested that if any change were to be made, Stavely should drop the second 'e.'[190]

Novelty postcard from Stavely, n.d. CALGARY PUBLIC LIBRARY PC 251

Steen River

Hamlet on Highway 35, approximately 120 kilometres north of High Level

This hamlet takes its name from the Steen River, itself named for A.S. Steen, the cook on J.R. Akins' survey party in 1915. The post office opened in 1957.

Stettler

Town on highways 12 and 56, approximately 74 kilometres east of Red Deer

Carl Stettler (1861–1919), observed Reverend Martin W. Holdom in

1909, was "the stoutest man I've ever seen."[191] Born in Berne, Switzerland, Stettler sojourned in the United States before homesteading west of the present town in 1903. There he established the Blumenau Swiss German colony, which opened the Blumenau post office in 1905. With the arrival of the Canadian Pacific Railway (CPR) in 1905, Stettler moved the post office (renamed Stettler) to the new townsite, where he became the CPR land agent. He was elected to Stettler's first village council in 1906, and built the National and Cosmopolitan hotels. Stettler became a town in 1906.

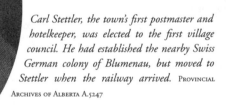

Carl Stettler, the town's first postmaster and hotelkeeper, was elected to the first village council. He had established the nearby Swiss German colony of Blumenau, but moved to Stettler when the railway arrived. PROVINCIAL ARCHIVES OF ALBERTA A.5247

Stirling

Village on Highway 4, approximately 30 kilometres southeast of Lethbridge

Stirling was named for British businessman John A. Stirling, managing director of a company that invested in the Alberta Railway and Irrigation Company, which built a narrow-gauge line between Lethbridge and Great Falls, Montana. Stirling became a village in 1901. Now a National Historic Site, Stirling is the best remaining example of the Mormon agricultural village pattern transplanted to southern Alberta from the United States. The spacious townsite pattern occupies 2.5 square kilometres, with the station outside the village.

Stony Plain

Town on Highway 16A, approximately 30 kilometres west of Edmonton

The traditional explanation for this town's name is that the Stoney people camped here historically. An alternative explanation comes from Dr. James Hector, a geologist on the Palliser expedition in the 1850s, who ascribed the name to the boulders he observed in the area. The present name was adopted in 1892 and in 1905 Stony Plain moved about three kilometres north, to its present site, when the Canadian Northern Railway arrived. It became a village in 1907 and a town in 1908.

Strathmore

Town on the Trans-Canada Highway (Highway 1), approximately 45 kilometres east of Calgary

In 1884, the Canadian Pacific Railway named this station on its transcontinental line for Claude Bowes-Lyon, 13th Earl of Strathmore (1824–1904). Fifty-five years later, his granddaughter—Queen Elizabeth, wife of King George VI—passed through Strathmore en route to Calgary as part of the Royal Tour of 1939. Strathmore was incorporated as a village in 1908 and as a town in 1911.

Streamstown

Hamlet south of Highway 45, approximately 20 kilometres northwest of Lloydminster

Reverend R. Smith suggested this name, after a town in Westmeath, Ireland, and it was adopted when the post office opened in September 1906.

Strome

Village on Highway 13, approximately 15 kilometres east southeast of Daysland

Max Knoll opened the first post office in 1905, and for one year the office was known as Knollton (although Knoll evidently called it Wavy City, at least unofficially).[192] When the Canadian Pacific Railway arrived in 1906, it was renamed Strome, believed to be for Stromeferry in Ross & Cromarty, Scotland. Strome became a village in 1910.

Sturgeon Valley

Hamlet east of Highway 28, approximately 18 kilometres north of Edmonton

Sturgeon Valley became a hamlet in 1985, and its name describes its position along the Sturgeon River.

Suffield

Hamlet on the Trans-Canada Highway (Highway 1), approximately 35 kilometres northwest of Medicine Hat

This hamlet began in 1883 as a Canadian Pacific Railway station on the railway's still-unfinished transcontinental line. One of the railway's backers had been banker Edward Charles Baring, 1st Lord Revelstoke. The station was named for Baring's brother-in-law Charles Harbord, 5th Baron Suffield (1830–1914). Nearby Canadian Forces Base Suffield shares the name.

Sundre

Town on Highway 27, approximately 77 kilometres southwest of Red Deer

In 1906, after a sojourn in Harvey, North Dakota, Norwegian émigrés Nels T. Hagen and his wife resettled in Alberta. Nels purchased a farm in the foothills, complete with a loghouse, from Alberta pioneer "Windy" Dave McDougall (the namesake for nearby McDougall Flats). The Hagens loaded their possessions on a wagon and travelled west from Olds. When they saw the desolate farmhouse, Mrs. Hagen told the drayman to leave everything on the wagon and resolved to go right back to North Dakota. But it was too late to return to Olds, and after a night on the farm, Mrs. Hagen changed her mind.[193] The Hagens opened a combined store, post office, dance hall and rooming house. Nels named the post office for his Norwegian birthplace, Søndre, meaning "south." Nels Hagen spent most of the rest of his life in Sundre, but moved to California in his final years. Sundre was incorporated as a village in 1949 and as a town in 1956.

Sunnybrook

Hamlet on Highway 39, approximately 27 kilometres west southwest of Calmar

Originally known as Stones Corners—presumably for A.I. Stone, who opened the post office in 1908—this creekside hamlet became Sunnybrook when the post office adopted the name in 1914. The name applies also to Sunnybrook Creek.

Sunnynook

Hamlet north of Secondary Highway 570, approximately 75 kilometres east southeast of Drumheller

Area settlers requested this optimistic, descriptive name. The post office opened in 1911.

Sunnyslope

Hamlet on Secondary Highway 582, approximately 20 kilometres west southwest of Three Hills

German-born postmaster Peter Giesbrecht, who held the post from 1903–1905, suggested *Sooniges Thale* "Sunny Valley," which was modified to Sunnyslope.

Swalwell

Hamlet west of Highway 21, approximately 16 kilometres south of Three Hills

When the Grand Trunk Pacific Railway's branch line from Tofield to Calgary reached Rawdonville in 1911, the railway company renamed the settlement for its Winnipeg auditor, James G. Swalwell. Both the origin of the name Rawdonville and the story of James Swalwell remain a mystery.

Swan Hills

Town on highways 32 and 33, approximately 75 kilometres southwest of Slave Lake

Following Home Oil's Swan Hills discovery in the late 1950s, the provincial government established a new town in 1959 in the midst of a northern forest, intended to house 1,500 oilfield workers and their families. It was one of several communities incorporated between 1956–1967 under the New Town Act. Oil discoveries led to the creation of instant boomtowns, and the New Town Act was intended to smooth the development of local government and infrastructure.[194]

An early suggestion for the town's name was Chalmers, after Thomas Chalmers, the Dominion Land surveyor who had cut a road though the Swan Hills six decades earlier. (Chalmers Avenue is named for him.) Instead, the town was named for Deer, House and Wallace mountains, some 30 kilometres to the west and collectively known as the Swan Hills. According to native legend, the birds that live in these hills had never been seen, but the flapping of their wings was heard as thunder. Swan Hills became a town in 1967.

Sylvan Lake

Town on Highway 11A, approximately 20 kilometres west of Red Deer

Natives and explorers knew the lake by a variety of names, including the Cree *wa-pi-sioo*, "Snake Lake," and Captain John Palliser's Swan Lake. By the dawn of the 20th century, people had begun camping by the

Owners, staff and guests gather outside the Sylvan Lake Hotel, 1923. Red Deer Archives P225-1

lake, and soon cottages started going up. Cottagers rejected the name Snake Lake and petitioned to change the lake's name to Sylvan (from the Latin *silvanus*, roughly meaning "of the woods").[195] The Sylvan Lake post office opened in 1907. The popular resort became a village in 1912 and a town in 1946.

Boating at Sylvan Lake, n.d. CALGARY PUBLIC LIBRARY PC1217

Taber

Town on Highway 3, approximately 40 kilometres east of Lethbridge

A persistent story about this name is that along with nearby Elcan (reverse of -nacle), it forms the word *tabernacle,* a nod to the district's prominent Mormon community. The post office opened in 1904 under the name Taber. However, both the village, incorporated in 1905, and its Canadian Pacific Railway station, were originally spelled Tabor and were reportedly named for the biblical Mount Tabor in Galilee.[196] When the village became a town in 1907, its spelling was changed to Taber. The surrounding municipal district, a provincial park and a nearby lake share the name. "Elcan" was probably someone's idea of a toponymic joke after the name Taber had been selected.

Taber's business district begins to take shape, n.d. CALGARY PUBLIC LIBRARY PC780

Taber Hotel and main street, n.d. CALGARY PUBLIC LIBRARY PC1204

Tangent

Hamlet on Highway 740, approximately 30 kilometres west northwest of Falher

As it passed between Culp, Watino and Tangent, the Edmonton, Dunvegan and British Columbia Railway took a sharp curve, nearly forming a loop. Westward from Tangent, however, the line followed a

56-kilometre tangent, or straight line, of track—and hence the name. The railway station at this point opened in 1916.

Tawatinaw

Hamlet east of Highway 2, approximately 29 kilometres northwest of Westlock

The Tawatinaw River flows though this eponymous village before reaching Tawatinaw Lake. The Cree word from which the name derives means "river which divides the hills." The post office opened in 1911.

Teepee Creek

Hamlet on Secondary Highway 674, approximately 30 kilometres north-east of Grande Prairie

Teepee, as the Sioux called their portable homes, became the generic term for aboriginal dwellings. The post office at this location took the name of a nearby creek when it opened in 1924.

Tees

Hamlet on Highway 12, approximately 27 kilometres southwest of Bashaw

When the Canadian Pacific Railway named its station here in 1905, it honoured the townsite's original owner—William E. Tees—instead of using the original post office name, Brook. Scottish-born brothers William (circa 1865–1929) and James Tees (1867–1955) emigrated with their parents to Iowa. In 1901 the brothers moved to central Alberta, where they ranched together until James moved to Clive in 1905. Will is buried in Lacombe, where he settled in 1912.

Telfordville

Hamlet south of Secondary Highway 622, approximately 52 kilometres southwest of Edmonton

The post office at Telfordville, opened in 1904, was named for Robert T. Telford (1860–1933), pioneer of nearby Leduc. Born in Quebec, Telford came west with the North-West Mounted Police in 1885 and settled with his wife in 1889 on the present Leduc townsite. Leduc pioneer C.H. Stout described Telford's significance:

> He was the first homesteader with his land containing all of Leduc for many years; was the first hotelman, first postmaster, first merchant, first sawmill operator, first lumberman, first justice of the peace, first mayor of the village, first school trustee, first real estate operator, first undertaker and, with the formation of the province in 1905, first member of the legislature for Leduc riding which he represented ten years…. It used to be when you thought of Leduc you thought of Telford, or it might be the other way round—when you thought of Telford you thought of Leduc.[197]

Thérien

Hamlet near Highway 881, approximately 28 kilometres north of St. Paul

In 1896, concerned by the corrupting influence of white society on the Métis people, Father Albert Lacombe (for whom the town of Lacombe was named) reestablished the defunct settlement of St. Paul des Métis (later renamed St. Paul) as a Métis enclave. Lacombe recruited his fellow member of the Oblate order, Reverend J. Adéot Thérien (1862–1936), to administer the colony. Despite Thérien's efforts, the second colony eventually met the fate of the original as its Métis settlers dispersed to other centres. This hamlet, located 28 kilometres north of Thérien's colony, adopted his name when its post office opened in 1909.

Thorhild

Village on Highway 827, approximately 24 kilometres north of Redwater

The childhood home of actor Leslie Neilsen and his brother Erik, who served as deputy prime minister in the 1980s, was reportedly named for the Norse god of strength, thunder and war. According to lore, Uno Glen Jardy's pioneer post office, a few kilometres east of the present village, was built on a hilltop frequently struck by lightning. In Norse mythology, lightning was created when Thor hurled his hammer in battle. Jardy called the hill Thor's Hill and styled the post office as the more Scandinavian-sounding Thorhild. It was incorporated as a village in 1949. The surrounding county shares Thorhild's name.

Thorsby

Village on Highway 778, approximately 49 kilometres southwest of Edmonton

Original postmaster August Sahlstrom hailed from Torsby, Sweden, and was one of many Scandinavians who settled this community. As with Thorhild, the name's origin lies with Thor, the son of Odin in Norse mythology. It was incorporated as a village in 1949.

Three Hills

Town on Highway 583, approximately 75 kilometres southeast of Red Deer

Arrayed northwest to southeast, the three hills that give this town its name can be seen to the west of Highway 21 and lie outside the town limits in Kneehills County. The Blackfoot-speaking people knew these hills as *nioka-etomox*, the Cree as *nis-to* and the Stoney as *ha-amni*. Besides the town, the name of this feature has also shifted to Threehills Creek, across which one of the province's oldest buffalo trails once passed. Three Hills became a village in 1912 and a town in 1929.

Three Hills Town Hall, circa 1915. The three hills for which the town are named lie outside its corporate limits. Calgary Public Library PC 1205

Thunder Lake

Hamlet west of Highway 18, approximately 21 kilometres west of Barrhead

This hamlet takes its name from the nearby shallow lake, so named by aboriginal people for the thunderous sound when its ice cracks.

Tilley

Village on Secondary Highway 876, approximately 83 kilometres northwest of Medicine Hat

Before the national holiday was renamed Canada Day in 1982, Dominion Day might have had special resonance in this farming village northwest of Medicine Hat. Sir John A. Macdonald, Canada's first prime minister, favoured calling the new nation the Kingdom of Canada. Others objected, fearing that the American republic to the south would resent a "kingdom" on its borders. Sir Leonard Tilley (1818–96), premier of New Brunswick and one of the Fathers of Confederation, suggested an alternative. From a line in Psalm 72—"His dominion shall be from sea to sea"—Tilley proposed the Dominion of Canada, and the term stuck. As the federal finance minister between 1878–85, Tilley reluctantly supported the Canadian Pacific Railway (CPR). Hence it seems more likely that, when the railway company established Tilley Station (later renamed Tilley) in 1884, it was not to honour Sir Leonard, but rather his brother, CPR director Sir Malcolm Tilley. Tilley became a village in 1940.

Tillicum Beach

Hamlet west of Highway 56, approximately 16 kilometres southeast of Camrose

The name for this hamlet along Driedmeat Lake was probably supplied by the developer.

Tofield

Town on Highway 14, approximately 57 kilometres east southeast of Edmonton

Yorkshire-born James H. Tofield (1840–1918) studied engineering at

Oxford, earned a medical degree and worked at St. George's Hospital in London before emigrating to Canada, where he arrived at Fort Edmonton in 1882. During the North-West Rebellion in 1885, Tofield served as an army doctor, and the small field hospital he established was the first military hospital in what is now Alberta.[198] Around 1893 Tofield settled southwest of Beaverhill Lake, where he strongly supported establishing a school district in the nascent community. Once formed, the school district was named Tofield, and in 1898 the local post office followed suit. (It was originally named Logan, for pioneer rancher Robert Logan.) The name falls neatly into the Grand Trunk Pacific Railway's alphabetical array: Ryley, Shonts, Tofield, Uncas although Deville spoils the sequence.

Tofield was incorporated as a village in 1907 and as a town two years later. Dr. Tofield died in September 1918, only weeks before the worldwide Spanish influenza pandemic, when his services would have been most needed. Both Dr. Tofield and his wife, Annie, are buried in Tofield Cemetery.

Dr. James H. Tofield established Alberta's first military hospital during the North-West Rebellion in 1885. The local school district was named for him, followed by the post office, railway station and municipality. Provincial Archives of Alberta B.8529

Tomahawk

Hamlet on Highway 759, approximately 24 kilometres north northeast of Drayton Valley

Before he settled southwest of Wabamun Lake, Ontario-born Lewis Shaw (1869–1950) had worked in lumber camps in Minnesota and Wisconsin. It was he who suggested the place name Tomahawk, after the city of Tomahawk, Wisconsin. The post office opened in 1907.

Torrington

Hamlet on Highway 27, approximately 26 kilometres west northwest of Three Hills

The Canadian Pacific Railway named this hamlet, possibly for the market town in Devon, England, where the renowned Rosemoor Gardens are a major tourist attraction. Since it opened in 1996, Alberta's Torrington has been known for its Gopher Hole Museum, where anthropomorphic dioramas showcase the rodent that farmers love to hate. Even the fire hydrants in Torrington are painted to look like Richardson's groundsquirrels, and a 3.66-metre-tall statue of the village mascot, Clem T. Go-Fur, attracts visitors from the highway. Torrington became a village in 1964, but has since reverted to hamlet status.

Travers

Hamlet east of Highway 845, approximately 60 kilometres north of Lethbridge

Teenage and pre-teen fans of Francine Pascal's Sweet Valley High books would be interested to know there once was a Sweet Valley, Alberta. When the post office opened in 1915, the name changed to Travers, but who or what Travers was has been forgotten.

Trochu

Town on Highway 21, approximately 62 kilometres south southeast of Red Deer

In 1905 a group of French cavalry officers settled in Alberta and established the St. Ann Ranch Trading Company. The group was led by

Colonel Armand Trochu (1857–1930), nephew of the Paris governor who had defended the city in the Franco-Prussian War of 1870–71. Trochu opened the eponymous Trochu Valley post office in 1906, and Trochu (as the village was incorporated in 1911) began to develop as a French, not French Canadian, settlement. With the outbreak of World War I in 1914, many of the French officers returned to fight for their mother country. Trochu himself returned in 1917, although in poor health. Trochu became a town in 1962.

Armand Trochu, left, and fellow settlers at the St. Ann ranchhouse, 1905. Trochu returned to his native France in 1917. Glenbow Archives NA-3018-38

Trout Lake

Hamlet on Secondary Highway 686, approximately 157 kilometres north of Slave Lake

The hamlet of Trout Lake is adjacent to a lake named Graham Lake, the hamlet's namesake is probably an unofficially named body of water in the area. The post office opened in 1973.

Tulliby Lake

Hamlet on Secondary Highway 641, approximately 52 kilometres east southeast of Elk Point

This small hamlet lies between Tulabi Lake to the north and the North Saskatchewan River to the south. It is named for the tullibee or cisco fish, a herring in Alberta's northern lakes. The post office opened in 1935.

Turin

Hamlet on Highway 25, approximately 35 kilometres northeast of Lethbridge

In 1908 the local school district was named for Turin, an imported Percheron stallion purchased by a group of eight area farmers. The names of cities were a popular choice in naming purebred horses. The Italian city of Turin is widely famed for the shroud housed in its St. John the Baptist Cathedral, which some argue is the burial shroud of Jesus. The post office opened in 1910, and the townsite was surveyed in 1925. The hamlet took the name of the school district.

Turner Valley

Town on Highway 22, approximately 40 kilometres south southwest of Calgary

For decades before the Leduc discovery in 1947, the name that epitomized Alberta's petroleum industry was Turner Valley. Scottish-born cousins Robert Turner (1861–1951), John Archibald Turner (1867–1935) and James Turner homesteaded near Millarville in 1887 and ran stock on lands in the valley (running south to the South Fork of the Sheep River) that became known as Turner's Valley. They imported and bred cattle and Clydesdale horses.

The Turner Valley post office opened in 1891. In May 1914 the discovery of oil and natural gas (including naphtha gas, natural gasoline) by the Dingman No. 1 well heralded Alberta's first petroleum boom and immortalized the Turner name. Turner Valley became a village in 1930 and a town in 1977.

James Turner left the area in 1894 for lands at Turner Siding south of Calgary, and moved later to Ontario. John and his wife, Williamina (Minnie), moved in 1904 to a ranch adjacent to the Sarcee Reserve next to Calgary. They later moved into Calgary and finally to Victoria. Robert and his wife, Catherine, moved to Okotoks, where they operated the Bar T Ranch, retiring to West Vancouver, where Catherine Turner lived to the age of 101.

Discoveries in 1914 and 1936 made the name Turner Valley synonymous with Alberta's oil industry.
CALGARY PUBLIC LIBRARY PC840

Twin Butte

Hamlet on Highway 6, approximately 90 kilometres southwest of Lethbridge

Two buttes—now separated by the highway—inspired the name for the local school district, organized in 1904. A post office opened under this name in 1905, and it moved to the present site two years later.

Two Hills

Town on Highway 45, approximately 117 kilometres east northeast of Edmonton

Before the Canadian Pacific Railway arrived in 1927–28, explains long-time resident Steve Miskiw, farmers from this area hauled their grain all the way to Vegreville, some 50 kilometres away. In the winter they travelled along the frozen Vermilion River, and on the return trip, two landmark hills signalled they were home. Fur trader Alexander Henry had stopped here in 1808 and referred to these hills as *les Deux Grosse Buttes*. Nearly a century after Henry's visit, another Henry—Henry Pozer—opened a post office and called it Pozerville. Mercifully, the present name was adopted in 1913. Two Hills became a village in 1929 and a town in 1955. The two hills lie southwest of the town limits in the County of Two Hills.

Valhalla Centre

Hamlet on Highway 59, approximately 42 kilometres northwest of Grande Prairie

In 1912 Lutheran pastor Halvor N. Ronning (1862–1950), a Norwegian-born missionary who had spent years in China, established a Scandinavian settlement in the south Peace River country. He called the settlement Valhalla, for the heavenly dwelling of the Norse god Odin and the destination of the souls of slain heroes. A post office named Valhalla opened a few kilometres away in 1916. When Ronning's brother-in-law Olaf Horte opened a nearer post office in 1923, it took the name Valhalla Centre.

Valleyview

Town on highways 34 and 43, approximately 111 kilometres east of Grande Prairie

Before 1929 this settlement was known as Red Willow, for nearby Red Willow Creek. It was reportedly farmer Oscar Adolphson who suggested the descriptive name Valleyview when the post office opened in 1929, and the name was officially adopted. North from Valleyview, Highway 43 eventually leads to the Mackenzie Highway. To the west, Highway 34 leads to the Alaska Highway. Valleyview became a village in 1955 and a town in 1957.

Vauxhall

Town on Highway 36, approximately 68 kilometres northeast of Lethbridge

This settlement had its origins as a camp of the Canada Land and Irrigation Co. Ltd., formed in London in 1906. In an apparent move to attract investment, it was named for a London suburb, once famed as the site of the Vauxhall Pleasure Gardens mentioned in William Makepeace Thackeray's *Vanity Fair*. Vauxhall was incorporated as a village in 1949 and as a town in 1961.

Vegreville

Town on highways 16 and 36, approximately 95 kilometres east of Edmonton

Vegreville's giant pysanka symbolizes its population's Ukrainian heritage. Hans-Ludwig Blohm, National Archives of Canada PA212539

Father Valentin Végréville (1829–1903), an Oblate missionary who mastered three native languages, served in the west for 50 years but never at the town that bears his name. He visited Batoche during the North-West Rebellion of 1885 and was briefly taken prisoner by Louis Riel's provisional government. The local post office established in 1895 was first known as Poulin, for original postmaster Eugene Poulin. The settlement and post office relocated a short distance to the northeast when the Canadian Northern Railway built its main line through the district in 1905. Vegreville became a village in April 1906 and was incorporated as a town four months later. Populated early on by French-speaking Roman Catholics from Kansas, Vegreville eventually became a largely Ukrainian Canadian community. Its giant *pysanka*, or Easter egg, was unveiled in 1978.

Veinerville

Hamlet on Highway 41A, just east of Medicine Hat

This hamlet is named for Saskatchewan-born Harry Veiner (1904–91), a Jewish farmer, businessman and philanthropist who served as mayor of Medicine Hat from 1952–66 and 1968–74. He was invested in the Order of Canada in 1982.

Vermilion

Town on Highway 41, approximately 57 kilometres west of Lloydminster

Red clay deposits in the Vermilion Lakes and Vermilion River provide the colour that inspired this name, translated from the Cree *wiyaman*. The main line of the Canadian Northern Railway arrived in 1905, and that year the post office opened. First known as Breage, for a Cornish village, it was renamed for the Vermilion River in 1906. Vermilion became a village in February 1906 and a town six months later.

Veteran

Village on Highway 12, approximately 26 kilometres east southeast of Coronation

This was one of several stations on the Canadian Pacific Railway's new Lacombe–Kerrobert branch named in 1911 to honour the coronation of

Vermilion Town Hall, circa 1911. The community was originally known as Breage. CALGARY PUBLIC LIBRARY PC787

King George V, which also included Fleet, Consort, Coronation, Loyalist and Throne, and possibly also Federal and Monitor.[199] In this context, Veteran refers to "those who have long been in the service of the British crown."[200] The post office was called Wheat Belt from 1910–1913. Veteran became a village on June 30, 1914—a significant date in retrospect, because it came two days after the assassinations in Sarajevo that triggered World War I and produced many, many more veterans.

Viking

Town on highways 14 and 36, approximately 70 kilometres east northeast of Camrose

Norwegian immigrants established this settlement and influenced the post office name, adopted in 1904. The main line of the Grand Trunk Pacific Railway reached Viking in 1908, and the following year it became a village. It was incorporated as a town in 1952.

Main Street in Viking, circa 1914. CALGARY PUBLIC LIBRARY PC493

Village at Pigeon Lake

See Pigeon Lake, Village at

Villeneuve

Hamlet on Highway 44, approximately 27 kilometres northwest of Edmonton

Lawyer, librarian and newspaper editor Frédéric-Edmond Villeneuve (1867–1915) arrived in St. Albert in 1898, and that year he set up a law practice, became the founding editor of *Ouest-canadien*, an Edmonton-based journal, and won election to the North-West Territories legislature as a Conservative. It was during his term that the new post office here adopted his name. Villeneuve returned to his native Montreal in 1902.[201]

Vilna

Village on highways 28 and 36, approximately 36 kilometres east of Smoky Lake

In 1919 forces from the newly independent Poland entered Lithuania to expel the Soviets, and again in 1920 Polish forces entered the Baltic state and occupied Vilna—the Polish form of Vilnius, the modern

Lithuanian capital. The Polish version was adopted in Alberta with the establishment of a Canadian National Railway station and the Vilna post office. The name is traditionally explained to have been the choice of Vilna's east European settlers. Vilna, Alberta, became a village in 1923 and since 1993 has boasted the world's largest mushrooms, a 6.10 metre tall steel sculpture set in Mushroom Park.

Vimy

Hamlet off Highway 2, approximately 17 kilometres southeast of Westlock

In April 1917, after both British and French efforts had failed, the Canadian Corps attacked and seized Vimy Ridge, a strategic position in northern France that formed part of the Germans' Hindenburg Line. Despite the battle's heavy price—nearly 3,600 Canadian dead—it was the nation's most stunning victory of World War I and it inspired lasting pride. Only weeks later Beart Benoit opened this post office. The Canadian Northern Railway had originally called its siding here Burrows in 1912 and later renamed it Dunrobin before adopting the name Vimy in 1917.[202]

Vimy Ridge memorial in France, 1988. Dunrobin, Alberta, was renamed Vimy shortly after the battle of Vimy Ridge in 1917. AUTHOR'S COLLECTION

Violet Grove

Hamlet north of Secondary Highway 620, approximately eight kilometres southwest of Drayton Valley

This hamlet's name describes the area's many violets. The post office opened in 1934.

Vulcan

Town on Highway 24, approximately 85 kilometres south southeast of Calgary

"When Vulcan, god of fire and patron saint of blacksmiths, pointed thunderbolts for Jupiter at the crater of Mount Etna," observed the *Vulcan Review* in 1912, "he was engaged in no grander occupation than are the people of the modern town of Vulcan who are making two blades grow where none grew before, and developing a grain belt and business centre that is phenomenal even for Alberta."[203] Vulcan was established with the construction of the Canadian Pacific Railway's Kipp–Aldersyde line, and townsite lots were sold in 1910. Street and avenue names in Vulcan originally included Apollo, Atlas, Juno, Jupiter, Mars, Neptune and Vulcan. They were later changed to numbers, but

Elevator Row in Vulcan, 1928. Vulcan was a major centre both for both the production and shipping of wheat. Glenbow Archives ND-8-219

the town readopted them in 1998 for Vulcan's 85th anniversary. Vulcan later embraced a Star Trek motif, capitalizing on the name of Mr. Spock's home planet. A starship model similar to the U.S.S. *Enterprise* greets motorists from the highway. The tourist centre is called the Vulcan Trek and Tourist Station, and Vulcan's annual rodeo has been termed Spock Days. Vulcan was incorporated as a village in 1912 and as a town in 1921.

Baseball teams provided boosters with an opportunity to promote their town and its reputation. Southern Alberta teams like Vulcan's would have included both local players and American talent that had been recruited. CALGARY PUBLIC LIBRARY PC544

Wabamun

Village south of Highway 16, approximately 65 kilometres west of Edmonton

In 1903 Wabamun post office opened on the north shore of Wabamun Lake, whose name comes from the Cree word for "mirror." The name has also shifted to Wabamun Creek, two Wabamun native reserves and Wabamun Lake Provincial Park. The original village of Wabamun, incorporated in 1912, was dissolved in 1946 and returned to the municipal district of Stony Plain. Its records, sadly, were destroyed in 1930, when the home of R.C. Kirkpatrick, village secretary-treasurer and justice of the peace, burned to the ground. The present village dates from 1980.

Wabasca–Desmarais

Hamlet west of Secondary Highway 754, approximately 90 kilometres northeast of Slave Lake

The Wabasca river took its name from the native *wapuskau*, possibly a Cree term for a body of water with whitecaps. The post office that opened in 1908 on the eastern shore of North Wabasca Lake adopted the name. The Wabasca native reserves, as well as South Wabasca Lake, share the name. The hamlets of Wabasca and Desmarais merged in 1982. Desmarais had been named for Father Alphonse Desmarais (1850–1940), who had visited the nearby Wabasca Settlement in 1891. The Desmarais post office opened in 1927.

Wagner

Hamlet north of Highway 2, approximately 18 kilometres northwest of Slave Lake

The Edmonton, Dunvegan and British Columbia Railway named this station in 1914 for one of its engineers.

Wainwright

Town on highways 14 and 41, approximately 75 kilometres southwest of Lloydminster

In its original 1906 location on what would become the site of the Wainwright Regional Training Area, this post office and settlement was first known as Denwood. Grand Trunk Pacific Railway (GTP) executive William Wainwright (1840–1914) made frequent trips to the area when the company built its main line through the province in 1908. That year Denwood's residents pulled up stakes and resettled on the nearby railway townsite, which the GTP named for its fourth vice-president. Born in England, Wainwright worked as a clerk for the Manchester, Sheffield and Yorkshire Railway before emigrating to Canada in 1862. In his 52 years with the Grand Trunk and Grand Trunk Pacific railways, Wainwright rose from chief clerk in the accounting office to senior vice-

William Wainwright, acting president of the Grand Trunk Railway System, 1912. The Wainwright Star eulogized him as the town's "best friend on the railway board". National Archives of Canada PA-213784

president of both railway systems. Wainwright died in Atlantic City, New Jersey, where he had travelled to recuperate from ailing health, and is buried in Mount Royal Cemetery in Montreal. The entire GTR and GTP network ground to a brief halt to mark Wainwright's passing.[204] His death was felt locally as well, for Wainwright's interest in the town lasted long after its establishment. "It was fitting that the town should observe the death of so prominent a benefactor by flying flags at half mast," opined the *Wainwright Star,* "for his loss may not be felt here until some future time when railway officials are in a position to favor it in some way, and when that time comes Wainwright will not have its best friend on the railway board to speak for it."[205]

Grand Trunk Pacific Railway train in Wainwright, 1909. When the railway bypassed Denwood, Alberta, its residents pulled up stakes and moved to the new railway townsite. Calgary Public Library PC61

Wainwright was incorporated as a village in 1909 and as a town the following year. To the general public, the name Wainwright was once inseparable from the adjacent Buffalo National Park and its massive bison herd. During World War II, however, the disease-ridden animals were either destroyed or relocated, and the national park was dismantled and replaced by Canadian Forces Base Wainwright.

Walsh

Hamlet on the Trans-Canada Highway (Highway 1), approximately 45 kilometres east of Medicine Hat

After cutting his military teeth in Fenian raids of 1866, Prescott, Ontario, native James Morrow Walsh (1840–1905) joined the newly formed North-West Mounted Police in 1873. He recruited men for the force, led them in their Great Trek across the prairies in 1874 and, with the rank of Inspector, established and named Fort Walsh in what is now Saskatchewan. His command took on an international character in 1876. Following Custer's defeat at the Battle of the Little Bighorn in present-day Montana, Sitting Bull and his Sioux followers crossed the Canada–U.S. boundary. Walsh handled the tense situation gracefully and befriended Sitting Bull during his four-year sojourn while encouraging him to lead his people back to the United States. Walsh left the force in 1883, but returned during the Klondike gold rush, when he

North-West Mounted Police Inspector James Morrow Walsh, commander of Fort Walsh, deftly handled a tense international situation when Sitting Bull and his Sioux followers entered Canada after the Battle of the Little Bighorn in 1876. Walsh later served as commissioner of the Yukon Territory.
GLENBOW ARCHIVES NA-1771-1

served briefly as commissioner of the Yukon Territory in 1897–98. This station on the Canadian Pacific Railway's transcontinental line was established in 1882–83 and named for the fort.

Wandering River

Hamlet on Highway 63, approximately 58 kilometres north northwest of Lac La Biche

This hamlet is named for the nearby river, whose name describes its meandering path. The post office opened in 1932.

Wanham

Hamlet north of Highway 49, approximately 69 kilometres north northeast of Grande Prairie

As with several place names along the former Edmonton, Dunvegan and British Columbia Railway, Wanham was named in 1918 by office engineer Ben James Prest (1883–1967). Prest was born in Richmond, Surrey, England, and evidently drew on its geography in naming such places as Wanham (Wonham in England), Woking and Surbiton (a former railway point later renamed Bracburn, located between Woking and Grande Prairie). For years Prest kept detailed diaries of his railway work. Had they survived, they might have yielded the mysteries of toponymy along what became the Northern Alberta Railways. Sadly, Prest's widow discarded them after his death.[206] The village of Wanham, incorporated in 1958, was dissolved in 1999 and returned to Birch Hills County as a hamlet.

Warburg

Village on Highway 39, approximately 50 kilometres southwest of Edmonton

Swedish émigrés settled this area around 1906, and when the post office was established a few years later, they requested the name Varberg, for a town in their home province of Halland. Postal authorities obliged, but changed the spelling. Warburg became a village in 1953.

Wardlow

Hamlet east of Secondary Highway 876, approximately 115 kilometres northwest of Medicine Hat

This name was evidently chosen by Canadian National Railways for its station in 1920, but is of uncertain origin. By one tradition, Wardlow was the daughter of James R. Sutherland, Dominion Land and Timber agent at Calgary, who had an interest in an irrigation project here. (Sutherland's daughters were Marjorie, Catherine and Eva.[207]) By another tradition, Wardlow was the gathering place of the Cameron clan in Scotland.

Warner

Village on highways 4 and 36, approximately 60 kilometres southeast of Lethbridge

This village was originally known as Brunton Siding when a narrow gauge railway—known as the Turkey Track Trail because of its meandering route—was constructed. It was renamed in 1906 for Alfred L. Warner, a Minneapolis land agent who encouraged Dakota farmers to resettle here in conjunction with the Alberta Railway and Irrigation Company. Warner became a village in 1908.

Warspite

Hamlet on Highway 28, approximately 10 kilometres west of Smoky Lake

At the suggestion of its second postmaster, E.R. Powell, the Smoky Lake Centre post office was renamed Warspite in 1916, to honour HMS *Warspite,* a British dreadnought battleship that had recently participated in the Battle of Jutland during World War I. Known as "the Old Lady," *Warspite* served in both world wars and sank in 1947 while being towed for scrap. In Alberta, a mountain, falls and creek are also named for *Warspite.* The post office moved to the new Canadian National Railways townsite in 1919, and Warspite became a village in 1951. Mount Warspite in the Kananaskis was named for the ship in 1922.

Waskatenau

Village on Highway 28, approximately 22 kilometres west of Smoky Lake

The Cree term from which this village's name derives—"opening in the banks"—describes a cleft in the ridge through which the Waskatenau Creek flows into the North Saskatchewan River. Canadian National Railways arrived in 1919, and that year the Waskatenau post office opened. Waskatenau became a village in 1932.

Water Valley

Hamlet on Secondary Highway 579, approximately 32 kilometres south of Sundre

This evidently descriptive name was first used in the 1920s by the school district and became the new post office's name in 1937. According to lore, when the school opened the teacher asked students to write down their suggestions and place them in a hat. Student Bernice Howard supplied the winning name.

Waterton

Hamlet on Highway 5, approximately 50 kilometres south of Pincher Creek

Following his travels and explorations in Antilles, the United States and South America (and even once riding an alligator), naturalist and conservationist Charles Waterton (1782–1865) retired to his estate in West Yorkshire, where he established what is said to have been the world's first nature reserve. Waterton never set foot in Canada. Fellow naturalist Thomas Blakiston (1832–91), a lieutenant in the Royal Artillery, admired Waterton and branded his name indelibly in southern Alberta. As part of the Palliser expedition that explored western Canada in the 1850s, Blakiston gave his hero's name to a chain of lakes in what is now Waterton Lakes National Park. The post office that opened in 1915 is called Waterton Park; the townsite is known simply as Waterton. Blakiston's name survives through Blakiston Creek, Blakiston Falls and Mount Blakiston, all within the national park.

Tourist facilities at Waterton Lakes National Park were largely developed in 1920s, and this dance hall was one of many new recreational amenities. In 1932 the park became part of the Waterton–Glacier International Peace Park, dedicated by U.S. President Herbert Hoover. CALGARY PUBLIC LIBRARY PC1207

Watino

Hamlet on Highway 49, approximately 98 kilometres northeast of Grande Prairie

Before the Edmonton, Dunvegan and British Columbia Railway arrived in 1915, a cable ferry crossed the Smoky River at Pruden's Crossing. The railway and its new bridge drew people from Pruden's Crossing to the new settlement of Smoky, on the river's west side. It was reportedly two railway agents—A.P. "Bert" Bott of Smoky and Frank Eagan of Enilda—who chose a new name to replace Smoky, a common element in area place names. Watino was reportedly formed by shortening the Cree word for "valley."[208]

Watts

Hamlet on Secondary Highway 855, approximately 11 kilometres west of Hanna

Sometime in the 1970s, a woman from Toronto showed up in this former village to see the place that had been named for her father, a onetime Canadian Northern Railway official.[209] The name had previously been thought to have honoured an early resident. The woman's name went unrecorded, but the 1914 Toronto city directory lists Charles E. Watts, an engineer with Canadian Pacific—the wrong railway. Watts, Alberta, came into being when the CNoR built its Saskatoon–Calgary branch in 1914.

Wayne

Hamlet on Highway 10x, approximately 10 kilometres southeast of Drumheller

History is a precious commodity in any ghost town, which by definition has a past far more dramatic than any possible future. The walls of the historic Rosedeer Hotel— named for one of the area's once-thriving coal mines— are lined with photographs and memorabilia of Wayne's colourful past as a teeming collection of coal mining camps. The Canadian Northern Railway arrived in 1914 and provided this name, but its origin is a mystery.

Wedgewood

Hamlet west of Resources Road, directly south of Grande Prairie

Wedgewood was created in 1989 as a controlled district with strict covenants within the county of Grande Prairie. It is adjacent to Grande Prairie and uses city water and services. The name was evidently provided by the developer.

Welling

Hamlet on Highway 5, approximately 24 kilometres south of Lethbridge

In 1904 officials of the Church of Jesus Christ of Latter-day Saints organized a branch west of Raymond and agreed unanimously to name it for Job Welling of Farmington, Utah. Job's son, civil engineer Horace Welling, had moved to Alberta in 1902 and homesteaded near the future site of this hamlet's railway station. Horace returned to Utah in 1910 and married. Though he loved Alberta, his wife would not move here, and they remained in the Beehive State.

Welling Station

Hamlet on Highway 5, approximately 21 kilometres south of Lethbridge

The Canadian Pacific Railway did not pass through Welling. This railway hamlet, being the nearest station to Welling, was named Welling Station.

Wembley

Town on Highway 43, approximately 19 kilometres west of Grande Prairie

When the Edmonton, Dunvegan and British Columbia Railway (ED&BC) pushed west from Grande Prairie in 1924, it bypassed the existing settlement of Lake Saskatoon and established a new townsite some eight kilometres to the south. It was reportedly the Lake Saskatoon Board of Trade that chose a new name for the settlement: Wembley, for the London suburb famed at the time as the venue of the British Empire Exhibition in 1924–25. Perhaps the best-known legacy of that exhibition is Wembley Stadium, which soccer icon Pele once termed the "Church of Football." The name was reportedly suggested by Ben Prest, an ED&BC engineer who drew on the geography of his native Britain in choosing names for railway centres in Alberta. For years, Prest kept detailed diaries of his railway work; had they survived, they might have yielded the mysteries of toponymy along what became the Northern

Northern Alberta Railways employee Ben Prest named Wembley, among other communities in northern Alberta. He is the namesake for Prest Creek and for Prestville, a tiny community that is no longer on the map. COURTESY OF GORDON PREST

Alberta Railways. Sadly, Prest's widow discarded them after his death. Wembley was incorporated as a village in 1928 and as a town in 1980.

Westerose

Hamlet on Highway 13, approximately 40 kilometres west of Wetaskiwin

Swedish army veteran John Norstrom and his wife, Johanna, arrived in the Pigeon Lake area in 1906, a few months after their son, Axel. During their first year in the area, John regularly walked to Falun to bring the mail. When the local post office opened in May 1907, it was named for the Norstroms' hometown of Vasterås, a city northwest of Stockholm. (Edmonton Oilers goalie Tommy Salo formerly played hockey in Vasterås, which is also the birthplace of Detroit Red Wings defenceman Nicklas Lidstrom.) Axel Norstrom's home served as a stopping house and church before the Westerose Gospel Church was built.

Westlock

Town on highways 18 and 44, approximately 75 kilometres north northwest of Edmonton

In its original location a few kilometres to the east, this post office was first called Edison. The current name dates from 1912, when the present townsite was acquired from two local families, the Westgates and the Lockharts. The Lockharts moved away early on, but Quebec-born William Westgate (1853–1918) and his wife Esther (died 1927) remained in Westlock for the rest of their lives, and are buried in Hazel Bluff Cemetery. Westlock was incorporated as a village in 1916 and as a town in 1947.

Westward Ho

Hamlet on Highway 27, approximately 16 kilometres east southeast of Sundre

The title of an historical adventure novel by British clergyman Charles Kingsley, published in 1855, provided the name for this hamlet. (The novel is partly set in Devon, England, where another town also took the name of Kingsley's novel and where Rudyard Kipling attended school as a boy.) Westward Ho was suggested by Captain Thomas, an early settler who had served in the British army. Perhaps this was Turberville Thomas, who homesteaded along the Red Deer River south of Westward Ho in 1906.

Wetaskiwin

City on Highway 2A, approximately 63 kilometres south of Edmonton

When the Calgary and Edmonton Railway (C&E) reached the Peace Hills area south of Edmonton in 1891, the company designated its station unimaginatively as Siding 16, marking its position as the sixteenth station north of Calgary. At the invitation of Sir William Cornelius Van Horne—president of the Canadian Pacific Railway, which operated the C&E—Father Albert Lacombe (for whom the town of Lacombe was named) reportedly chose names for a handful of the numbered sidings.[210] For Siding 16, Lacombe chose Wetaskiwin, commemorating the Cree *wi-ta-ski-winik*, meaning "place of peace." In the Blackfoot language it is *inustisti-tomo*, "peace hills." The name refers to an incident that took place around 1860 on a hill north of what is now Wetaskiwin. A band of Blackfoot on way south from a hunt camped on the north side of the hill. At the same time, a band of Cree were camped on the south side. The Cree and Blackfoot had a history of warfare, but each camp sent a chief to meet on a hilltop where they smoked a pipe of peace together. But the peace agreement was short lived, and it took until 1867 before the two groups agreed to a permanent peace.[211] Wetaskiwin was incorporated as a village in 1899, as a town in 1902 and as a city in 1906.

Whitecourt

Town on Highway 43, approximately 158 kilometres west northwest of Edmonton

In 1908 former Kansas Governor John Whitlah Leedy (1849–1935) and his extended family moved from Alaska to the growing Alberta settlement of Sagitawah (from the Cree *sak-de-wah*, meaning "where the waters come together"), which was becoming more commonly known as McLeod River Flats. While in Alaska the former governor served as mayor of Valdez, and it was there that his daughter Alice met and married an army medical orderly named Walter E. White. When the family moved to Alberta, Walter White became the mail carrier, bringing the mail from Green Court, some 40 kilometres away. By 1909 residents applied for a post office of their own, but before they could meet to choose a name, they learned it had been named Whitecourt. "This office was probably named after me," White explained to the chief geographer of the Department of the Interior in 1904, "or my name may have had something to do with the naming, although the intention in naming it was to make it conform with 'Green Court'."[212] Settlers who had been there longer than White resented the name, and many would have preferred the name Saquatemau, using an aboriginal word believed to mean "big bird," referring to the pattern of merging streams that looked like an eagle's foot. Whitecourt was incorporated as a village in 1959 and as a new town in 1961. It was one of several communities incorporated between 1956–1967 under the New Town Act. Oil discoveries led to the creation of instant boomtowns, and the New Town Act was intended to smooth the development of local government and infrastructure.[213] Whitecourt became a town in 1971.

Whitelaw

Hamlet on Highway 2, approximately 20 kilometres east northeast of Fairview

J.D. McArthur's Central Canada Railway, built through the Peace River country, established this station in 1924 and named it for car service accountant Wilkie T. Whitelaw of Edmonton.

Whitford

Hamlet on Highway 45, approximately 32 kilometres southeast of Smoky Lake

In the 1890s much of the population in this lakeside Métis settlement was related, and two-thirds—including the second postmaster—shared the same family name: Whitford. Both the hamlet and the lake were named for the Whitfords. By World War I most of the family had died or moved away. The Canadian Pacific Railway bypassed Whitford in 1927 and created the railway village of Willingdon.

Widewater

*Hamlet north of Highway 2, approximately 18 kilometres northwest of
Slave Lake*

Widewater is a descriptively named hamlet south of the very wide
Lesser Slave Lake, established in 1914 as a station along the Edmonton,
Dunvegan and British Columbia Railway.

Wildwood

Hamlet on Highway 16, approximately 38 kilometres south of Mayerthorpe

In 1929 Wildwood was known as Junkins. Resident Horace Thompson
judged the name unattractive. A petition was soon circulated to have it
changed, and citizens were asked for suggestions. Thompson favoured
Cloverdale, but the final choice, proffered by Ruby Lord, was
Wildwood, which described of the area's bushy character.

Willingdon

*Village on Highway 45, approximately 97 kilometres east northeast of
Edmonton*

Freeman Freeman-Thomas, first Marquess of Willingdon (1866–1941),
served as governor of Bombay and Madras in India before he became

Governor-General and Lady Willingdon visit Waterhole, 1928. Glenbow Archives NA-3564-12

Canada's thirteenth governor-general since Confederation, a post he held from 1926–31. When the Canadian Pacific Railway built its Edmonton to Lloydminster line in 1927, it bypassed the existing community of Whitford and established a new railway settlement named for the governor-general. Willingdon became a village in 1928. Viscount Willingdon, as Freeman-Thomas was eventually styled, later served as viceroy of India.

Wimborne

Hamlet on Secondary Highway 805, approximately 25 kilometres west of Trochu

This hamlet was probably named for the town in Dorset, in southern England, where novelist Thomas Hardy once lived. The post office opened in 1909.

Winfield

Hamlet on highways 13 and 20, approximately 47 kilometres southeast of Drayton Valley

Vernor Winfield Smith was minister of railways and telephones when this railway hamlet was named for him. Courtesy of V.W.M. Smith

In the province's first upset election in 1921, the United Farmers of Alberta swept to power and consigned the governing Liberal party to oblivion. One of the farmers elected was Vernor Winfield Smith (1864–1932), a transplanted Prince Edward Islander who had worked as a schoolteacher and railway accountant before he took up farming at Camrose in 1915. Smith's previous political experience was as a councilman in Prince Rupert, British Columbia, the Grand Trunk Pacific Railway's terminus, where he also served as secretary of the school board.[214] Smith was the provincial minister of railways and telephones when the Lacombe and Northwestern Railway named this siding for him. Smith's appointment as provincial secretary and minister of industries was pending when he died of a heart attack. He is buried in Edmonton.

Withrow

Hamlet north of Highway 11, approximately 11 kilometres northwest of Eckville

Nearly four decades before the United Church of Canada was formed in 1925, Dr. William H. Withrow (1839–1908), longtime editor of the *Canadian Methodist Magazine*, had advocated church union. Born in Toronto, Dr. Withrow entered the ministry in 1866 and became editor of the church periodical in 1874. He travelled widely and wrote prolifically. Withrow's titles include *The Underground Railroad, The Bible and the Temperance Question, Prohibition, The Duty of the Hour, Is Alcohol Food?, The World's Fair Through a Camera and How I Made My Pictures, The Catacombs of Rome and Their Testimony Relative to Primitive Christianity,* and *China and Its People.* The Canadian Northern Railway branch line to Rocky Mountain House reached Withrow in 1912.

Woking

Hamlet on Highway 677, approximately 45 kilometres north of Grande Prairie

As with several place names along the former Edmonton, Dunvegan and British Columbia Railway, Woking was named by Office Engineer Ben James Prest in 1916. The original Woking, a town 40 kilometres southwest of London, is famed as the home of H.G. Wells—it was where he wrote *The War of the Worlds* in 1898—and as the launching point for the Spice Girls' pop music career in 1994.

Woodhouse

Hamlet on Highway 2, approximately 57 kilometres northwest of Lethbridge

Master mechanic William E. Woodhouse, at one time the Canadian Pacific Railway's superintendent of motive power, was living in Calgary when the railway named this station for him in 1909. Little is know of Woodhouse or his wife—they left the city by 1910—except that their young son, Earl Clifford, is buried in Calgary's Union Cemetery.

Woolford

Hamlet on Secondary Highway 503, approximately 60 kilometres southwest of Lethbridge

At the beginning of the 20th century, English-born Thomas Henry Woolford (1856–1944), his wife, Hanna, and their children, late of Utah, settled near a ford on the St. Mary River southwest of Cardston. The ford became known as Woolford Ford, and the settlement that developed was called Woolford. Thomas and Hanna were active in the Church of Jesus Christ of Latter-day Saints, and in 1911 they returned to Utah. Woolford Provincial Park shares this hamlet's name.

Worsley

Hamlet on Secondary Highway 726, approximately 66 kilometres northwest of Fairview

There are two explanations for Worsley's name: that it honours Captain Eric Worsley, a onetime Peace River fur trader who trained an army in India and died in World War I as a British cavalry officer, or that it is named for a Lancashire village.

Wostok

Hamlet south of Highway 45, approximately 76 kilometres northeast of Edmonton

In 1896 a group of Ukrainian settlers from Galicia, then part of the Austro-Hungarian Empire, arrived in Strathcona (now part of Edmonton). Many of them homesteaded in an area then known as Mole Lake, and when Theodore Nemirsky opened the post office in 1899, he named it for the Slavic word for "east" or "eastern," perhaps referring as much to the eastern faith—the Orthodox Church—as to the compass direction.

Wrentham

Hamlet south of Highway 61, approximately 50 kilometres east southeast of Lethbridge

When the Canadian Pacific Railway (CPR) built its Lethbridge to Weyburn line from 1909–13, it established several new communities, one of which was Wrentham, named for a coastal village in Suffolk, England. (Local myth has a different explanation: early homesteaders could lease clothing from a female storekeeper for the trip to Lethbridge; hence, at her shop, one could "rent 'em.") As with other CPR townsites, Wrentham's streets were originally named. They included such colourful examples as Bedient and Cady streets and Carrigan and Speaker avenues.

Youngstown

Village on Highway 9, approximately 50 kilometres east southeast of Hanna

Soon after their marriage in 1907, Ontario-born Joseph Victor Young (died 1952) and his wife, Hilda (died 1974), homesteaded in a newly settled district southeast of Hanna. By 1912 the Canadian Northern Railway reached the area, and Joseph sold part of his land to the railway for townsite development. The Youngs had a large family—10 of their children survived infancy—and all grew up listening and singing along as Joseph played his violin and harmonica. During the Great Depression, Joseph supplemented his farming income by becoming a

Business street in Youngstown, 1913. Calgary Public Library PC499

mortician. Drought forced the Youngs off their land in 1931, and the family left Youngstown permanently for Elk Point. However, two of Joseph and Hilda's small children, Annetta and Margaret, remained behind in Youngstown's cemetery. Incorporated as a village in 1913, Youngstown became a town in 1921 but reverted to village status in 1936.

Zama City

Hamlet on Zama Road west of Highway 35, approximately 115 kilometres northwest of High Level

The now famous 1965 oil discovery near Rainbow Lake prompted the growth of this northern prospecting hamlet, named for the Zama River. The Slavey name for the river, *K'olaa Zahéh*, "Old Man River," possibly refers to a chief of the Slaveys, the most northerly native group in the province. Zama City is adjacent to the Zama Oilfield, and north of Zama Lake and Hay–Zama Lakes Wildland Provincial Park.

Notes

1 Geographical Board of Canada, *Place-Names of Alberta* (Ottawa: Department of the Interior, 1928) 8.

2 Aritha van Herk, *Mavericks: An Incorrigible History of Alberta* (Toronto: Penguin Group, 2001) 210.

3 "Princess Louise, 91, Dies; Alberta Named After Her," *Edmonton Journal* 4 Dec. 1939: 3.

4 Hamlets are defined by the Municipal Government Act and generally include five or more dwellings, parcels of land used for nonresidential purposes, accepted boundaries and a name.

5 William B. Hamilton, *The Macmillan Book of Canadian Place Names* (Toronto: Macmillan of Canada, 1978) 6.

6 Thorhild History Book Committee, *Building and Working Together: A Study of the Thorhild Area* (Thorhild, AB: Thorhild and District Historical Society, 1985) 35.

7 Stephen Wilk, *100 Years of Nose Creek Valley History* (Calgary: Nose Creek Historical Society, 1997) 64. Dixon has been spelled alternatively as Dickson.

8 Jeff Alcombrack, telephone interview, May 2002.

9 "What's In A Name? 20—Aldersyde," *Calgary Daily Herald* 5 Jan. 1937: 16.

10 Michael Dawe, Red Deer City Archivist, telephone interview, 16 March 2003.

11 "What's In A Name? 6—Alix," *Calgary Daily Herald* 16 December 1936: 12.

12 *Dreams and Destinies: Andrew and District* (Andrew, AB: Andrew Historical Society, 1980) 4.

13 James G. MacGregor, *Paddle Wheels to Bucket-wheels on the Athabasca* ([Toronto]: McClelland and Stewart, [1974?]) 151–52; L. Hastie, *Anzac: A Community Profile* (n.p.: Ekistic Design Consultants Ltd., 1975) 5.

14 "Death Came Gently to Former Well Loved Ardrossan Pioneer," *Edmonton Journal* 14 Mar. 1927: 8.

15 Audrey Highet, telephone interview, 2002; Marguerite Styner, telephone interview, 2002.

16 From 1902–1948 the name Athabasca was officially changed to Athabaska, to follow the rules of orthography then in vogue with the Geographic Board, adopted from the Royal Geographical Society. But the spelling "Athabasca" had long been in popular use, and the change was eventually reversed.

17 Bashaw History Committee, *Beautiful Fields* (Bashaw, AB: The Committee, 1974) 29, 35.

18 "Bashaw's Founder Dies," *Bashaw Star* 4 Jan. 1939.

19 *Bawlf Sun* 16 Aug. 1907.

20 J.M. Bumsted, *Dictionary of Manitoba Biography* (Winnipeg: University of Manitoba Press, 1999) 18.

21 Harold Fryer, *Ghost Towns of Alberta* (1976; Langley, B.C.: Mr. Paperback, 1981) 19–20.

22 Ruth Kerr, "Our Towns: Beiseker's colonizing dreams," *Calgary Real Estate News* 29 June 2001.

23 Ken Liddell, "Furrows and Foothills: They Made It Home And Call It Home," *Calgary Herald* 24 Apr. 1954: 5.

24 *Pas-ka-poo: An Early History of Rimbey and the Upper Blindman Valley* (Rimbey: Rimbey Record, 1962) 21.

25 Edith J. Lawrence Clark, *Trails of Tail Creek Country* [N.p.: n.p., 1968?] 85, 103.

26 "Stettler's First Reeve Dead," *Stettler Independent* 8 Mar. 1945; "First Stettler Reeve Dies in U.S. Aged 82," *Albertan* 19 Mar. 1945: 7; *Long Beach Argus* 3 Dec. 1947.

27 A. Maynard Bezanson, *Peace River Trail* (Edmonton: Journal Co., [1907]) 14.

28 Provincial Archives of Alberta (PAA), Legislature Library fonds, Accession 74.350.

29 Canada, Department of the Interior, Office of the Geographer, reply to circular sent to the post office at Blackfalds, circa 1905, Alberta Community Development, Geographical Names Program.

30 Christina Blackie, *A Dictionary of Place-Names, Giving Their Derivations* (Detroit: Gale Research Company Book Tower, 1968) ix.

31 Glenbow Archives (GA), Eric Holmgren fonds (M8857), Ambassador Matthys Izak Botha to Holmgren, 28 May 1974.

32 PAA, Legislature Library fonds, Accession 74.350.

33 GA, Eric Holmgren fonds (M8857). The same information appears in Eric J. Holmgren and Patricia Holmgren, *Over 2000 Place Names of Alberta*, 3rd ed. (Saskatoon: Western Producer Prairie Books) 34.

34 "Judge Boyle Taken by Death," *Albertan* 17 February 1936.

35 "What's In A Name? 85—Bragg Creek," *Calgary Daily Herald* 25 Mar. 1937: 23.

36 Henry J. Morgan, ed., *The Canadian Men and Women of their Time*, 2nd ed. (Toronto: William Briggs, 1912) 1032.

37 *Packhorse to Pavement* (Buck Lake, Alberta: Buck Lake History, 1981) 35–36; *Rimbey Record* 1 Sept. 1955.

38 Canada, Department of the Interior, Office of the Geographer, reply to circular sent to the post office at Buford, circa 1906, Alberta Community Development, Geographical Names Program.

39 Ken Liddell, *Exploring Southern Alberta's Chinook Country*, Frontier Series No. 6 (1977; Surrey, B.C.: Heritage House Publishing Co. Ltd., 1981) 40.

40 Hugh A. Dempsey, *Calgary: Spirit of the West* (Calgary: Glenbow and Fifth House Publishers, 1994) 30, 156.

41 Dempsey, *Calgary: Spirit of the West* 31.

42 City of Calgary Archives, City Clerk's fonds, file 2210, J.M. Mackenzie to City Clerk Frank A. Thorpe, 24 May 1943.

43 "Beloved Campsie Old Timer Passes in 80th Yr.," *Barrhead Leader* 4 June 1942: 1.

44 Rae Bruce Fleming, *The Railway King of Canada: Sir William Mackenzie, 1849–1923* (Vancouver, B.C.: UBC Press, 1991) 178. Fleming's source was his 1977 interview with Elizabeth (McKenzie) Brodie.

45 *Camrose Canadian* 24 Nov. 1927.

46 James White, *Place-Names in the Rocky Mountains Between the 49th Parallel and the Athabasca River*, Trans. R.S.C., Section II, 1916: 510.

47 Paul Voisey, "Boosting the Small Prairie Town, 1904-1931: An Example From

Southern Alberta," *Town and City: Aspects of Western Canadian Urban Development*, ed. Alan F.J. Artibise (Regina: University of Regina, Canadian Plains Research Centre, 1981) 148.

48 "Action This Day," *Finest Hour* No. 102 (1999), 16 Mar. 2003 <http://www.winstonchurchill.org/>.

49 "Castor, the Youngest Town in the Province," *Morning Albertan* 9 June 1909: 1.

50 Ted Byfield, ed., *The Great West Before 1900*, Alberta in the 20th Century Vol. 1 (Edmonton: United Western Communications, 1991) 259.

51 "Walter Butler Cheadle," *Who Named It?* (2001) 16 Mar. 2003 <www.whonamedit.com/doctor.cfm/1119.html.>

52 "Transforming Chestermere Lake into Summer Resort," *Calgary News Telegram* 28 Sept. 1911: 1; "Chestermere Lake," *Calgary Herald* 20 May 1969: 64.

53 Pierre Berton, *Klondike: The Life and Death of the Last Great Gold Rush* (1958; Toronto: McClelland & Stewart, 1961) 293.

54 *Trails and Rails North: History of McLennan and District*, vol. 1 (McLennan, AB: McLennan History Book Committee, 1981) 147–48; Ena Schneider, *Ribbons of Steel: The Story of the Northern Alberta Railways* (Calgary: Detselig Enterprises Ltd., 1989) 19.

55 Alan Rayburn, *Dictionary of Canadian Place Names* (Toronto: Oxford University Press, 1997) 77.

56 "Clandonald Founder Dies in Montreal," *Edmonton Journal* 6 Nov. 1944: 11; "Clandonald Project Brought 100 Farmers From Britain," *Edmonton Journal* 2 Sept. 1955: 11.

57 "J. Niblock Died Today in Victoria," *Calgary Daily Herald* 30 July 1914: 1.

58 "Mrs. Niblock Dies, Claresholm Was Named After Her," *Calgary Herald* 8 Dec. 1942: 9.

59 David Blyth Hanna, *Trains of Recollection, Drawn From Fifty Years of Railway Service in Scotland and Canada, and Told to Arthur Hawkes* (Toronto: Macmillan, 1924) 189.

60 "How Tom Clover, California Forty-Niner, Came to Edmonton, Giving Name to Clover Bar," *Edmonton Bulletin* 19 May 1917: 15.

61 *Westlock Witness* 10 Aug. 1955.

62 *Pioneer Heritage of Kirriemuir, Altario and Compeer* (N.p.: Wheatsheaf Women's Institute, [197?]) 46.

63 "Coronation Will Send Cable To King George VI, Relating How Name Was First Obtained," *Calgary Daily Herald* 7 Apr. 1937: 8. Neither Federal nor Throne meet the criteria for hamlet status and so have no separate entries. In the context of its naming, according to the source cited here, *federal* refers to the relationship of the components of the British Empire. An alternative explanation is that it refers to Canada's federal structure. Throne, whose post office was originally called Hamilton Lake, referred either to the physical throne or to the power it symbolized. Not all sources include Federal and Monitor among the names selected to honour the coronation.

64 *Calgary Daily Herald* 7 Apr. 1937: 8. Neither Federal nor Throne meet the criteria for hamlet status and so have no separate entries here (see footnote 63).

65 *Calgary Daily Herald* 7 Apr. 1937: 8.

66 "Coronation Cashes In On 42-Year-Old Name," *Calgary Herald* 2 June 1953: 26.

67 *Coronation Review* 19 Feb. 1953.

68 Ken Liddell, *Exploring Southern Alberta's Chinook Country* (Surrey, B.C.: Frontier Books, 1977) 40.

69 Delia and District Historical Society, *The Delia Craigmyle Saga* (Lethbridge, AB: Southern Print. Co., 1970) 591–92.

70 Alice Whitlow, compiler, *Under The Chinook Arch* (N.p.: n.p., 1979) 16–17.

71 "Cremona visits Cremona?" *Calgary Rural Times* 6 Aug. 1991: 15.

72 Alternatively, it was Fleutot himself who made this statement. William James Cousins, *A History of the Crow's Nest Pass* (N.p.: The Historic Trails Society of Alberta, 1981) 46.

73 Lenny Bruce, *How to Talk Dirty and Influence People* (Chicago: Playboy Press, 1963) 5; John Fox, "*Israelite* columnist visits the Frank Slide to find his roots," *American Israelite* [Cincinnati] 29 June 1989: 7.

74 Canada, Department of the Interior, Office of the Geographer, reply to circular sent to the post office at Hillcrest Mines, 1909, Alberta Community Development, Geographical Names Program. The Idaho community is properly spelled Posthill.

75 Jack Masson, *Alberta's Local Governments and Their Politics*, Local Government Series (Edmonton: Pica Pica Press, 1985) 101–02.

76 "New Town To Rise In Pembina Oilfield," *Calgary Herald* 24 Aug. 1956: 34.

77 "Name Central Alberta Town After Man Who Owned Land," *Edmonton Journal* 22 Sept. 1958: 34.

78 "Major Day Dead," *Daysland Press* 13 Feb. 1919.

79 "Update: The beaus of Dorothy revisited," *Calgary Herald* 13 Jan. 1979: D1.

80 Jack Deakin, "Pioneer Woman Prefers Old Methods," *Edmonton Journal* n.d.

81 Masson 101–02.

82 PAA, Legislature Library fonds, Accession 74.350/81. Other sources indicate that a contest produced Eckville's name, with the winning suggestion by Hattie Mitzner (later Mrs. Hattie Stephens).

83 *Homesteads and Happiness* (Eckville, AB: Eckville and District Historical Society, 1979) 97–100; Thomas Eckford, telephone interview, 8 August 2002.

84 Some sources indicate that George Sutherland, and not Tomison, built Edmonton House, and that it was named to honour his clerk, John Pruden, who like James Winter Lake had come from Edmonton. However, former Edmonton city archivist Bruce Ibsen has demonstrated that Sutherland and Pruden were not associated with Edmonton House until after it was named. Alex Mair, *Gateway City: Stories from Edmonton's Past* (Calgary: Fifth House Ltd., 2000) 11–12.

85 The name honoured Canadian Pacific Railway General Superintendent Reuben Rupert Jamieson (1856–1911), who came from Beverly in Wentworth County, and who served as mayor of Calgary from 1909–11.

86 M.A. Kostek, *A Century and Ten: The History of Edmonton Public Schools* (Edmonton: Edmonton Public Schools, 1992) 214–215.

87 "'Pop' Kemiston Dead in England," *Edmonton Bulletin* 21 Aug. 1948: 3.

88 Schneider 115–116.

89 "What's In A Name? 73—Elnora," *Calgary Daily Herald* 12 Mar. 1937: 9.

90 Ted Byfield, ed., *The Birth of the Province 1900–1910*, Alberta in the 20th Century vol. 2 (Edmonton: United Western Communications, 1992) 115.

91 "What's In A Name? 81—Erskine," *Calgary Daily Herald* 22 Mar. 1937: 5.

92 Schneider, 38, 134, 188.

93 *Calgary Daily Herald* 7 Apr. 1937: 8. Neither Federal nor Throne meet the criteria for hamlet status and so have no separate entries here (see footnote 63).

94 *Calgary Daily Herald* 7 Apr. 1937: 8.

95 "What's In A Name? 79—Forestburg," *Calgary Daily Herald* 19 Mar. 1937: 10.

96 Masson 101–02.

97 Masson 101–02.

98 Previous works suggest it was a person named M.F. Gadsby of Ottawa, but he does not appear in city directories, and only Henry Franklin Gadsby appears in contemporary *Who's Who* publications.

99 *Reflexions: Histoire Girouxville-Culp*, vol. II (Girouxville, AB: Girouxville Historical Society, 1990) 10.

100 Canada, Department of the Interior, Office of the Geographer, Reply to circular sent to the post office at Gleichen, 16 Sept 1905, Alberta Community Development, Geographical Names Program.

101 Grande Cache was one of several communities incorporated between 1956 and 1967 under the New Town Act. Oil discoveries led to the creation of instant boomtowns.

102 *Land of Hope and Dreams: A History of Grimshaw and Districts* (Grimshaw, AB: Grimshaw and District Historical Society, 1980) 287.

103 Hanna 3.

104 Duke Hartell, telephone interview, 11 March 2003.

105 "New Resort Town Opens This Year Near Banff," *Calgary Herald* 2 June 1951: 1; "Hidden Treasure," *Calgary Herald* 19 Aug. 1995: B10.

106 *Early Furrows: A Story of Our Early Pioneers in Provost, Hayter, Bodo, Alberta and Surrounding Districts* (Provost, AB: Senior Citizen's Club of Provost, 1977) 249.

107 *Wagon Trails in the Sod: A History of the Heisler Area* (Heisler: Heisler Historical Society, 1982) 19, 21, 265–66.

108 Lorna Bell, telephone interview, July 2002.

109 Masson 101–02.

110 Hugh A. Dempsey, *Indian Names for Alberta Communities*, Occasional Paper No. 4 (Calgary: Glenbow-Alberta Institute, 1969) 12.

111 Canadian Permanent Committee on Geographic Place Names, correspondence files on microfiche 1897–1979 (Toronto: Micromedia Ltd., 1985–1987), Robert Douglas, Secretary of the Geographic Board of Canada to G.H. Lash, Publicity Representative, Western Region, Canadian National Railways, Winnipeg, 27 Aug. 1926.

112 "Protest Town Name," *Drayton Valley Tribune* 7 Feb. 1957: 1.

113 Masson 101–02.

114 James G. MacGregor, *Father Lacombe* (Edmonton: Hurtig Publishers, 1975) 289.

115 Jack Deakin, "Pioneer's Birthday Recalls 53 Years Of Alberta History," *Edmonton Journal* 3 Oct. 1951.

116 Merrily K. Aubrey, ed., *Place Names of Alberta*, vol. 4 (Calgary: University of Calgary Press, 1996) 104.

117 Holmgren 144–45.

118 "What's In A Name? 36—Kathyrn," *Calgary Daily Herald* 25 Jan. 1937: 17.

119 Aubrey 113.

120 "Moses Smith Kelsey," obituary, *Camrose Canadian* 8 Dec.1927: 1.

121 MacGregor, *Father Lacombe* 289.

122 *Dreams Become Realities: A History of Lafond and Surrounding Area* (N.p: Lafond Historical Committee, 1981) 503–04.

123 "What's In a Name? 75—Lanfine," *Calgary Daily Herald* 15 Mar. 1937: 13.

124 Delon Shurtz, "Leavitt cairn dedicated to pioneer," *Lethbridge Herald* 17 May 1994.

125 Aphrodite Karamitsanis, ed., *Place Names of Alberta*, vol. 2 (Calgary: University of Calgary Press, 1992) 71.

126 *CNR Magazine* August 1927.

127 E.T. Russell, *What's in a Name: The Story Behind Saskatchewan Place Names* (Saskatoon: Western Producer Prairie Books, 1984) 179.

128 Byfield, *The Birth of the Province 1900–1910* 162.

129 Masson 101–02.

130 *Calgary Daily Herald* 7 Apr. 1937: 8. Neither Federal nor Throne meet the criteria for hamlet status and so have no separate entries here (see footnote 63).

131 *Calgary Daily Herald* 7 Apr. 1937: 8.

132 Karen Buckley, *No Ordinary Prairie Town: A Researcher's Guide and Historical Inventory to the Towns of Southern Alberta* (Karen Buckley, 1998) 83.

133 Barrhead and District Historical Society, *Trails Northwest: A History of the District of Barrhead, Alberta ... 1867–1967* (Barrhead, AB: The Society, 1967) 94.

134 "Dr. C.P. Marker Looks Back On 50 Years' Dairying Work," *Edmonton Journal* 14 July 1934: 7.

135 "Andrew—Willingdon—Derwent—Marwayne: Representing Progress and Production On Willingdon Branch of C.P.R.," *Edmonton Journal* 24 Mar. 1934: 13. Ontario's Wainfleet Township is also named for the Lincolnshire port town.

136 Canada, Department of the Interior, Office of the Geographer, reply to circular sent to the post office at Marwayne, 1909, Alberta Community Development, Geographical Names Program.

137 "Early Days Treasure House Is Feature At Mayerthorpe," *Edmonton Journal* 25 Aug. 1958; "Mayerthorpe Founder Dies At Age Of 81," *Edmonton Journal* 22 Apr. 1965.

138 "Founder Of Town Dies In Edmonton," *Edmonton Journal* 16 Oct. 1937.

139 The name was formerly spelled Athabaska. For an explanation, see the footnote for Athabasca (16).

140 Dempsey, *Indian Names for Alberta Communities* 14.

141 Alan Rayburn, *Naming Canada: Stories About Canadian Place Names* (Toronto: Oxford University Press, 1977) 196.

142 Rayburn 196–97.

143 Canadian Permanent Committee on Geographic Place Names, correspondence files on microfiche 1897–1979 (Toronto: Micromedia Ltd., 1985–1987), A.A. Tisdale, General Manager, Canadian National Railways, Western Division, to all concerned, 15 August 1930.

144 Holmgren 185.

145 MacGregor, *Father Lacombe* 289.

146 "Funeral Tuesday For City Teacher Miss M. Burns," *Ottawa Journal* 9 May 1960.

147 Richard D. Woollatt, "Origins of Mirror," *Alberta History* Summer 1984: 22–23.

148 *Calgary Daily Herald* 7 Apr. 1937: 8. Neither Federal nor Throne meet the criteria for

hamlet status and so have no separate entries here (see footnote 63).

149 *Calgary Daily Herald* 7 Apr. 1937: 8.

150 *Furrows of Time: A History of Arrowwood, Shouldice, Mossleigh and Farrow, 1883–1982* (N.p.: Arrowwood-Mossleigh Historical Society, 1982) 593.

151 Canadian Permanent Committee on Geographic Place Names, correspondence files on microfiche 1897–1979 (Toronto: Micromedia Ltd., 1985–1987), Douglas to Lash, 27 Aug. 1926.

152 Canadian Permanent Committee on Geographic Place Names, correspondence files on microfiche 1897–1979 (Toronto: Micromedia Ltd., 1985–1987), Christian to Douglas, 1924.

153 Canada, Department of the Interior, Office of the Geographer, reply to circular sent to the post office at New Norway, 1906, Alberta Community Development, Geographical Names Program.

154 PAA, Legislature Library fonds, Accession 74.35081.

155 "Jones Meets New Sarepta," *Edmonton Journal* 5 Jan. 1963.

156 Schneider 115–16.

157 Conrad Sarnecki, telephone interview, 10 Aug. 2002.

158 "He Used His Head," *Calgary Albertan* 8 July 1957: 4.

159 Martin Nordegg, *To the Town That Bears Your Name: A Young Woman's Journey to Nordegg in 1912*, trans. Maria Koch (Edmonton: Brightest Pebble, 1995) 54.

160 Nordegg 107.

161 William Morrow, telephone interview, June 2002.

162 "Village of Oyen Named After Norwegian Pioneer Andy Oyen; Was One of First Settlers in East," *Hanna Herald and East Central Alberta News* 25 August 1955; Rose Jardine and Harriet Austen, *Many Trails Crossed Here: A Story of Oyen, Alberta, and The Surrounding Districts* (Oyen, AB: Oyen and District Historical Society, 1981) 218.

163 Georgina Helen Thomson, *Crocus and Meadowlark Country: Recollections of a Happy Childhood and Youth on a Homestead in Southern Alberta* (Edmonton: Institute of Applied Art, 1963) 229–30; "What's In A Name? 22—Parkland," *Calgary Daily Herald* 8 January 1937: 9.

164 Canada, Department of the Interior, Office of the Geographer, reply to circular sent to the post office at Penhold, 1905, Alberta Community Development, Geographical Names Program.

165 Larry Speers, ed., *Rolling Hills & Whispering Pines: A Peek at the Past: A History of the Nestow, Tawatinaw, Rochester and Perryvale Districts as Remembered and Recorded by Their People* (N.p.: Nestow, Tawatinaw, Rochester, Perryvale History Book Committee, 1986) 200–01, 849–51, 1175–76.

166 Karamitsanis 96.

167 Radway and Area Historical Archives Association, *In Search of Greener Pastures: A History of Radway and Area* (Radway, AB: Radway and Area Historical Archives Association, 1993) 873.

168 Masson 101–02.

169 Jesse Knight, personal interview, 27 July 2002.

170 Karamitsanis 101.

171 Don Rimbey, telephone interview, 10 March 2003.

172 Rivercourse, Alta. Sewing Circle, *Rivercourse Centennial* ([Rivercourse, AB?]: n.p., 1967) 1.

173 GA, Peter Addison Robb fonds inventory.

174 Vera A. Holt, ed., *The Lantern Era: A History of Cherhill, Rochfort Bridge, Sangudo and Surrounding School Districts* ([Sangudo, AB]: Sangudo and District Historical Society, 1979) 533.

175 "Former Banker Dies in East," *Calgary Herald* 22 Jan. 1947: 3.

176 *Regina Leader* 26 Sept. 1929.

177 PAA, Northern Alberta Railways fonds, accession 86.587, file 999.

178 Sandy Isaac, ed., *Wheatfields and Wildflowers. A History of Rycroft & Surrounding School Districts* (Rycroft, AB: Rycroft History Book Committee, 1984) 1–3; "Grandmother Likens West To Norway," *Albertan* 17 July 1957.

179 Katherine Hughes, *Father Lacombe: The Black-Robe Voyageur* (1911; Toronto: W. Briggs, 1914) 82.

180 Between 1957–1962, St. Albert was classified as a new town.

181 Canadian Permanent Committee on Geographic Place Names, correspondence files on microfiche 1897–1979 (Toronto: Micromedia Ltd., 1985–87), T. Bond, Director of Postal Services, Canada Post Office, Post Office Facilities Division, to Canadian Permanent Committee on Geographical Names, Geographical Branch, Department of Mines and Technical Surveys, Ottawa, 15 July 1964.

182 *St. Lina and Surrounding Area* (St. Lina: St. Lina History Book Club, 1978) 126. Other sources suggest that St. Lina was named for Lectande's wife. Emile Mageau had a son named Lionel, and it is possible to speculate that his name influenced the suggestion.

183 *Souvenirs: Saint Vincent 1906–1981* (Saint Vincent, AB: Saint Vincent Historical Club, [1981?]) 10–11.

184 Canadian Permanent Committee on Geographic Place Names, correspondence files on microfiche 1897–1979 (Toronto: Micromedia Ltd., 1985–87), Postmaster E.J. Thibert's reply to Douglas' circular, 30 June 1926, and correspondence between Rayburn and Lillian A. Coulson, Sangudo and District History Committee, September-October 1977.

185 Sexsmith to the Smoky Historical Society, *Wagon Trails Grown Over: Sexsmith to the Smoky* (Sexsmith, AB: Sexsmith to the Smoky Historical Society, 1980) 573.

186 *Sibbald Community History, 1908–1980* (Sibbald, AB: Sibbald Community Club, 1980) 35.

187 Schneider 20.

188 Schneider 17.

189 GA, Eric Holmgren fonds (M8857).

190 "Incorrect Spelling of Town Name Gave Rise to Concern in High Circles," *Calgary Daily Herald* 3 March 1937: 9.

191 Martin W. Holdom, *A Preacher's Frontier: the Castor, Alberta Letters of Rev. Martin W. Holdom, 1909–1912* (Calgary: Historical Society of Alberta, 1996) 18.

192 *Lanterns on the Prairie: Strome Diamond Jubilee, 1905–1980* (Strome, AB: Strome Senior Citizens Club, 1980) 242.

193 "Sundre Heart Of The Back-Country," *Calgary Herald* 5 May 1962.

194 Masson 101–02.

195 Sheila Jarvin, ed., *Reflections of Sylvan Lake* (Sylvan Lake, AB: Sylvan Lake Historical Society, 1984) 65; Tracey Harrison, ed., *Place Names of Alberta*, vol. 3 (Calgary: University of Calgary Press, 1994) 241.

196 Canadian Permanent Committee on Geographic Place Names, correspondence files on microfiche 1897–1979 (Toronto: Micromedia Ltd., 1985–1987), J.A. Jackson to Hon. Senator W.A. Buchanan, 7 July 1943.

197 C.H. Stout, "Saddle Notches, Candles and Oil: Early Days in Leduc," *Alberta History* Autumn 1958: 17.

198 *Alberta Medical Bulletin* Vol. 30, No. 1: 39.

199 *Calgary Daily Herald* 7 Apr. 1937: 8. Neither Federal nor Throne meet the criteria for hamlet status and so have no separate entries here (see footnote 63).

200 *Calgary Daily Herald* 7 Apr. 1937: 8.

201 Gloria M. Strathern, *Alberta Newspapers, 1880–1982: An Historical Directory* (Edmonton: University of Alberta Press, 1988) 80, 446.

202 Dale Holtslander, "Railway to Athabasca," *Alberta History* Winter 1978: 27.

203 "As Others See Us: Vulcan The Town Upon Which the Gods Descended," *Vulcan Review* 19 Mar. 1912: 1.

204 "Wm. Wainwright, Vice-Pres. G.T.P. Has Passed Away," *Wainwright Star* 20 May 1914: 1.

205 "Wainwright's Loss in Death of Railway Official," editorial, *Wainwright Star* 20 May 1914: 4.

206 Gordon Prest, personal interview, July 2002.

207 Archibald Oswald MacRae, *History of the Province of Alberta* (Calgary: Western Canada History, 1912) 635.

208 Schneider 43–44.

209 GA, Eric J. Holmgren fonds (M8857).

210 MacGregor, *Father Lacombe* 289.

211 GA, George Gwynne Mann fonds (M809).

212 Canada, Department of the Interior, Office of the Geographer, reply to circular sent to the post office at Whitecourt, Alberta Community Development, Geographical Names Program.

213 Masson 101–02.

214 "The Late Hon. V. W. Smith," *Camrose Canadian* 30 July 1932.

Selected Bibliography

Primary Sources

Canada. Department of the Interior. Office of the Geographer. James White correspondence with Alberta postmasters. 1905–08. Alberta Community Development, Geographical Names Program.

Canadian Permanent Committee on Geographic Names. Correspondence files on microfiche 1897–1979. Toronto: Micromedia Ltd., 1985–87.

Glenbow Archives, Eric Holmgren fonds (M8857).

Provincial Archives of Alberta (PAA), Eric J. Holmgren fonds, Accessions 91.313, 94.137.

PAA, Legislature Library fonds, Accession 74.350.

PAA, Northern Alberta Railways fonds, Accession 86.587

Secondary Sources

Aubrey, Merrily K. *Place Names of Alberta*, Vol. 4. Calgary: University of Calgary Press, 1996.

Bezanson, A. Maynard. *Peace River Trail*. Edmonton: Journal Co., 1907.

———. *Sodbusters Invade the Peace*. Toronto: Ryerson Press, 1954.

Buckley, Karen. *No Ordinary Prairie Town: A Researcher's Guide and Historical Inventory to the Towns of Southern Alberta*. Karen Buckley, 1998.

Bumsted, J.M. *Dictionary of Manitoba Biography*. Winnipeg: University of Manitoba Press, 1999.

Byfield, Ted, ed., *The Great West Before 1900*. Alberta in the 20th Century Vol. 1. Edmonton: United Western Communications, 1991.

———. *The Birth of the Province 1900–1910*. Alberta in the 20th Century Vol. 2. Edmonton: United Western Communications, 1992.

———. *The Boom and the Bust 1910–1914*, Alberta in the 20th Century Vol. 3. Edmonton: United Western Communications, 1994.

———. *The Great War and its Consequences 1914–1920*, Alberta in the 20th Century Vol. 4. Edmonton: United Western Communications, 1994.

———. *Brownlee and the Triumph of Populism 1920–1930*, Alberta in the 20th Century Vol. 5. Edmonton: United Western Communications, 1996.

Cheadle, Walter Butler. *Cheadle's Journal of a Trip Across Canada, 1862–1863*. Ottawa: Graphic Publishers, 1931.

Douglas, Robert. *Place-Names of Alberta*. Ottawa: Geographic Board of Canada, 1928.

Dempsey, Hugh A. *Indian Names for Alberta Communities*. Occasional Paper No. 4. Calgary: Glenbow-Alberta Institute, 1969.

Dirk, Marcel. *But Names Will Never Hurt Me: Why Medicine Hat? Legends Behind the Naming of the City*. Medicine Hat, AB: Curly Dagger Productions, 1993.

Fryer, Harold. *Ghost Towns of Alberta*. 1976; Langley, BC: Mr. Paperback, 1981.

Hamilton, William B. *The Macmillan Book of Canadian Place Names*. Toronto: Macmillan of Canada, 1978.

Hanna, David Blyth. *Trains of Recollection, Drawn From Fifty Years of Railway Service in Scotland and Canada, and Told to Arthur Hawkes*. Toronto: Macmillan, 1924.

Harrison, Tracey. *Place Names of Alberta*, Vol. 3. Calgary: University of Calgary Press, 1994.

Hill, Alexander Staveley. *From Home to Home: Autumn Wanderings in the North-West, in the Years 1881, 1882, 1883, 1884.* London: S. Low, Marston, Searle, & Rivington, 1885.

Holmgren, Eric J., and Patricia M. Holmgren. *Over 2000 Place Names of Alberta,* 3rd ed. Saskatoon: Western Producer Prairie Books, 1976.

Humber, Donna Mae. *What's in a Name ...Calgary? A Look at the People Behind Place Names in Calgary.* Calgary: Detselig Enterprises Ltd., 1995.

————. *What's in a Name ...Calgary?,* Vol. 2. Calgary: Detselig Enterprises Ltd., 1995.

Jeffords, A. Norman, ed. *Cowper Selected Poems and Letters.* London:Oxford University Press, 1963: 70

Johnston, Alex, and Barry R. Peat. *Lethbridge Place Names.* Occasional Paper No. 14. Lethbridge: Whoop-Up Country Chapter, Historical Society of Alberta, 1987.

Karamitsanis, Aphrodite. *Place Names of Alberta,* Vol. 2. Calgary: University of Calgary Press, 1992.

————. *Place Names of Alberta,* Vol. 1. Calgary: University of Calgary Press, 1991.

Kerfoot, H., and W.B. Yeo. "Chief Geographer's Place Name Survey 1905–1909, I. British Columbia." *CANOMA* July 1978: 1–10.

Landelius, Otto Robert. *Swedish Place-Names in North America.* Carbondale: Southern Illinois University Press, 1985.

MacGregor, James G. *A History of Alberta.* 1972; Edmonton: Hurtig Publishers, 1981.

MacRae, Archibald Oswald. *History of the Province of Alberta.* Calgary: Western Canada History, 1912.

Mardon, Ernest G. and Austin A. *Community Names of Alberta,* Expanded Second Edition. Edmonton: Golden Meteorite Press, 1998.

Milton, William Fitzwilliam, and W.B. Cheadle. *The North-West Passage by Land: Being the Narrative of an Expedition From the Atlantic to the Pacific.* London: Cassell, Petter and Galpin, 1865.

Morgan, Henry J., ed. *The Canadian Men and Women of their Time,* 2nd ed. Toronto: William Briggs, 1912.

Nordegg, Martin. *The Possibilities of Canada are Truly Great: Memoirs, 1906–1924.* Ed. T.D. Regehr. Toronto: Macmillan, 1971.

Nordegg, Martin. *To the Town That Bears Your Name: A Young Woman's Journey to Nordegg in 1912.* Trans. Maria Koch. Commentary by W. John Koch. Edmonton: Brightest Pebble, 1995.

Palmer, Howard, with Tamara Palmer. *Alberta: A New History.* Edmonton: Hurtig Publishers, 1990.

Rayburn, Alan. *Oxford Dictionary of Canadian Place Names.* Toronto: Oxford University Press, 1997.

Rayburn, Alan. *Naming Canada: Stories About Canadian Place Names.* Toronto: Oxford University Press, 1977.

Schneider, Ena. *Ribbons of Steel: The Story of the Northern Alberta Railways.* Calgary: Detselig Enterprises Ltd., 1989.

Service, Robert. *The Complete Poems of Robert Service.* New York: Dodd, Mead & Company, 1940: 239

Swan, Annie S. *Aldersyde: A Border Story of Seventy Years Ago.* 1884; Toronto: W. Briggs, 1982.

Thomson, Georgina Helen. *Crocus and Meadowlark Country: Recollections of a Happy Childhood and Youth on a Homestead in Southern Alberta.* Edmonton: Institute of Applied Art, 1963.

Yeo, W.B. "When Banff was somewhere else down the track." *CANOMA* July 1985: 5–7

Index

About the Author

Harry Sanders is a Calgary-based freelance writer, historical consultant and reference archivist. He studied history at the University of Calgary and has worked for the Calgary Public Library, the City of Calgary Archives, the Glenbow Library and Archives and the Jewish Historical Society of Southern Alberta. He is a past president of the Chinook Country Historical Society, the Calgary and district chapter of the Historical Society of Alberta. This is his third book.